ULTIMATE POCKET
BOOK OF THE
WORLD

ATLAS

A DORLING KINDERSLEY BOOK

Project Cartography and Design
Julia Lunn, Peter Winfield

Cartographic Research Michael Martin

Project Editor and Index-Gazetteer
Jayne Parsons

Digital base maps produced on DK Cartopia by
Simon Lewis, Rob Stokes, Thomas Robertshaw

Production Controller Hilary Stephens

Editorial Director Andrew Heritage

Art Director Chez Picthall

Published in the United States by Dorling Kindersley Publishing Inc.,
95 Madison Avenue, New York, New York 10016
First published in this version 1998

A CIP catalog record for this book is available from the Library of Congress

ISBN 07894-3623-X

*Film output in England, by Euroscan
Printed and bound in Italy, by L.E.G.O*

ULTIMATE POCKET
BOOK OF THE
WORLD
ATLAS

DK

KEY

～～	*International border*
– –	*Disputed border*
– –	*Claimed border*
～	*International border along river*
～	*State border*
～	*State border along river*
～	*River*
～	*Lake*
～	*Canal*
～	*Seasonal river*
～	*Seasonal lake*
─┼─	*Waterfall*
───	*Road*
───	*Railway*
●	*Capital city*
◎	*Major town*
○	*Minor town*
●	*Major port*
●	*Minor port*
✈	*International airport*
▲	*Spot height – feet*
•	*Spot depth – feet*

CONTENTS

CONTINENTAL NORTH AMERICA 14-15

CONTINENTAL SOUTH AMERICA 36-37

CONTINENTAL AFRICA 48-49

CONTINENTAL EUROPE 60-61

NORTH & WEST ASIA 92-93

EAST & SOUTH ASIA 104-105

AUSTRALASIA & OCEANIA 124-125

THE PHYSICAL WORLD

ARCTIC OCEAN

Svalbard
Franz Josef Land
Severnaya Zemlya
New Siberia

Greenland Sea
Novaya Zemlya
Kara Sea
Laptev Sea
Khrebet Cherskogo

North Cape
Barents Sea

Norwegian Sea
Scandinavia
Lapland
Ob'
Yenisey
Central Siberian Plateau
Lena

Iceland
Denmark Strait
North Sea
Baltic Sea
Volga
Ural Mts.
Siberia
Kamchatka

British Isles
EUROPE
ASIA
L. Baikal
Sea of Okhotsk
Sakhalin

Bay of Biscay
Alps
Danube
Black Sea
Aral Sea
L. Balkhash
Altai Mts.
Tien Shan
Gobi
Manchurian Plain
Sea of Japan
Hokkaido

Iberia
Mediterranean Sea
Anatolia
Caspian Sea
Zagros Mts.
Iranian Plateau
Hindu Kush
Plateau of Tibet
Himalayas
Yellow R.
Yellow Sea
Honshu

Madeira
Atlas Mts.
Kyūshū

Canary Is.
Sahara
Arabian Peninsula
Thar Desert
Yangtze
East China Sea
Taiwan

Cape Verde Is.
AFRICA
Red Sea
Ganges
Deccan
Mekong

Sahel
Ethiopian Highlands
Horn of Africa
Arabian Sea
Bay of Bengal
South China Sea
Philippine Sea

Niger
L. Chad
Nile
Great Rift Valley
Somali Basin
Sri Lanka
Borneo
Philippine Islands
Melanesia

Gulf of Guinea
Congo
Congo Basin
L. Victoria
L. Tanganyika
Seychelles
Sumatra
East Indies
New Guinea

Mid-Atlantic Ridge
Angola Basin
Zambezi
L. Nyasa
INDIAN
Java Sea
Java
Timor
Arnhem Land

Namib Desert
Mozambique Channel
Mauritius
Réunion
Timor Sea
AUSTRALIA

Cape Basin
Kalahari Desert
Drakensberg
Madagascar
OCEAN
Great Victoria Desert
Darling

Cape of Good Hope
Southwest Indian Ridge
Bass Strait

Tasmania

Kerguelen

South Sandwich Is.

Dronning Maud Land
ANTARCTICA
Wilkes Land

6

THE POLITICAL WORLD

For full list of abbreviations see page 134.

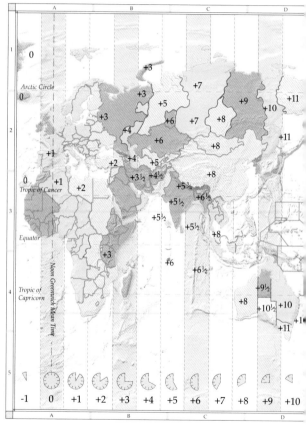

Numbers on the map show the number of hours ahead of, or behind, GMT.

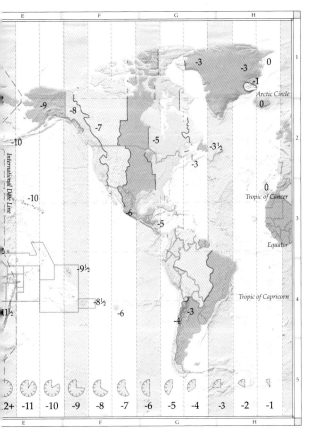

Tiksi

Laptev Sea

Lomonosov (Harris) Ridge

ASIA

New Siberian Is.
(Russ. Fed.)

East Siberian Sea

ARCTIC OCEAN

Fram (Angara) Basin

Pevek

Wrangel I.
(Russ. Fed.)

Arctic Circle

Chukchi Sea

Limit of permanent pack ice

Canada (Laurentian) Basin

Bering Strait

NORTH AMERICA

Beaufort Sea

Tuktoyaktuk

Mackenzie

Banks I.
(Canada)

Prince Patrick I.
(Canada)

Melville I.
(Canada)

Bathurst I.
(Canada)

Queen Elizabeth Is.
(Canada)

0 km   500

0 miles   500

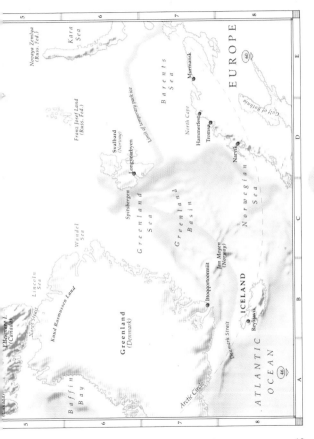

CONTINENTAL NORTH AMERICA

ARCTIC OCEAN

12

Limit of permanent pack-ice

Chukchi Sea

Beaufort Sea

9,059ft

Melville

Viscount Melville Sou

Banks I.

Victor

Amundsen Gulf

Brooks Range

92

Arctic Circle

ASIA

Bering Strait

Yukon

Denali 20,333ft

Mackenzie

Great Bear Lake

USA (Alaska)

Alaska Range

St Lawrence I.

Nunivak I.

Mt. Logan 19,850ft

Great Slave Lake

Alaska Peninsula

Kodiak I.

Queen Charlotte Is.

Bering Sea

Queen Charlotte Sound

Aleutian Islands

Gulf of Alaska

A l e u t i a n   T r e n c h

122

Vancouver I.

Mt. Rainier 14,410ft

Mt St Helens 8,366ft

Cascade Range

Great Basin

Great Salt Lake

B

PACIFIC

OCEAN

Mt. Whitney 14,492ft

Death Valley 282ft

Colorado Plateau

Sonoran Desert

Gulf of California

Co 14,2

Tropic of Cancer

Baja California

USA (*Hawaiian Is.*)

ROCKY MOUNTAINS

Great Rocky Mts.

C A N A D A

U

Gr

0 km   1000

0 miles   1000

Axel
Heiberg I.
Ellesmere I.
Queen Elizabeth Is.
Knud Rasmussen Land
Devon I.
Lancaster Sound
ince of
Somerset I.
Greenland
Baffin I.
Baffin Bay
(Denmark)
Wales I.

Gunnbjørn Field▲
12,139ft
Arctic Circle

Davis Strait

Denmark Strait
Iceland

Southampton I.
Hudson Strait
EUROPE
60

Hudson
Bay
Ungava
Peninsula
Ungava
Bay
Labrador
Sea

Reindeer
Lake
Belcher Is.
Labrador Basin

D   A
James
Bay

L. Winnipeg

A
L. Superior
Laurentian Plateau
Strait of Belle Isle
Newfoundland

Great Lakes
L. Huron
St Lawrence
Gulf of
St Lawrence

L. Ontario
St Pierre
& Miquelon
(France)
C. Race
Grand
Banks

L. Michigan
L. Erie
Niagara
Falls
Cape Cod

Missouri
Ohio
6,683ft
Sohm Plain

Arkansas
Appalachian Mts.
Cape
Hatteras
Azores
(Portugal)

Red R.

Mississippi

Mississippi
Delta
Bermuda
(UK)
46

The
Everglades
Nares Plain
ATLANTIC

MEXICO
Gulf
of
Mexico
Straits of Florida
OCEAN
Tropic of Cancer

▲ Citlaltépetl
18,701ft
opocatépetl
17,375ft
Cayman Is.
(UK)
BAHAMAS

CUBA
Turks & Caicos Is. (UK)
DOMINICAN REP.
Puerto Rico (USA)
British Virgin Is. (UK)

BELIZE
JAMAICA
HAITI
(USA) Virgin Is.
Anguilla (UK)
ANTIGUA & BARBUDA

GUATEMALA
HONDURAS
ST KITTS & NEVIS
Guadeloupe (France)
DOMINICA
Montserrat (UK)
48

EL SALVADOR
Caribbean
Sea
ST LUCIA
Martinique (France)

NICARAGUA
Aruba
(Neth.)
GRENADA
BARBADOS
ST VINCENT &
THE GRENADINES

COSTA RICA
PANAMA
Neth. Antilles
(Neth.)
36
TRINIDAD
& TOBAGO

SOUTH AMERICA

WESTERN CANADA & ALASKA

RUSSIAN
FEDERATION

Wrangel I.

A R C

O C E

Attu I.

*Bering
Sea*

Bering Strait

Kiska I.

St. Lawrence I.

Brooks Range

Pru
Bay

Aleutian Islands

Nunivak I.

Yukon

ALASKA
(USA)

Fairbanks

Umnak I.

Dutch Harbor

Unalaska I.

Alaska Range

Anchorage

Daw

Aleutian Trench

Kodiak I. Kodiak

Valdez

Cordova

YUKO
TERRI

WHITEHORSE

JUNEAU

Gulf
of
Alaska

PACIFIC

OCEAN

Ketchikan

Prince Rupert

Queen Charlotte I

*Queen Charlotte
Sound*

Port Alice

Vancouver I.

VICTO

0 km   400

0 miles   400

C

160°   140°   120°   100°   80°   60°   40°

Ellesmere I.

Greenland
(Denmark)

40°   1

Axel Heiberg I.

Queen Elizabeth Is.

Bathurst I.   Devon I.   Baffin Bay

Parry Is.

Melville I.   Lancaster Sound   Davis Strait

Viscount   Resolute
Banks I.   Melville   Somerset I.   Baffin I.   2
Sound   Prince
of   60°
Beaufort   Wales I.
Sea   Amundsen   Victoria I.
Gulf   King
William I.   Arctic Circle   Iqaluit

Coppermine

Great Bear L.   Hudson Strait   60°

NORTHWEST TERRITORIES   Southampton I.   3

Mackenzie   YELLOWKNIFE
Great Slave L.   Rankin   QUÉBEC
Inlet   Hudson
Hay River   Fort Smith   Bay
L. Athabasca   Churchill

Fort   Fort   MANITOBA
St. John   McMurray   C A N A D A   4

Grande Prairie   SASKATCHEWAN   Flin   Thompson   80°
EDMONTON   Flon

Leduc   Prince Albert   L. Winnipeg   ONTARIO

Red Deer   Saskatoon   L. Winnipegosis
Calgary   Yorkton   5
Kelowna   REGINA   Brandon   WINNIPEG
Vancouver   Lethbridge   Estevan
120°   Kamloops   USA   100°

18

20

17

EASTERN CANADA

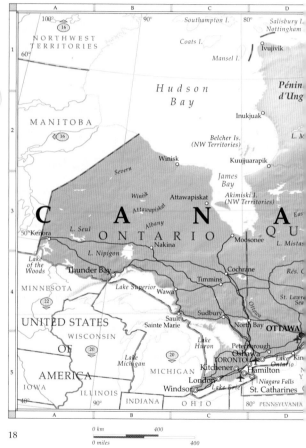

0 km   400

0 miles   400

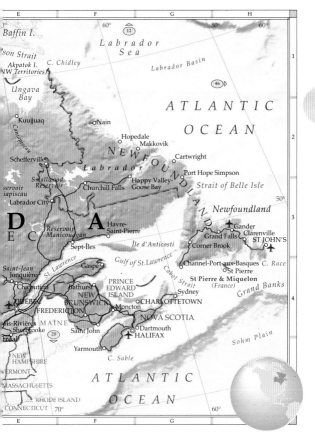

USA: THE NORTHEAST

0 km 200

0 miles 200

USA: CENTRAL STATES

0 km   200

0 miles   200

USA: THE WEST

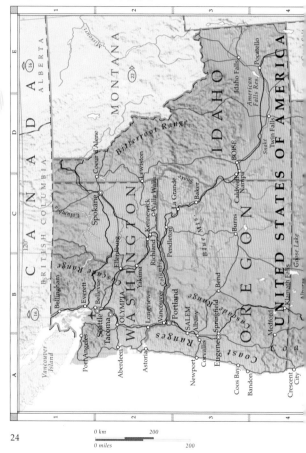

0 km   200

0 miles   200

UTAH

NEVADA

ARIZONA

CALIFORNIA

MEXICO

Ely

Tonopah

Hawthorne

Bishop

Fallon

Reno Sparks
Lake Tahoe
CARSON CITY

Chico
Yuba City
Santa Rosa
Auburn
SACRAMENTO
Stockton
Concord
Oakland
San Francisco
San Jose
Santa Cruz
Salinas
Monterey

Modesto
Merced
Fresno
Visalia

Bakersfield

Mojave
Lancaster
Barstow

San Bernardino
Pasadena
Santa Ana
Riverside
Palm Springs
Los Angeles
Oceanside
Long Beach

Santa Barbara
Oxnard

San Diego

Las Vegas
North Las Vegas

Lake Mead

Death Valley

Mojave Desert

Salton Sea

Colorado

Sierra Nevada

Coast Ranges

San Joaquin

PACIFIC OCEAN

Santa Rosa I.
Santa Catalina I.
San Nicolas I.
San Clemente I.
Channel Islands

120°

40°

PitmanLake

22

26

30

5   6   7   8

B   C   D   E

25

USA: The Southwest

0 km   200

0 miles   200

27

USA: The Southeast

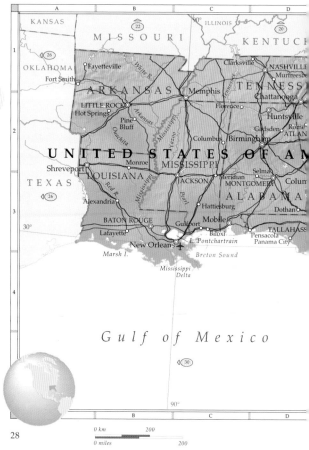

0 km   200

0 miles   200

Mexico

0 km   200
0 miles   200

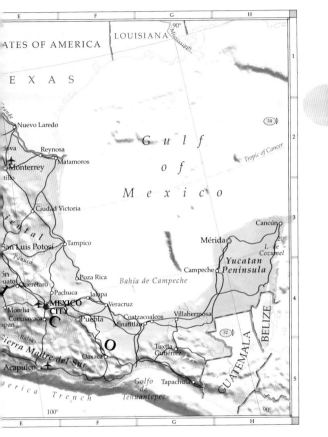

CENTRAL AMERICA

	A	B	C	D

90°

M E X I C O

30

1

Usumacinta

Belize City

BELMOPAN

Flores

San Ignacio

BELIZE

Islas de la Bah

GUATEMALA

Huehuetenango

Cobán

Lago de Izabal

Puerto Barrios

Gulf of Honduras

Puerto Cortés

Trujillo

Quezaltenango

Zacapa

San Pedro Sula

La Ceiba

2

GUATEMALA CITY

Mazatenango

Santa Rosa de Copan

Comayagua

HONDURAS

Juticalpa

Escuintla

La Esperanza

TEGUCIGALPA

Santa Ana

San Miguel

SAN SALVADOR

San Lorenzo

EL SALVADOR

Choluteca

Somoto

NIC

Gulf of Fonseca

Jinotega

3

Estelí

Matagalpa

Chichigalpa

Corinto

León

Juigalpa

MANAGUA

Middle America Trench

Granada

Lago de Nicaragua

Rivas

10°

P A C I F I C

Peninsula de Nicoya

Liberia

4

Puntarenas

Ala

SAN J

O C E A N

122

Golfo de Nicoya

90°

	B		C		D

0 km   200

0 miles   200

80°

Cayman Trench

Greater Antilles

HAITI

JAMAICA

s Santanilla
onduras)

Bajo Nuevo
(Colombia)   34

Cayos Miskitos
(Nicaragua)

C a r i b b e a n

I. de Providencia
(Colombia)

S e a

I. de San Andrés
(Colombia)

Islas del Maíz (Nicaragua)
fields

OSTA
ICA
Limón
go

10°

Colón

PANAMA   PANAMA CITY   Gulf
                                  of
            Penonomé   Panama   Darien
                        Canal   Isla del
David   Rey
    Golfo   Santiago   COLOMBIA
    de   Chitré
Chiriquí   Las Tablas   Golfo
                          de
                          Panamá

80°   38

THE CARIBBEAN

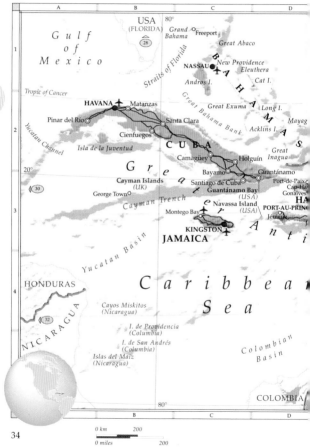

Gulf of Mexico

USA (FLORIDA)

Grand Bahama   Freeport
Great Abaco

NASSAU   New Providence
Eleuthera
Andros I.   Cat I.

Tropic of Cancer

HAVANA   Matanzas
Pinar del Rio
Santa Clara
Cienfuegos
CUBA
Isla de la Juventud
Camagüey   Holguín

Great Bahama Bank
Great Exuma   Long I.   Mayag
Acklins I.

Great Inagua

Straits of Florida

Yucatán Channel

Cayman Islands (UK)
George Town

Cayman Trench

Bayamo   Guantánamo
Santiago de Cuba   Port-de-Paix
Guantánamo Bay (USA)   Cap-Ha
Gonaïves
HA
PORT-AU-PRINC
Jérémie

Montego Bay
Navassa Island (USA)
KINGSTON
JAMAICA

Anti

HONDURAS

NICARAGUA

Yucatan Basin

Caribbean Sea

Cayos Miskitos (Nicaragua)

I. de Providencia (Columbia)
I. de San Andrés (Columbia)
Islas del Maíz (Nicaragua)

Colombian Basin

COLOMBIA

| 0 km | 200 |
| 0 miles | 200 |

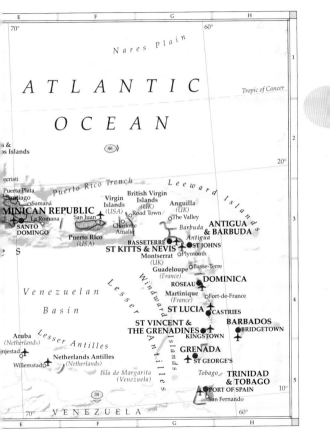

CONTINENTAL SOUTH AMERICA

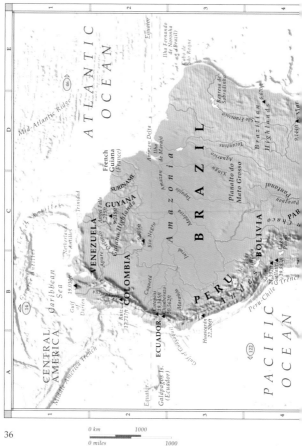

0 km 1000

0 miles 1000

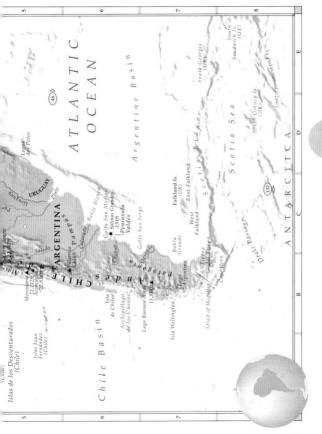

NORTHERN SOUTH AMERICA

0 km   200

0 miles   200

PERU, BOLIVIA & NORTH BRAZIL

0 km 400

0 miles 400

PARAGUAY, URUGUAY & SOUTH BRAZ

0 km   200

0 miles   200

CHILE & ARGENTINA

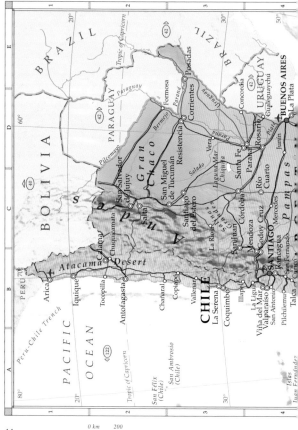

0 km   200

0 miles   200

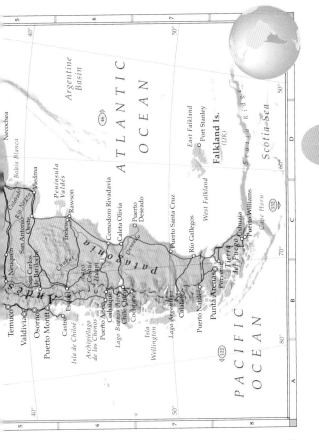

Necochea

Argentine Basin

Bahía Blanca

Colorado

Río Negro

Viedma

San Antonio Oeste

Península Valdés

A T L A N T I C   O C E A N

Rawson

Trelew

46

East Falkland

Port Stanley

Falkland Is.
(UK)

West Falkland

Comodoro Rivadavia

Caleta Olivia

Puerto Deseado

Chubut

Deseado

Puerto Santa Cruz

Río Gallegos

Neuquén

San Carlos de Bariloche

Temuco

Valdivia

Osorno

Puerto Montt

Castro

Isla de Chiloé

Archipiélago de los Chonos

Puerto Aisén

Coihaique

Chile Chico

Lago Buenos Aires

Cochrane

Isla Wellington

Lago Argentino

Puerto Natales

Calafate

Punta Arenas

Porvenir

Tierra del Fuego

Ushuaia

Puerto Williams

Cape Horn

Scotia Ridge

Scotia Sea

Esquel

Bariloche

Lago Colhué Huapi

P a t a g o n i a

A n d e s

P A C I F I C   O C E A N

122

135

45

THE ATLANTIC OCEAN

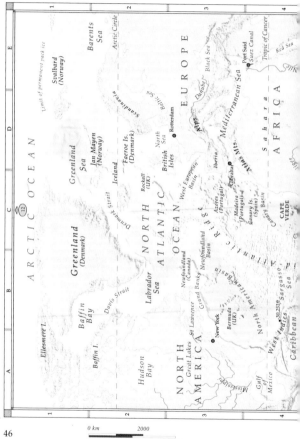

ARCTIC OCEAN

Barents
Sea

Arctic Circle

Spitsbergen
(Norway)

Limit of permanent pack ice

EUROPE

Black Sea

Port Said
Suez Canal

Tropic of Cancer

Red Sea

Greenland
Sea

Jan Mayen
(Norway)

Scandinavia

Baltic Sea

North Sea

Alps

Mediterranean Sea

Sahara

AFRICA

Ellesmere I.

Greenland
(Denmark)

Faeroe Is.
(Denmark)

Iceland

British
Isles

Rotterdam

Atlas Mts.

Danube

Baffin
Bay

Denmark Strait

Rockall
(UK)

West European
Basin

Iberia

Gibraltar

Madeira
(Portugal)

Azores
(Portugal)

Atlantic Ridge

Baffin I.

Davis Strait

Labrador
Sea

NORTH
ATLANTIC
OCEAN

Newfoundland
(Canada)

Newfoundland
Basin

CAPE
VERDE

Canary Is.
(Spain)

Canary Basin

Hudson
Bay

Great Lakes

St Lawrence

Grand Banks

New York

Bermuda
(UK)

North
American Basin

30,251 ft

Sargasso
Sea

West Indies

NORTH
AMERICA

Gulf of
Mexico

Mississippi

North

Caribbean

0 km   2000

0 miles   2000

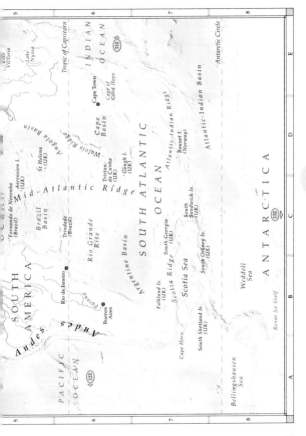

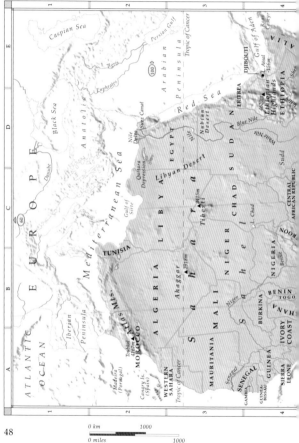

0 km   1000

0 miles   1000

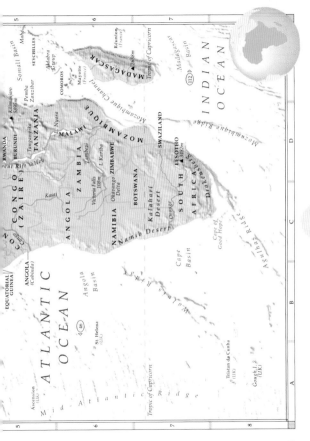

SPAIN

72

ATLANTIC

OCEAN

46

Madeira
(Portugal)

Tanger
Ceuta
(Spain)
Tétouan
Melilla
(Spain)

Mostaganem Blid
Oran

ALGIE

Kénitra
RABAT
Casablanca
Khouribga
Safi
Beni
Mellal
Essaouira

Fès
Tlemcen
Oujda

Meknès

Sidi
Bel Abbe

Tia

Lagho

Atlas Mountai

MOROCCO

Marrakech
Agadir

Er Rachidia
Figuig
Béchar

Ghar

Canary Islands
(Spain)
La Palma
Tenerife

Lanzarote

30°

Gran
Canaria

Fuerte-
ventura

Grand Erg
Occidenta

Tan-Tan

LAÂYOUNE

Semara

Tindouf

A L G E R

In S

3

WESTERN
SAHARA
(occupied by Morocco)

Reggane

Ad Dakhla

Tropic of Cancer

S

a

Guerguerat

20°

52

MAURITANIA

M A L I

52

10°

0°

0 km   400

0 miles   400

Tropic of Cancer

ATLANTIC
OCEAN

20°

WESTERN
SAHARA
(occupied by Morocco)

Zouérat

S

Râs
Nouâdhibou

Nouâdhibou

Atâr

MAURITANIA

NOUAKCHOTT

L. Rkîz
Rosso   Aleg   Kiffa

Saint-Louis   Senegal   Kaédi

Nioro

CAPE VERDE

PRAIA

DAKAR   Thiès   Diourbel

Kaolack   SENEGAL   Kayes

GAMBIA   Georgetown

BANJUL   Kolda

Ziguinchor

BISSAU   Bafatá

GUINEA-BISSAU

Labé   Siguiri   Bougouni   Sik

GUINEA

Kindia   Kankan   Kor

CONAKRY   Odienné   IVO

COA

FREETOWN   Makeni   Boua

Bo   Nzérékoré   Man   Dal

SIERRA LEONE   Kénema

Tubmanburg   YAMOUSSOUKR

MONROVIA   Zwedru   Buya

Buchanan   Gagnoa

LIBERIA

Harper

Ségou

BAMA

ATLANTIC
OCEAN

20°

10°

0 km   250

0 miles   250

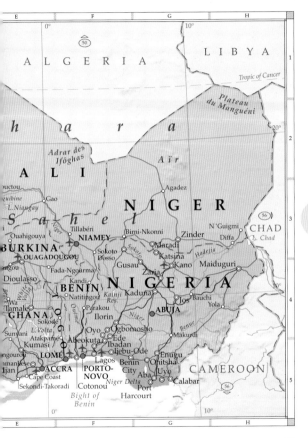

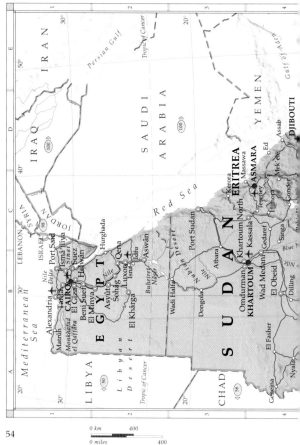

0 km 400

0 miles 400

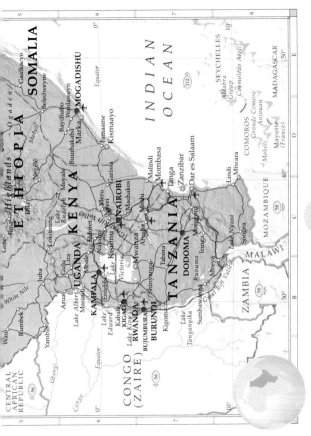

CENTRAL AFRICA

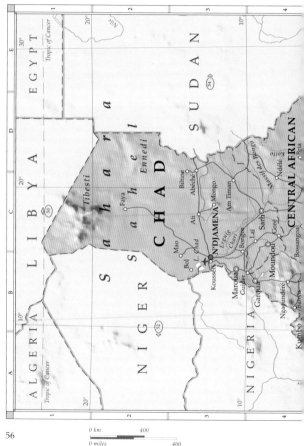

0 km   400

0 miles   400

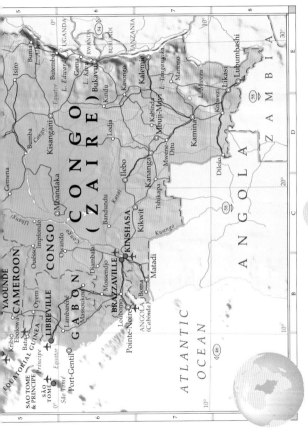

0 km   400

0 miles   400

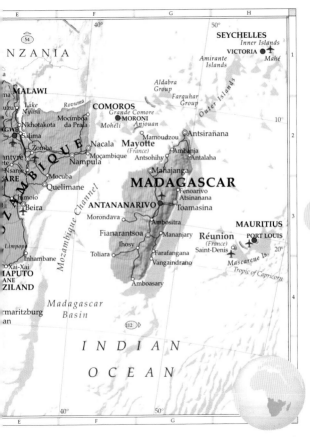

CONTINENTAL EUROPE

ARCTIC OCEAN

Norwegian Basin

Arctic Circle

Norwegian Sea

ICELAND

Faeroe-Iceland Ridge

Faeroe Islands (Denmark)

Shetland Is.

8,101ft▲

NORWAY

Orkney Is.

SWE

Outer Hebrides

North Sea

DENMARK

ATLANTIC

UNITED KINGDOM

IRELAND

NETHERLANDS

Elbe

GERMAN

OCEAN

Thames

BELGIUM

Rhine

LUX.

English Channel

Seine

FRANCE

Meuse

Loire

AU

Biscay Plain

6,188ft▲

Massif Central

Mont Blanc
15,771ft

SWITZ.

LIECH

SLO

ITALY

SAN MARINO

Bay of Biscay

Garonne

11,168ft▲

Pyrenees

MONACO

C. Finisterre

ANDORRA

Corsica

VATICAN CITY

PORTUGAL

SPAIN

Balearic Is.

Sardinia

Tyrrh.
Sea

Guadalquivir

Mulhacén

C. St Vincent

Mediterranean Sea

Gibraltar (UK)

AFRICA

MAL

0 km   600

0 miles   600

THE NORTH ATLANTIC

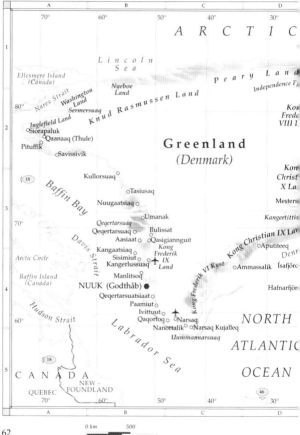

0 km   500

0 miles   500

O C E A N

_andel
Sea_

_Greenland
Sea_

Danmarkshavn

Svalbard
(Norway) Nordaustlandet 80°

Spitsbergen Pyramiden

Barentsburg ○ ○Longyearbyen

Edgeøya

Greenland Basin

neborg

Mohns Ridge

rtoormiit

Jan Mayen
(Norway)

North Cape

70°

_Norwegian
Sea_

Arctic Circle

○Húsavík
yri ○Seydhisfjördhur
JAVIK ○
_ss_ Djúpivogur

Faeroe Islands
(Denmark)

○Tórshavn

CELAND

64

NORWAY

60°

FINLAND

_Shetland
(UK)_

SWEDEN

ESTONIA

le-Thomson Ridge

_Orkney
(UK)_

LATVIA

_Hebrides
(UK)_

(68)

DENMARK

(66)

LITH.

UNITED
KINGDOM

IRELAND 10°

NETH. GERMANY POLAND
0° 10°

SCANDINAVIA & FINLAND

ARCTIC OCEAN

Barents Sea

RUSSIAN FEDERATION

Norwegian Sea

North Cape

Arctic Circle

Vardø
Kirkenes
Sodankylä
Hammerfest
Kemijärvi
Rovaniemi
Tornio
Kemi
Oulu
Tromsø
Gällivare
Kiruna
Luleå
Piteå
Skellefteå
Harstad
Narvik
Lofoten
Bodø
Mo
Ångermanälven
Kuusamo

FINLAND

0 km   150
0 miles   150

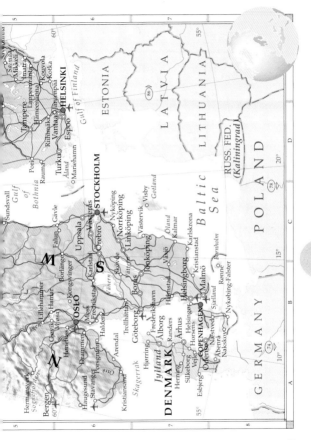

THE LOW COUNTRIES

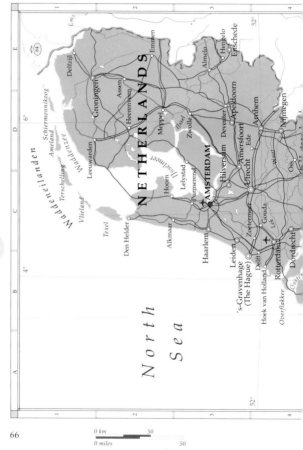

THE BRITISH ISLES

0 km   100

0 miles   100

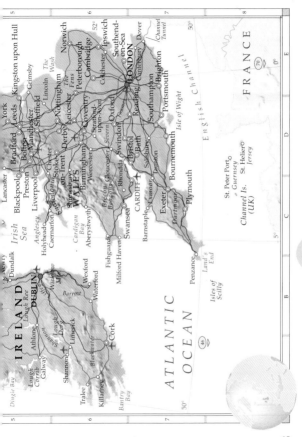

Administrative border

FRANCE & ANDORRA

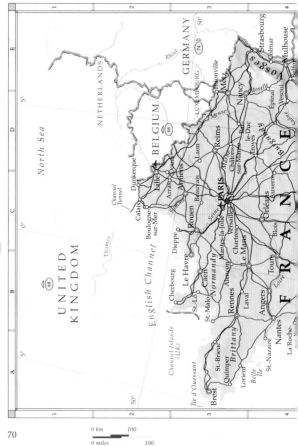

0 km   100

0 miles   100

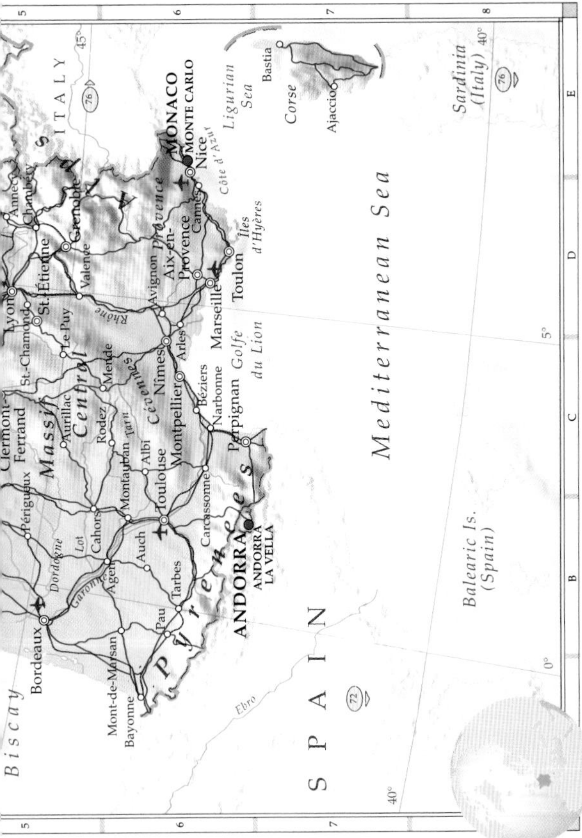

Biscay

Bordeaux

Mont-de-Marsan
Bayonne
Pau
Tarbes
Agen
Auch
Cahors
Montauban
Toulouse
Albi
Carcassonne

ANDORRA
ANDORRA
LA VELLA

Pyrenees

SPAIN

Dordogne
Garonne
Lot

Périgueux

Clermont-
Ferrand
Aurillac
Rodez
Mende

Massif
Central

Cévennes

Béziers
Narbonne
Perpignan

Montpellier
Nîmes
Arles

Marseille
Toulon

Golfe
du Lion

Mediterranean Sea

Balearic Is.
(Spain)

Ebro

40°

Annecy
Chambéry
Lyon
St-Étienne
St-Chamond
Le Puy
Valence

Grenoble

Provence

Avignon
Aix-en-
Provence
Cannes
Nice

MONACO
MONTE CARLO

Côte d'Azur

Îles
d'Hyères

Rhône

ITALY

Ligurian
Sea

Corse
Bastia
Ajaccio

Sardinia
(Italy) 40°

45°

40°

5°

0°

76
72
76

5 6 7 8

71

SPAIN & PORTUGAL

0 km   100

0 miles   100

GERMANY, SWITZERLAND & AUSTR

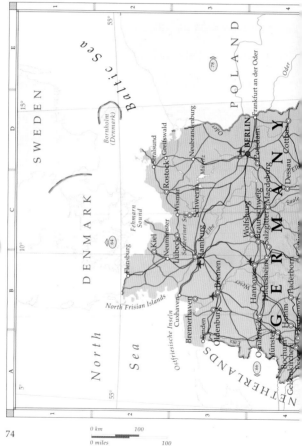

0 km 100

0 miles 100

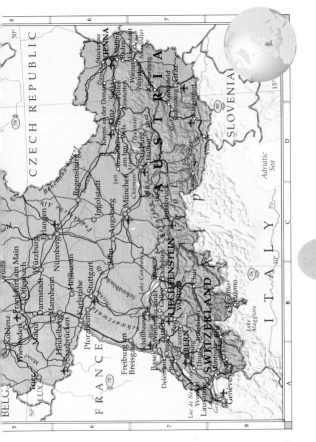

ITALY & MALTA

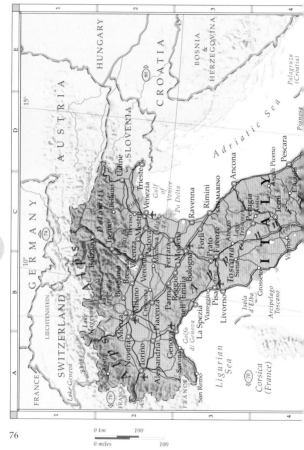

0 km   100

0 miles   100

CENTRAL EUROPE

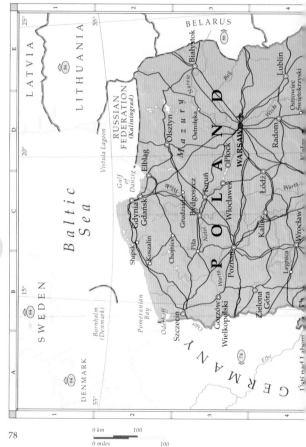

0 km   100

0 miles   100

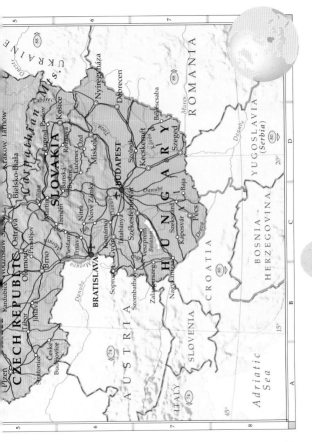

THE WESTERN BALKANS

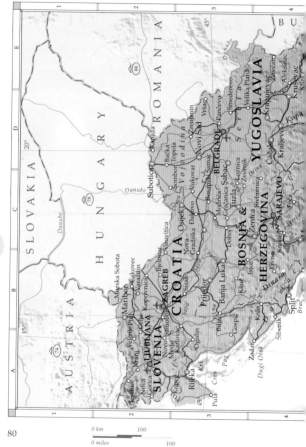

0 km   100

0 miles   100

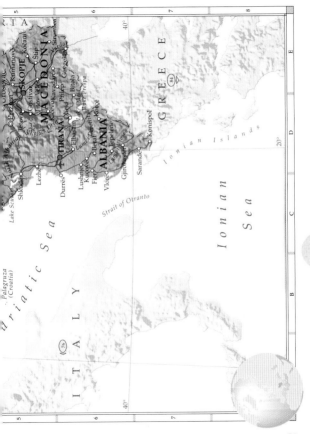

THE MEDITERRANEAN

ATLANTIC

OCEAN

Thames

English Channel

Seine

Rhine

E

Danube

Loire

Bay
of
Biscay

Dordogne

Massif
Central

L. Geneva
Mt. Blanc
15,772ft

Rhône

Alps Alp

Garonne

Marseille

Genoa

Apennin

Po

C. Finisterre

Pyrenees
11,168ft

Golfe
du
Lion

Livorno

Ebro

Corsica

Iberian

Barcelona

Valencia

Sardinia

Na

Peninsula

Balearic Is.

Tagus

Guadalquivir

C. St Vincent

11,168ft

Algiers

Med

Tell Atlas

Tunis

Tyrrh
Se

Gibraltar

Strait of Gibraltar

Oran

Rif

638ft

Sfax

Atlas Mountains

Chott el Jerid

Tripo

46

13,665ft

Grand Erg
Occidental

Canary Is.
(Spain)

Grand Erg
Oriental

A F R I

48

S a h a

0 km   400

0 miles   400

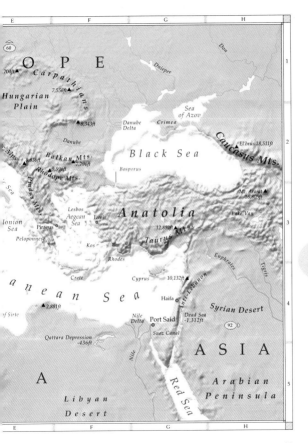

E F G H

60

704ft▲ *Carpathians*

Hungarian Plain

7,556ft▲

8,343ft▲

Danube

Dnieper

Sea of Azov

Danube Delta

Crimea

Black Sea

Caucasus Mts.

El'brus 18,511ft

Alps

8,836ft▲ *Balkan* Mts.

9,596ft▲ 7,796ft▲

Rhodope Mts.

Pindus Mts.

Sea

Bosporus

Anatolia

Mt. Ararat ▲ 16,805ft

Lesbos

Aegean Sea

İzmir

12,852ft▲ *Taurus* Mts.

Lake Van

Ionian Sea

Piraeus

Peloponnese

Kos

Rhodes

Crete

Cyprus

10,132ft▲

Euphrates

Tigris

Anti-Lebanon

ean Sea

Haifa

Dead Sea -1,312ft

Syrian Desert

of Sirte

▲ 2,881ft

Nile Delta

Port Said

92

Suez Canal

ASIA

Qattara Depression -436ft

A

Libyan Desert

Nile

Red Sea

Arabian Peninsula

E F G H

1

2

3

4

5

BULGARIA & GREECE

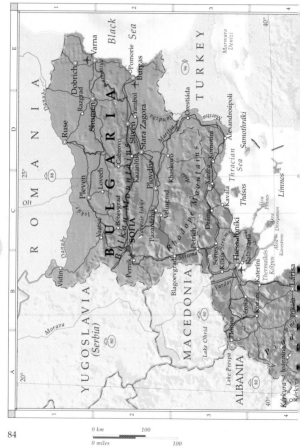

0 km 100

0 miles 100

Aegean
Sea

Chíos   Chíos

Sámos

Ikaría

D o d e k á n i s o s

Kos

Ródos
Ródos

Kárpathos

Tínos   Mýkonos

Ándros

K y k l á d e s

Náxos   Amorgós   Astypálaia

Páros

Íos

Kéa

Thíra

Sea of Crete

Iráklio

Milos

Mírtóo Pélagos

Chaniá

Kríti

Mediterranean Sea

Chalkída
ATHENS
Acharnés
Peiraiás
Dírfiga
Korínthou

Levídia

Agrínio

Kerkínia

Pátra
Korinthiakós Kólpos
Korinthos

Árgoli

P e l o p ó n n i s o s

Kalámata

Spárti

Kýthira

Iónioi Nísoi

Ionian
Sea

Zákynthos

Kefllínia

L I B Y A

THE BALTIC STATES & BELARUS

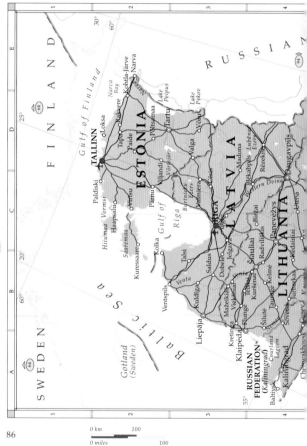

0 km   100

0 miles   100

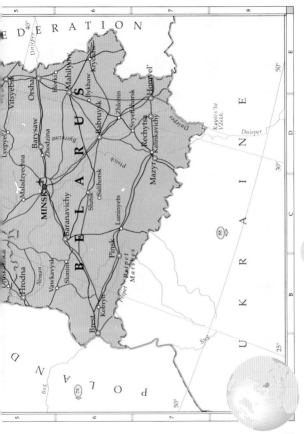

UKRAINE, MOLDOVA & ROMANIA

0 km   100

0 miles   100

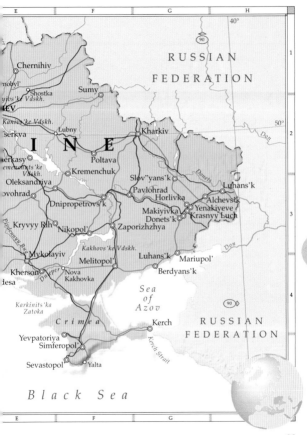

0 km 400

0 miles 400

CONTINENTAL NORTH & WEST AS

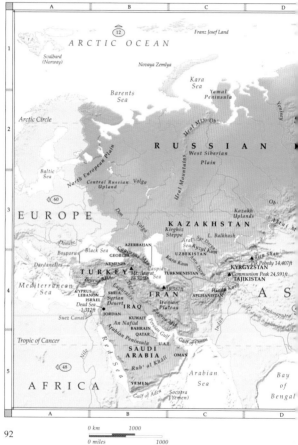

ARCTIC OCEAN

Franz Josef Land

Svalbard
(Norway)

Novaya Zemlya

Kara
Sea

Yamal
Peninsula

Barents
Sea

Arctic Circle

R U S S I A N

West Siberian
Plain

Ob'

North European Plain

Baltic
Sea

Central Russian
Upland

Volga

Ural Mountains

EUROPE

Don

Volga

KAZAKHSTAN

Kazakh
Uplands

Altai M

Kirghiz
Steppe

Aral
Sea

L. Balkhash

Ob'

Danube

Black Sea

AZERBAIJAN

Caucasus Mts

GEORGIA

ARMENIA

Syr Darya

Kyzyl Kum

Tien Shan

Bosporus

Dardanelles

T U R K E Y

Mt. Ararat
16,805ft

Caspian
Sea

UZBEKISTAN

Kara Kum

Amu Darya

KYRGYZSTAN
Pik Pobedy 14,407ft

TURKMENISTAN

Communism Peak 24,591ft
TAJIKISTAN

Mediterranean
Sea

CYPRUS
LEBANON
ISRAEL

18,387ft

Euphrates

I R A N

AFGHANISTAN

Hindu Kush

A S

SYRIA

Dead Sea
-1,312ft

Syrian
Desert

Tigris

Iranian
Plateau

Indus

Brahmaputra

Suez Canal

JORDAN

IRAQ

Zagros Mts

Tropic of Cancer

KUWAIT

An Nafud

BAHRAIN

Persian Gulf

Gulf of Oman

Nile

QATAR

U.A.E.

Arabian Peninsula

SAUDI
ARABIA

OMAN

AFRICA

Red Sea

Rub' al Khali

Arabian
Sea

Bay
of
Bengal

YEMEN

Gulf of Aden

Socotra
(Yemen)

0 km   1000

0 miles   1000

ARCTIC OCEAN

New Siberian Islands

Limit of permanent pack-ice

Laptev Sea

East Siberian Sea

Wrangel I.

Chukchi Sea

Arctic Circle

Bering Strait

a Zemlya

yr sula

d Siberian ateau

e r i a

E R A T I O N

Pri Verhoyansk Range

Lena

Cherskiy Range

Kolyma Range

Bering Sea

Kamchatka
▲4750m

Stanovoy Range

Dzhugdzhur Range

Sea of Okhotsk

Sakhalin

Aleutian Islands (USA)

L. Baikal

Amur

Sikhote-Alin Range

Sea of Japan

Hokkaidō

Honshū

PACIFIC OCEAN

Kyūshū

ver

Yangtze

Taiwan

Hawaiian Is. (USA)

Tropic of Cancer

Hainan Dao

South China Sea

Luzon

Northern Marianas (USA)

Mariana Trench

Guam (USA)

RUSSIA & KAZAKHSTAN

DENMARK

NORWAY

SWEDEN

RUSSIAN
FEDERATION
(Kaliningrad)

POLAND

FINLAND

⊙Murmansk

Barents Sea

ARCTIC

Novaya Zemlya

Karskoye Mo

LAT⊙EST.

LITH.

Pskov⊙

⊙St Petersburg

⊙Arkhangel'sk

BELARUS

Novgorod⊙

Cherepovets⊙

⊙Vologda

MOSCOW

Bryansk⊙

Tula⊙

⊙Yaroslavl'

⊙Vorkuta

Salekhard

⊙Syktyvkar

Nakhodkao

No

UKRAINE

Ryazan⊙

Voronezh⊙

Nizhniy
Novgorod⊙

Kazan⊙

⊙Kirov

Ural Mountains

Ob'

Rostov-
na-Donu⊙

Izhevsk⊙

⊙Perm'

⊙Serov

*West Siberian
Plain*

R U

⊙Volgograd

Sochi⊙

Samara⊙

⊙Ufa

⊙Yekaterinburg

Nizhnevarto

F E D

Stavropol⊙

Nal'chik⊙

Ural'sk⊙

⊙Orenburg

Chelyabinsk⊙

GEORGIA

Volga

Ural

⊙Orsk

Rudnyy⊙

⊙Kustanay

Petropavlovsk⊙

Krasno

Groznyy⊙

⊙Kokchetav

Omsk⊙

Tomsk⊙

Makhachkala⊙

Kirghiz Steppe

⊙Novosibirsk

Aktau⊙

K A Z A K H S T A N

⊙Akmola

Pavlodar⊙

Kemer

Barnaul⊙

Novokuzn

Caspian Sea

*Aral
Sea*

Zhezkazgan⊙

⊙Karaganda

Semipalatins

Ust'-
Kamenogo

Kzyl-Orda⊙

⊙Balkhash

*Ozero
Balkhash*

TURKMENISTAN

UZBEKISTAN

Shymkent⊙

Zhambyl⊙

Taldy-Kurgan⊙

IRAN

Kapshagay⊙

ALMA-ATA

CHINA

KYRGYZSTAN

0 km   500

0 miles   500

TURKEY, CYPRUS & THE CAUCASUS

0 km   200

0 miles   200

■ ■ ■ *Cyprus - 1974 ceasefire line*

THE NEAR EAST

0 km   100

0 miles   100

SAUDI ARABIA

100

OCCUPIED TERRITORIES

The West Bank, Gaza Strip and Golan Heights
have been occupied by Israel since the Six Day
War in 1967.

Palestinians gained home rule of the Gaza Strip
and Jericho in 1994.

Irbid

Az Zarqā

AMMAN

Madaba

As Salt

West Bank

Jordan

Tel Aviv-Yafo
Holon

ISRAEL

Bethlehem

JERUSALEM

JORDAN

Al Karak

At Tafilah

Ma'ān

Gaza Strip

Gaza Strip

Be'ér Sheva'

Ha Negev

Petra

Elat Al 'Aqabah

EGYPT

Gulf of Aqaba

Red Sea

Gulf of Suez

54

30°

35°

30°

THE MIDDLE EAST

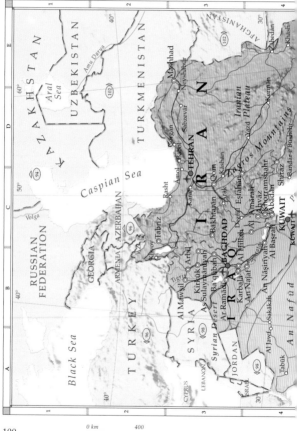

0 km   400

0 miles   400

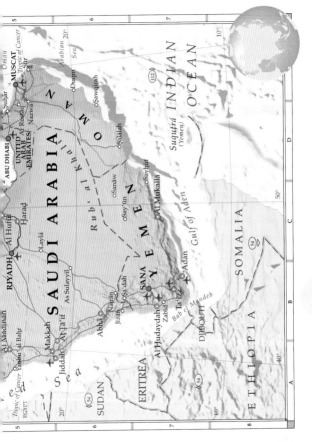

CENTRAL ASIA

0 km   200

0 miles   200

Aksai Chin
Occupied by China,
claimed by India.

Jammu & Kashmir
A "line of control" was agreed
between India and Pakistan in
1972

Demchok/Dêmqog
Claimed by India
and China.

EAST & SOUTH ASIA

A
B
C
D

Lake Baikal

92

ASIA

Aral Sea

Altai Mountains
4362m
MONGOLIA

Caspian Sea

Tien Shan
7439m
Turpan Depression
-154m
Takla Makan

Gobi

Hindu Kush

Altun Mts.

Iranian Plateau

K2
8582m

Kunlun Mts.

C H I N A

Plateau of Tibet

Great of Ch

PAKISTAN

Himalayas

BHUTAN

Indus

Thar Desert

NEPAL

Mt Everest
8848m
Ganges Plain

Ganges

Yangtze

Tropic of Cancer

BANGLADESH

INDIA

Ganges Delta

MYANMAR

Arabian Peninsula

Arabian Sea

Indus Delta

Godavari

Deccan

Western Ghats

Bay of Bengal

Haine
Dae

Irrawaddy

Mekong

VIETN

THAILAND

LAOS

Lakshadweep (India)

Eastern Ghats

Andaman Is. (India)

Andaman Sea

Gulf of Thailand

Sou
Chi
Se

MALDIVES

SRI LANKA

Nicobar Is. (India)

CAMBO

BRUN

MALAYSIA

Equator

48

SINGAPORE

Str of Malacca

3800m

Borr

Sumatra

I N D

INDIAN OCEAN

112

Krakatau
813m

Java

Java Sea

Sunda Trench

Bal

A
B
C
D

0 km   1000

0 miles   1000

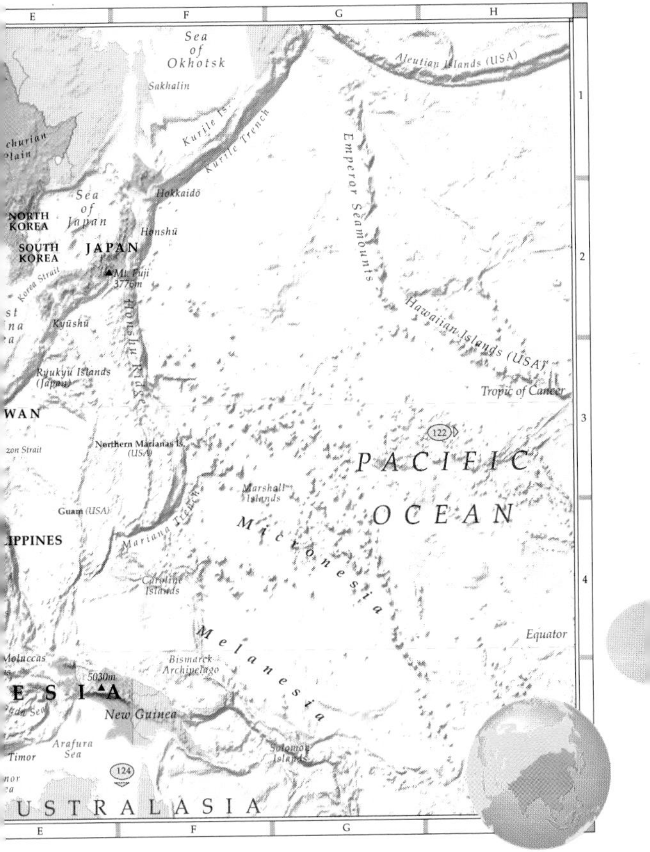

E   F   G   H

Sea of Okhotsk

Sakhalin

Aleutian Islands (USA)

Kurile Is.

Kurile Trench

Emperor Seamounts

NORTH KOREA

Sea of Japan

Hokkaidō

SOUTH KOREA

Honshū

Korea Strait

JAPAN

Mt. Fuji
3776m

Kyūshū

Hawaiian Islands (USA)

Ryukyu Islands
(Japan)

Tropic of Cancer

TAIWAN

zon Strait

Northern Marianas Is.
(USA)

(122)

PACIFIC

PPINES

Micronesia

Marshall Islands

OCEAN

Guam (USA)

Mariana Trench

Caroline Islands

Melanesia

Equator

Moluccas

Bismarck Archipelago

5030m

da Sea

ESIA

New Guinea

Timor

Arafura Sea

(124)

Solomon Islands

nor a

USTRALASIA

E   F   G

WESTERN CHINA & MONGOLIA

RUSSIAN F

KAZAKHSTAN

Lake
Balkhash

KYRGYZSTAN

Altay
Hovd
Ulaangom

Hövsgöl
Nuur
Hyargas
Nuur
Altay

M O

Karamay
Dzungaria
Yining
Kuytun
ÜRÜMQI
Irtysh

Tsetserle

G

Tien Shan
Korla
Hami

Kashi
XINJIANG
Tarim He

Tarim Pendi
Taklimakan
Shamo

Lop Nur

Qilian Shan

Hotan
Altun Shan

Kunlun Shan
Golmud
Qing

PAKISTAN
Aksai Chin
Occupied by
China, claimed
by India.
Denchok/Demqog
Claimed by
India and China

C
Qing-Zang
Gaoyuan

Tongtian He

H

Yushu

Gar
T I B E T
Tanggula Shan
Saluu

INDIA
Tangra Yumco
Siling
Co
Nagqu
Qando

Xigaze
Brahmaputra
LHASA

Himalayas

Yamuna
NEPAL
BHUTAN
INDIA

MYANMAR

0 km   400

0 miles   400

Great Wall of China

EASTERN CHINA & KOREA

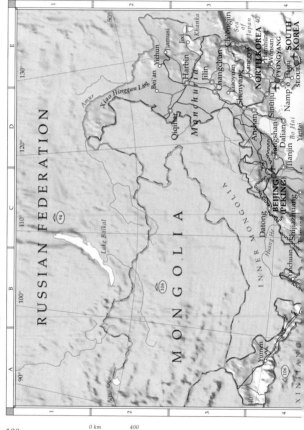

0 km   400

0 miles   400

JAPAN

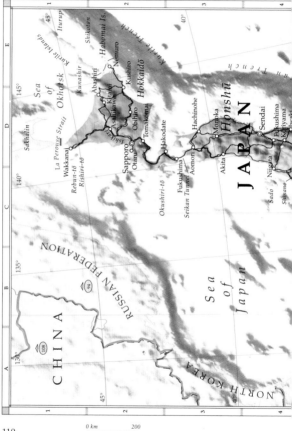

0 km   200

0 miles   200

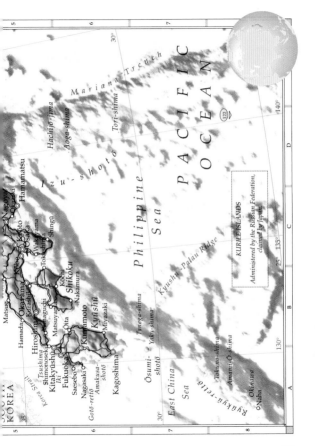

PACIFIC
OCEAN

Mariana Trench

Hachijō-jima

Aoga-shima

Tori-shima

Izu-shotō

Philippine

Sea

Kyushu-Palau Ridge

KURILE ISLANDS
Administered by the Russian Federation,
claimed by Japan.

Matsue

Okayama

Kobe

Kyōto

Wakayama

Osaka

Tokushima

Shingū

Nagoya

Hamamatsu

Shizuoka

Kōchi

Shikoku

Nakamura

Hamada

Hiroshima

Yamaguchi

Matsuyama

Ōita

Tanega-shima

Tsushima

Shimonoseki

Kitakyūshū

Fukuoka

Yaku-shima

Iki

Saesebo

Nagasaki

Kumamoto

Kyūshū

Miyazaki

Gotō-rettō

Amakusa-
shotō

Kagoshima

Ōsumi-
shotō

Tokuno-shima

Amami-Ō-shima

East China

Sea

Ryūkyū-rettō

Okinawa

Naha

Korea Strait

KOREA

35°

30°

25°

30°

130°

135°

140°

THE INDIAN OCEAN

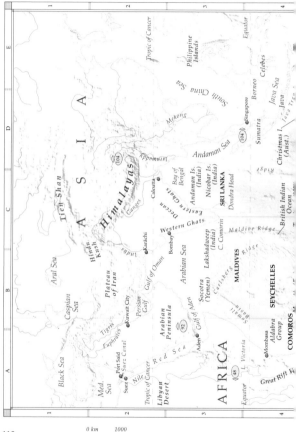

ASIA

AFRICA

Tien Shan

Himalayas

Hindu Kush

Plateau of Iran

Deccan

Western Ghats

Eastern Ghats

Libyan Desert

Arabian Peninsula

Aral Sea

Caspian Sea

Black Sea

Med. Sea

Philippine Islands

South China Sea

Celebes

Borneo

Java Sea

Java

Sumatra

Singapore

Christmas I. (Aust.)

Java Trench

Ninety East Ridge

Mekong

Andaman Sea

Bay of Bengal

Brahmaputra

Ganges

Calcutta

Indus

Karachi

Bombay

Andaman Is. (India)

Nicobar Is. (India)

SRI LANKA

Dondra Head

Lakshadweep (India)

C. Comorin

Arabian Sea

Gulf of Oman

Persian Gulf

Kuwait City

Tigris

Euphrates

Nile

Suez Canal

Port Said

Suez

Red Sea

Gulf of Aden

Aden

Socotra (Yemen)

Maldive Ridge

MALDIVES

Carlsberg Ridge

British Indian Ocean Territory

SEYCHELLES

COMOROS

Aldabra Group

Mombasa

L. Victoria

Great Rift Va

Equator

Tropic of Cancer

Tropic of Cancer

104

104

92

48

0 km   1000

0 miles   1000

AUSTRALIA

Fremantle
Cape Leeuwin
Nullarbor Plain

Southeast Indian Ridge

South Australian Basin

Broken Ridge

INDIAN OCEAN

Indian Ridge

Mozambique Plateau

MADAGASCAR
Faratanjana
Madagascar Basin

Southwest Indian Ridge

Madagascar Ridge

Prince Edward Is. (SA)

Crozet Is. (Fr.)

Crozet Basin

Kerguelen (Fr.)
Heard I. (Aust.)
Macdonald Is. (Aust.)
Kerguelen Plateau

South Indian Basin

Wilkes Land

ANTARCTICA

Amery Ice Shelf

Queen Maud Land

Atlantic-Indian Basin

Durban
Drakensberg
Tropic of Capricorn

NORTH INDIA, PAKISTAN & BANGLADE

0 km   200

0 miles   200

SOUTHERN INDIA

Arabian

Sea

Arabian Basin

70°

Thane   Nānded
Bombay
Pune   Nizāmābā
                        Dec
        Solāpur
                        Hydera
              Krishna
        IND
Belgaum   *Karnātaka*
Pānāji   Hubli
Goa   Dāvangere
                Kurnool
                Bangalore
Mangalore   Mysore
                        Ta
        Amīndīvi Is.   Salem
10°   **Lakshadweep**   Calicut   N
            (India)   Coimbator   Tiru
        Kavaratti I.   Ernākulam
                Kalpeni I.   Cochin
                        Kerala   Mad
                        Dham
        Minicoy I.   Trivandrum
                        Nāgercoil

⊲ 112

Thiladhunmathi
Atoll

MALDIVES
            MALE'

Kolhumadulu Atoll   *Maldive Ridge*

Equator   **IN**

Huvadhu Atoll

70°

0 km   300
0 miles   300

MAINLAND SOUTHEAST ASIA

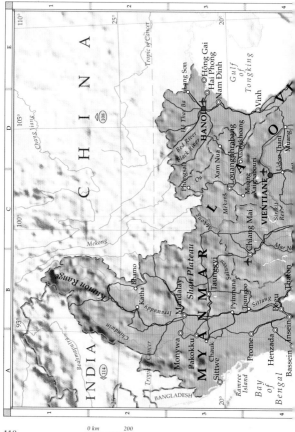

0 km   200

0 miles   200

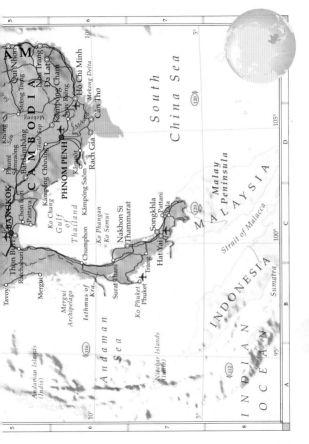

MARITIME SOUTHEAST ASIA

0 km 400

0 miles 400

The Pacific Ocean

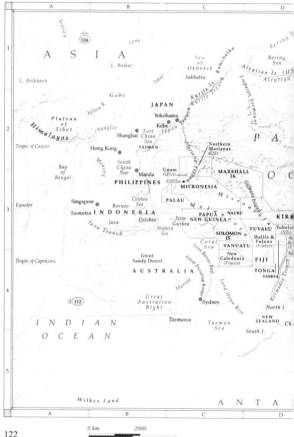

A S I A

Yenisey

104

Lena

L. Baikal

Bering

Bering Sea

Aleutian Is. (USA)

L. Balkhash

Amur

Sea of Okhotsk

Sakhalin

Kamchatka

Aleutian

Gobi

Yellow R.

Kurile Is.

Emperor Seamounts

JAPAN

Kurile Trench

Plateau of Tibet

Himalayas

Yangtze

Shanghai

East China Sea

Yokohama

Kōbe

Japan

P A

Tropic of Cancer

Hong Kong

South China Sea

Manila

TAIWAN

Guam (USA)

Northern Marianas (US)

MARSHALL IS.

O

Mariana Trench

Bay of Bengal

Mekong

PHILIPPINES

–1022m

MICRONESIA

Gilbert Islands

Singapore

Celebes Sea

PALAU

Micro

Equator

Sumatra

Borneo

I N D O N E S I A

Celebes

Mel

PAPUA NEW GUINEA

NAURU

KIRI

Java

Java Trench

New Guinea

SOLOMON IS.

TUVALU

Tokelau (NZ)

Arafura Sea

Wallis & Futuna (France)

Tropic of Capricorn

Great Sandy Desert

Coral Sea

VANUATU

FIJI

New Caledonia (France)

A U S T R A L I A

Great Barrier Reef

Great Dividing Range

TONGA

SAMOA

Kermadec Trench

112

Great Australian Bight

Murray

Sydney

Lord Howe Rise

North I.

I N D I A N

O C E A N

Tasmania

Tasman Sea

NEW ZEALAND

Ch

South I.

Wilkes Land

A N T A

0 km 2000

0 miles 2000

AUSTRALASIA & OCEANIA

Borneo
Celebes Sea
PALAU
MICRONE
Equator
104
M e l
A S I A
PAPUA NEW GUINEA
Celebes
Java Sea
Irian Jaya
Bismarck Archipelago
Java
Banda Sea
New Guinea
New Britain
Mt. Wilhelm 4509m
Flores
Arafura Sea
Solomon Sea
Sumba
Timor
SOL
Java Trench
Bathurst I.
Melville I.
Torres Strait
Timor Sea
Arnhem Land
Gulf of Carpentaria
Coral Sea Islands (Australia)
North Australian Basin
C. Londonderry
Victoria
Cape York Peninsula
Co ral Sea
Fitzroy
Ca
Great Sandy Desert
Great Barrier Reef
Tropic of Capricorn
L. Disappointment
L. Mackay
Macdonnell Ranges
Great Dividing Range
Dirk Hartog I.
Gibson Desert
Uluru 868m (Ayer's Rock)
L. Carnegie
Fraser I.
AUSTRALIA
L. Barlee
Great Victoria Desert
Lake Eyre -16m
Perth Basin
L. Torrens
Darling
Nullarbor Plain
L. Gairdner
Flinders Range
C. Leeuwin
Great Australian Bight
Murray
▲ Mt. Kosciusko 2228m
Kangaroo I.
Cape Howe
112
Bass Strait
Tasm
King I.
Flinders I.
Se
Tasmania
I N D I A N
O C E A N
South East Cape
Tasman Plateau
South Australian Basin

0 km   1000

0 miles   1000

MARSHALL IS.

Kingman Reef *(USA)*

Palmyra Atoll *(USA)*

Baker & Howland Is.
(USA)

Jarvis Island
(USA)

Equator

P A C I F I C

O C E A N

Gilbert Is.

K I R I B A T I

Phoenix Is.

Line Islands

Marquesas Is.

TUVALU

Tokelau
(New Zealand)

Northern
Cook Is.

SAMOA

Wallis & Futuna
(France)

Vanua Levu

American
Samoa
(USA)

Cook Islands
(New Zealand)

French Polynesia
(France)

Viti Levu

Niue
(New Zealand)

Tahiti

es Loyauté

FIJI

TONGA

Southern Cook Is.

Tropic of Capricorn

Society Islands

South Fiji
Basin

Norfolk I.
(Australia)

Kermadec
Islands
(NZ)

North Cape

Bay
of
Plenty

East Cape

PACIFIC

uth I.

NEW
ZEALAND

OCEAN

Cook Strait

ok
Chatham I.
(NZ)

Canterbury Bight

aveaux Strait

Southwest Pacific Basin

land I.

THE SOUTHWEST PACIFIC

MARSHALL ISLANDS

Micronesia

Caroline Islands

Guam — Agana
(USA)

Yap

Chuuk Is.

Pohnpei I.

PALIKIR

Kosrae

KOROR

PALAU

Equator

MICRONESIA

NAURU

PAPUA NEW GUINEA

Bismarck Archipelago New Ireland

INDONESIA

New Guinea Madang

Mendi Lae New Britain

Bougainville I.

New Georgia

Mela

PORT MORESBY

Solomon Sea

HONIARA Santa Cruz Is.

SOLOMON ISLANDS

Arafura Sea

Torres Str.

VANUATU

Arnhem Land

Gulf of Carpentaria

Coral Sea

Cooktown

NORTHERN TERRITORY

Cairns

Coral Sea Islands
(Australia)

POR

Normanton

New Caledonia
(France)

Tennant Creek

Townsville

Mount Isa Cloncurry Mackay

Nouméa

AUSTRALIA

Alice Springs Longreach Rockhampton

QUEENSLAND

Bundaberg

Great Barrier Reef

Great Dividing Range

120

128

130

0 km   400

0 miles   400

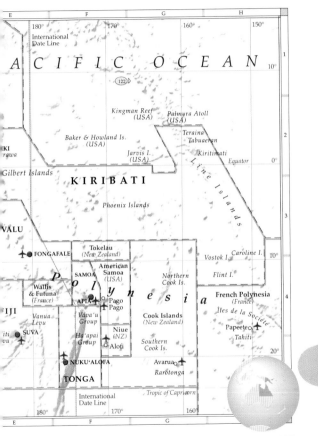

WESTERN AUSTRALIA

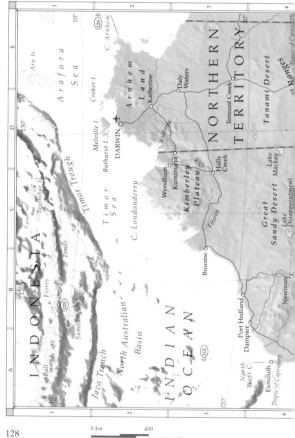

0 km   400

0 miles   400

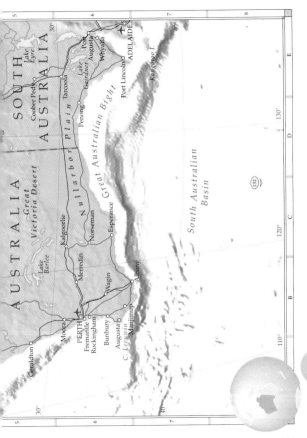

SOUTHEAST AUSTRALIA

Mount Isa
Cloncurry
Hughenden
Mackay
140°
150°
126
Tropic of Capricorn
Longreach
Diamantina
Rockhampton
Bundaberg
128
QUEENSLAND
Fraser I.
AUSTRALIA
Charleville
Roma
Miles
SOUTH
Toowoomba
BRISBANE
AUSTRALIA
Cunnamulla
Goondiwindi
Ipswich
Gold Coast
L. Eyre
Milparinka
Moree
Grafton
30°
Bourke
Armidale
Coffs Harbour
L. Torrens
L. Frome
Broken Hill
Wilcannia
Darling
NEW
Tamworth
Port Augusta
SOUTH
Dubbo
Whyalla
Ivanhoe
WALES
Orange
Newcastle
Bathurst
Port Lincoln
ADELAIDE
Mildura
Murrumbidgee
SYDNEY
Wollongong
Murray
Wagga Wagga
CANBERRA
Kangaroo I.
Keith
Albury
(AUSTRALIAN CAPITAL TERRITORY)
Bendigo
Shepparton
Mount Gambier
Ballarat
VICTORIA
Geelong
MELBOURNE
Sale
Cape Howe
40°
Bass Strait
King I.
Flinders I.
Tasman
Burnie
Devonport
Launceston
TASMANIA
Sea
HOBART
131
South East Cape
140°
150°
160°
132

0 km   400
0 miles   400

NEW ZEALAND

ANTARCTICA

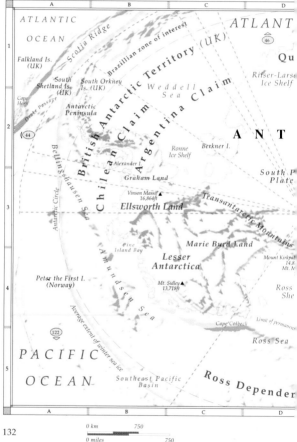

ATLANTIC
OCEAN

Scotia Ridge

ATLANT

Falkland Is.
(UK)

46

Qu

South
Shetland Is.
(UK)

South Orkney
Is. (UK)

Brazillian zone of interest

British Antarctic Territory (UK)

Ritser-Larse
Ice Shelf

Weddell
Sea

Cape
Horn

44

Drake Passage

Antarctic
Peninsula

Chilean Claim

Argentina Claim

ANT

Bellingshausen Sea

Ronne
Ice Shelf

Berkner I.

South P
Plate

Alexander I.

Graham Land

Vinson Massif ▲
16,864ft

Antarctic Circle

Ellsworth Land

Transantarctic Mountains

Pine
Island Bay

Marie Byrd Land

Mount Kirkpat
14,8
Mt. M

Peter the First I.
(Norway)

Amundsen Sea

Lesser
Antarctica

Mt. Sidley ▲
13,718ft

Ross
She

122

Average extent of winter sea ice

Cape Colbeck

Limit of permanen

Ross Sea

PACIFIC

OCEAN

Southeast Pacific
Basin

Ross Dependen

0 km   750

0 miles   750

OCEAN

Limit of permanent pack ice

Average extent of winter sea ice

Lutzow-Holm Bay

ud Land (Norway)

Enderby Land

CTICA

Cape Darnley

Lambert Glacier

Mackenzie Bay

Prydz Bay

Princess
Elizabeth Land

Greater
Antarctica

Antarctic Circle

Kerguelen
Plateau

Shackleton
Ice Shelf

Davis
Sea

Erebus
48ft

Cape Poinsett

INDIAN

▲ Mt. Shafer 11,811ft

Terre Adélie (France)

Wilkes
Land

OCEAN

34

alian Antarctic Territory

Victoria Land

Z)

Balleny Is.

Southwest
Pacific Basin

GLOSSARY OF ABBREVIATIONS

This glossary provides a comprehensive guide to the abbreviations used in this Atlas.

abbrev. abbreviation
Afgh. Afghanistan
Amh. Amharic
anc. ancient
Ar. Arabic
Arm. Armenia/Armenian
Aus. Austria
Aust. Australia
Az. Azerbaijan/Azerbaijani

Bas. Basque
Bel. Belorussian
Belg. Belgium
Bos. & Herz. Bosnia & Herzegovina
Bul. Bulgarian
Bulg. Bulgaria
Bur. Burmese

C Central
C. Cape
Cam. Cambodian
Cast. Castilian
Chin. Chinese
Cord. Cordillera (Spanish for mountain range)
Cz. Czech
Czech Rep. Czech Republic

D.C. District of Columbia
Dan. Danish
Dominican Rep. Dominican Republic

E East
Emb. Embalse
Eng. English
Est. Estonia/Estonian

Faer. Faeroese
Fin. Finnish
Flem. Flemish
Fr. France/French
ft feet

Geo. Georgia
Geor. Georgian
Ger. Germany/German
Gk. Greek

Heb. Hebrew
Hung. Hungary/Hungarian
I. Island
Ind. Indonesian
Is. Islands
It. Italian

Kaz. Kazakh
Kep. Kepulauan (Indonesian/Malay for island group)
Kir. Kirghiz
Kor. Korean
Kurd. Kurdish
Kyrgy. Kyrgyzstan

L. Lake, Lago
Lat. Latvia
Latv. Latvian
Leb. Lebanon
Liech. Liechtenstein
Lith. Lithuania/Lithuanian
Lux. Luxembourg

Mac. Macedonia
Med. Sea Mediterranean Sea
Mold. Moldova
Mt. Mount/Mountain
Mts. Mountains

N North
N. Korea North Korea
Neth. Netherlands
NW Northwest
NZ New Zealand

P. Pulau (Indonesian/Malay for island)
Peg. Pegunungan (Indonesian/Malay for mountain range)
Per. Persian
Pol. Poland/Polish
Port. Portuguese
prev. previously

R. River, Rio, Río
Res. Reservoir
Rom. Romania/Romanian
Rus. Russian
Russ. Fed. Russian Federation

S South
S. Korea South Korea
SA South Africa
SCr. Serbo-Croatian
Slvka. Slovakia

Slvna. Slovenia
Som. Somali
Sp. Spanish
St, St. Saint
Str. Strait
Swed. Swedish
Switz. Switzerland

Tajik. Tajikistan
Th. Thai
Turk. Turkish
Turkm. Turkmen
Turkmen. Turkmenistan

U.A.E. United Arab Emirates
UK United Kingdom
Ukr. Ukrainian
USA United States of America
Uzb. Uzbek
Uzbek. Uzbekistan

var. variant
Vdkhr. Vodokhranilishche (Russian for reservoir)
Vdskh. Vodoskhovyshche (Ukrainian for reservoir)
Ven. Venezuela

W West
W. Sahara Western Sahara
Wel. Welsh

Yugo. Yugoslavia

Dorling Kindersley Cartography would like to thank the following for their assistance in producing this Atlas:

James Anderson, Laura Porter, Margaret Hynes, Ruth Duxbury, Roger Bullen, Julie Phillis, Robin Giddings and Tony Chambers.

Albury Australia 130 B3

Alcácer do Sal Portugal 72 C4

Alcalá de Henares Spain 73 E3

Alchevs'k Ukraine 89 G3

Aldabra Group *Island group* Seychelles 59 G1

Aleg Mauritania 52 C3

Aleksandriya *see* Oleksandriya

Aleksandropol' *see* Gyumri

Aleksinac Yugoslavia 80 E4

Alençon France 70 B3

Alessandria Italy 76 A2

Ålesund Norway 65 A5

Aleutian Islands *Islands* Alaska, USA 16 A3

Aleutian Trench *Undersea feature* Pacific Ocean 122 D1

Alexander Island *Island* Antarctica 132 B2

Alexandretta *see* İskenderun

Alexandria Egypt 54 B1

Alexandria Louisiana, USA 28 B3

Alexandroúpoli Greece 84 D3

Al Fāshir *see* El Fasher

Alföld *Plain* Hungary 79 D7

Algarve *Region* Portugal 72 C4

Algeciras Spain 72 D5

Algeria *Country* N Africa 50-51

Alghero Italy 77 A5

Algiers *Capital of* Algeria 50 D1

Al Ḥasakah Syria 98 D2

Al Ḥillah Iraq *var.* Hilla 100 B3

Al Ḥudaydah Yemen 101 B7

Al Ḥufūf Saudi Arabia 101 C5

Alicante Spain 73 F4

Alice Springs Australia 126 A5 128 E4

Al Jawf Saudi Arabia 100 B4

Al Jazīrah *Region* Iraq/Syria 98 E2

Al Jīzah *see* El Gîza

Al Karak Jordan 99 B6

Al Khārijah *see* El Khârga

Al Khums Libya 51 F2

Al Khurṭum *see* Khartoum

Alkmaar Netherlands 66 C2

Al Kufrah Libya 51 H4

Al Lādhiqīyah Syria *Eng.* Latakia 98 B3

Allahābād India 114 C4

Allenstein *see* Olsztyn

Allentown Pennsylvania, USA 21 F4

Alma-Ata *Capital of* Kazakhstan *Rus. / Kaz.* Almaty 95 C5

Al Madīnah Saudi Arabia *Eng.* Medina 100 A5

Al Mafraq Jordan 99 B5

Almalyk Uzbekistan *Uzb.* Olmaliq 103 E2

Al Manāmah *see* Manama

Al Marj Libya 51 G2

Almaty *see* Alma-Ata

Al Mawṣil Iraq *Eng.* Mosul 100 B3

Almelo Netherlands 66 E3

Almería Spain 73 E5

Al Mukallā Yemen 101 C7

Alofi *Capital of* Niue 127 F5

Alor, Kepulauan *Island group* Indonesia 121 E5

Alps *Mountain range* C Europe 60 D4

Al Qāhirah *see* Cairo

Al Qāmishlī Syria *var.* Kamishli 98 E1

Al Qunayṭirah Syria 98 B4

Altai Mountains *Mountain Range* C Asia 106 C2

Altamura Italy 77 E5

Altay China 106 C2

Altay Mongolia 106 D2

Altun Shan *Mountain Range* China 106 B4

Alturas California, USA 24 B4

Al Wajh Saudi Arabia 100 A5

Alytus Lithuania *Pol.* Olita 87 B5

Amakusa-shotō *Island group* Japan 111 A6

Amami-Ō-shima *Island* Japan 111 A8

Amara *see* Al 'Amārah

Amarillo Texas, USA 27 E2

Amazon *River* South America 36 C2

Amazon Delta *Wetland* Brazil 36 D2

Amazonia *Region* C South America 40 C2

Ambanja Madagascar 59 G2

Ambarchik Russian Federation 95 G2

Ambato Ecuador 38 A4

Amboasary Madagascar 59 F4

Ambon Indonesia 121 F4

Ambositra Madagascar 59 G3

Ambriz Angola 58 B1

Ameland *Island* Netherlands 66 D1

American Falls Reservoir *Reservoir* Idaho, USA 24 E4

American Samoa *External territory* USA, Pacific Ocean 122 D3

Amersfoort Netherlands 66 D3

Amiens France 70 C3

Amīndīvi Islands *Island group* India 116 C2

Amirante Islands *Island group* Seychelles 59 H1

Amman *Capital of* Jordan 99 B5

Ammassalik Greenland *var.* Angmagssalik 62 C4

Ammochostos *see* Gazimağusa

Āmol Iran 100 C3

Amorgós *Island* Greece 85 D6

Amritsar India 114 D2

Amsterdam *Capital of* Netherlands 66 C3

Amstetten Austria 75 D6

Am Timan Chad 56 C3

Amu Darya *River* C Asia 102 D3

Amundsen Gulf *Sea feature* Canada 17 E2

Amundsen Sea Antarctica 132 B4

Amur *River* E Asia 93 F3 105 E1

Anadolu Dağları *see* Doğu Karadeniz Dağları

Anadyr' Russian Federation 95 H1

Anápolis Brazil 41 F4

Anatolia *Region* SE Europe 83 G3

Anchorage Alaska, USA 16 C3

Ancona Italy 76 C3

Andalucía *Region* Spain 72 D4

Andaman Islands *Island group* India 117 H2 119 H3

Andaman Sea Indian Ocean 112 D3

Andaman-Nicobar Ridge *Undersea feature* Indian Ocean 117 H3

Andes *Mountain range* South America 37 B6

Arnhem Land *Region* Australia 128 E2

Arno *River* Italy 76 B3

Ar Ramādī Iraq 100 B3

Arran *Island* Scotland, UK 68 C4

Ar Raqqah Syria 98 C2

Arras France 70 C2

Ar Riyāḍ *see* Riyadh

Ar Rustāq Oman *var.* Rostak 101 D5

Artesia New Mexico, USA 26 D3

Artigas Uruguay 42 B4

Aru, Kepulauan *Island group* Indonesia 121 G5

Arua Uganda 55 B6

Aruba *External territory* Netherlands, West Indies 35 E5

Arun *River* India/Nepal 115 F3

Arusha Tanzania 55 C7

Asad, Buḩayrat al *Reservoir* Syria 98 C2

Asadābād Afghanistan 103 E4

Asahikawa Japan 110 D2

Asamankese Ghana 53 E5

Ascension *Island* Atlantic Ocean 47 C5

Ascoli Piceno Italy 76 C4

Ashburton New Zealand 131 F4

Asheville North Carolina, USA 29 E1

Ashgabat *Capital of* Turkmenistan *prev.* Ashkhabad, Poltoratsk 102 B3

Ashkhabad *see* Ashgabat

Ash Shāriqah *see* Sharjah

Asia 92-93 104-105

Asmara *Capital of* Eritrea *Amh.* Asmera 54 C4

Asmera *see* Asmara

Assab Eritrea 54 D4

'Assal, Lac *see* Lake Assal

Assal, Lake *Lake* Djibouti *var.* Lac 'Assal 48 E4

As Salṭ Jordan *var.* Salt 99 B5

Assen Netherlands 66 E2

Assisi Italy 76 C4

As Sulaymānīyah Iraq 100 B3

As Sulayyil Saudi Arabia 101 B6

As Suwaydā' Syria 99 B5

Astoria Oregon, USA 24 A2

Astrakhan' Russian Federation 91 B7 95 A4

Astypálaia *Island* Greece 85 D6

Asunción *Capital of* Paraguay 42 B3

Aswân Egypt 54 B2

Asyût Egypt 54 B2

Atacama Desert *Desert* Chile 44 B2

Atakpamé Togo 53 F4

Atâr Mauritania 52 C2

Atbara Sudan 54 C3

Athabasca, Lake *Lake* Canada 17 F4

Athens *Capital of* Greece *Gk.* Athína, *prev.* Athínai 85 C5

Athens Georgia, USA 29 E2

Athína *see* Athens

Athínai *see* Athens

Athlone Ireland 69 B5

Ati Chad 56 C3

Atlanta Georgia, USA 28 D2

Atlantic City New Jersey, USA 21 F4

Atlantic Ocean 46-47

Atlantic-Indian Basin *Undersea feature* Indian Ocean 113 A7

Atlantic-Indian Ridge *Undersea feature* Atlantic Ocean 47 D7

Atlas Mountains *Mountain range* Morocco 50 C2

Aṭ Ṭafīlah Jordan 99 B6

Aṭ Ṭā'if Saudi Arabia 100 B6

Attapu Laos 119 E5

Attawapiskat Canada 18 C3

Attawapiskat *River* Canada 18 B3

Attersee *Lake* Austria 75 D7

Attu Island *Island* Alaska, USA 16 A2

Auburn California, USA 25 B5

Auch France 71 B6

Auckland New Zealand 131 G2

Augsburg Germany 75 C6

Augusta Italy 77 D7

Augusta Georgia, USA 29 E2

Augusta Maine, USA 20 G2

Aurillac France 71 C5

Aurora Colorado, USA 22 D4

Aurora Illinois, USA 20 B3

Aussig *see* Ústí nad Labem

Austin Texas, USA 27 G4

Australasia 124-125

Australia *Country* Pacific Ocean 126-130

Australian Antarctic Territory *Territory* Antarctica 132-133

Australian Capital Territory *Territory* Australia *abbrev.* A.C.T. 130 C3

Austria *Country* C Europe 75

Auxerre France 70 C4

Avarua *Capital of* Cook Islands 127 G5

Aveiro Portugal 72 C3

Avignon France 71 D6

Ávila Spain 72 D3

Avilés Spain 72 D1

Awbārī Libya 51 F3

Axel Heiberg Island *Island* Canada 17 F1

Axios *see* Vardar

Ayacucho Peru 40 B4

Aydarkul', Ozero *Lake* Uzbekistan 102 D2

Aydın Turkey 96 A3

Ayer's Rock *see* Uluru

'Ayn ath Tha'lab Libya 51 G3

Ayr Scotland, UK 68 C4

Ayutthaya Thailand 119 C5

Ayvalık Turkey 96 A3

A'zāz Syria 98 B2

Azerbaijan *Country* SW Asia 97 G2

Azores *Islands* Portugal, Atlantic Ocean 46 C3

Azov, Sea of Black Sea *Ukr.* Azovs'ke More, *Rus.* Azovskoye More 91 A6

Azovs'ke More *see* Azov, Sea of

Azovskoye More *see* Azov, Sea of

Azul Argentina 44 D4

Azur, Côte d' *Coastal region* France 71 E6

Az Zarqā' Jordan 99 B5

Az Zāwiyah Libya 51 F2

B

Baabda Lebanon 98 B4

Baalbek Lebanon *var.* Ba'labakk 98 B4

Bab el Mandeb *Sea feature* Djibouti/Yemen 101 B7

Baracaldo Spain 73 E1

Baranavichy Belarus *Rus.* Baranovichi, *Pol.* Baranowicze 87 C6

Baranovichi *see* Baranavichy

Baranowicze *see* Baranavichy

Barbados *Country* West Indies 35 E4

Barbuda *Island* Antigua & Barbuda 35 G3

Barcelona Spain 73 G2

Barcelona Venezuela 39 E1

Bareilly India 115 E3

Barentsburg Svalbard 63 G2

Barents Sea Arctic Ocean 64 E1

Bari Italy 77 E5

Barinas Venezuela 38 D2

Barisan, Pegunungan *Mountains* Indonesia 120 B4

Bar-le-Duc France 70 D3

Barito *River* Indonesia 120 D4

Barlee, Lake *Lake* Australia 124 B3 129 B 5

Barnaul Russian Federation 94 D4

Barnstaple England, UK 69 C7

Barquisimeto Venezuela 38 D1

Barra *Island* Scotland, UK 68 B3

Barranquilla Colombia 38 B1

Barrow *River* Ireland 69 B6

Barstow California, USA 25 C7

Bartang *River* Tajikistan 103 F3

Bartica Guyana 39 G2

Barysaw Belarus *Rus.* Borisov 87 D5

Basarabeasca Moldova 88 D4

Basel Switzerland 75 A7

Basque Provinces *Region* Spain *Sp.* País Vasco 73 E1

Basra *see* Al Baṣrah

Bassein Myanmar 118 A4

Basse-Terre *Capital of* Guadeloupe 35 G4

Basseterre *Capital of* St Kitts & Nevis 35 G3

Bass Strait *Sea feature* Australia 130 R4

Bastia Corse, France 71 E7

Bastogne Belgium 67 D7

Bata Equatorial Guinea 56 A5

Batangas Philippines 121 E1

Bătdâmbâng Cambodia 119 D5

Bath England, UK 69 D7

Bathurst Australia 130 C3

Bathurst Canada 19 F4

Bathurst Island *Island* Australia 128 D2

Bathurst Island *Island* Canada 17 F2

Batman Turkey *var.* İluh 97 F2

Batna Algeria 51 E1

Baton Rouge Louisiana, USA 28 B3

Batticaloa Sri Lanka 117 E3

Bat'umi Georgia 97 F2

Bauchi Nigeria 53 G4

Bauru Brazil 42 D2

Bavarian Alps *Mountains* Austria/Germany 75 C7

Bayamo Cuba 34 C2

Bay City Michigan, USA 20 C3

Baydhabo Somalia 55 D6

Baykal, Ozero *Lake* Russian Federation *Eng.* Lake Baikal 93 E3 95 F4

Bayonne France 71 A6

Bayramaly Turkmenistan 102 C3

Bayrūt *see* Beirut

Beaufort Sea Arctic Ocean 17 E2

Beaufort West South Africa 58 C5

Beaumont Texas, USA 27 H4

Beauvais France 70 C3

Béchar Algeria 50 D2

Be'ér Sheva' Israel 99 A6

Beijing *Capital of* China *var.* Peking 108 C4

Beira Mozambique 59 E3

Beirut *Capital of* Lebanon *var.* Beyrouth, Bayrūt 98 B4

Beja Portugal 72 C4

Béjaïa Algeria 51 E1

Bek-Budi *see* Karshi

Békéscsaba Hungary 79 D7

Belarus *Country* E Europe *var.* Belorussia 87

Belau *see* Palau

Belcher Islands *Islands* Canada 18 C2

Beledweyne Somalia 55 D5

Belém Brazil 41 F2

Belfast Northern Ireland, UK 69 B5

Belfort France 70 E4

Belgaum India 116 C1

Belgium *Country* W Europe 6

Belgorod Russian Federation 91 A5

Belgrade *Capital of* Yugoslavia *SCr.* Beograd 80 D3

Belitung, Pulau *Island* Indone 120 C4

Belize *Country* Central America 32

Belize City Belize 32 C1

Bella Unión Uruguay 42 B4

Belle Île *Island* France 70 A4

Belle Isle, Strait of *Sea feature* Canada 15 G3 19 H3

Bellevue Washington, USA 24 B2

Bellingham Washington, USA 24 B1

Bellingshausen Sea Antarctica 47 A8 132 A3

Bello Colombia 38 B2

Belluno Italy 76 C2

Bellville South Africa 58 C5

Belmopan *Capital of* Belize 32

Belo Horizonte Brazil 41 G5 43 F1

Belorussia *see* Belarus

Belostok *see* Białystok

Beloye More Arctic Ocean *Eng.* White Sea 61 F1 90 C3

Bend Oregon, USA 24 B3

Bendery *see* Tighina

Bendigo Australia 130 B4

Benevento Italy 77 D5

Bengal, Bay of *Sea feature* Ind Ocean 112 C3

Benghazi *see* Banghāzī

Bengkulu Indonesia 120 B4

Benguela Angola 58 B2

Beni *River* Bolivia 40 C4

Benidorm Spain 73 F4

Beni Mellal Morocco 50 C2

Benin *Country* N Africa *prev.* Dahomey 53

Benin, Bight of *Sea feature* W Africa 53 F5

Benin City Nigeria 53 F5

Beni Suef Egypt *var.* Banī Suwayf 54 B1

Benue *River* Cameroon/Niger 53 G4

Beograd *see* Belgrade

C

143

Cape Coast Ghana 53 E5
Cape Town South Africa 58 C5
Cape Verde Country Atlantic Ocean 52 A3
Cape Verde Basin Undersea feature Atlantic Ocean 46 C4
Cape York Peninsula Peninsula Australia 124 C2
Cap-Haïtien Haiti 34 D3
Capri, Isola di Island Italy 77 C5
Caquetá River Colombia 38 C4
CAR see Central African Republic
Caracas Capital of Venezuela 38 D1
Carazinho Brazil 42 C3
Carbondale Illinois, USA 20 B5
Carcassonne France 71 C6
Cardiff Wales, UK 69 C7
Cardigan Bay Sea feature Wales, UK 69 C6
Caribbean Sea Atlantic Ocean 34-35
Carlisle England, UK 68 D4
Carlsbad New Mexico, USA 26 D3
Carlsberg Ridge Undersea feature Indian Ocean 112 B3
Carnavon Australia 128 A4
Carnegie, Lake Lake Australia 129 C5
Carolina Brazil 41 F3
Caroline Island Island Kiribati 127 H3
Caroline Islands Island group Micronesia 126 B1
Caroní River Venezuela 39 F2
Carpathian Mountains Mountain range E Europe var. Carpathians 61 E4
Carpathians see Carpathian Mountains
Carpaţii Meridionali Mountain range Romania Eng. South Carpathians, Transylvanian Alps 88 B4
Carpentaria, Gulf of Sea feature Australia 126 A4
Carson City Nevada, USA 25 C5
Cartagena Colombia 38 B1
Cartagena Spain 73 F4
Cartago Costa Rica 33 E4
Cartwright Canada 19 G2
Carúpano Venezuela 39 E1

Casablanca Morocco 50 C2
Casa Grande Arizona, USA 26 3
Cascade Range Mountain range Canada/USA 24 B3
Cascais Portugal 72 B4
Caseyr, Raas Coastal feature Somalia 48 E4
Casper Wyoming, USA 22 C3
Caspian Sea Inland sea Asia/Europe 94 A4
Castellón de la Plana Spain 73 F3
Castelo Branco Portugal 72 C3
Castries Capital of St Lucia 35 G4
Castro Chile 45 B6
Cat Island Island Bahamas 34 D1
Catania Italy 77 D7
Catanzaro Italy 77 D6
Cauca River Colombia 38 B2
Caucasus Mountains Asia/Europe 61 G4 92 B3
Cauquenes Chile 44 B4
Caura River Venezuela 39 E2
Caviana, Ilha Island Brazil 41 F1
Cawnpore see Kānpur
Caxias do Sul Brazil 42 D4
Cayenne Capital of French Guiana 39 H3
Cayman Islands External territory UK, West Indies 34
Cayman Trench Undersea feature Caribbean Sea 34 B3
Cebu Philippines 121 E2
Cedar Rapids Iowa, USA 23 G3
Cedros, Isla Island Mexico 30 A2
Cefalù Italy 77 C7
Celebes see Sulawesi
Celebes Sea Pacific Ocean Ind. Laut Sulawesi 122 B3
Celje Slovenia 80 A2
Central African Republic Country C Africa abbrev. CAR 56-57
Central Makrān Range Mountains Pakistan 114 A3
Central Russian Upland Russian Federation 92 B3
Central Siberian Plateau Plateau Russian Federation 95 E3

Cephalonia see Kefallonía
Cernăuţi see Chernivtsi
Cēsis Latvia Ger. Wenden 86
České Budějovice Czech Republic Ger. Budweis 79
Ceuta External territory Spain N Africa 50 C1
Cévennes Mountains France 71 C6
Ceylon see Sri Lanka
Ceylon Plain Undersea feature Indian Ocean 117 F4
Chad Country C Africa 56
Chad, Lake Lake C Africa 48
Chāgai Hills Mountains Paki 114 A2
Chalándri Greece 85 C5
Chalkída Greece 85 C5
Châlons-sur-Marne France 70 D3
Chambéry France 71 D5
Champlain Seamount Undersea feature Atlantic Ocean 43 C
Chañaral Chile 44 B2
Chandigarh India 114 D2
Chang, Ko Island Thailand 119 C5
Changchun China 108 D3
Chang Jiang River China var. Yangtze 104 D4 109 B5
Changsha China 109 C6
Changzhi China 109 C5
Chaniá Greece 85 C7
Channel Islands Islands UK 69 D8
Channel-Port-aux-Basques Canada 19 G4
Channel Tunnel France/UK 69 E7
Chapala, Lago de Lake Mexic 30 D4
Chardzhev Turkmenistan pre Chardzhou, prev. Leninsk, Turkm. Chärjew 102 D3
Chardzhou see Chardzhev
Chari River C Africa 56 C3
Chārīkār Afghanistan 103 E4
Chärjew see Chardzhev
Charleroi Belgium 67 C7
Charleston South Carolina, US 29 F2
Charleston West Virginia, USA 20 D5

Clermont-Ferrand France 71 C5

Cleveland Ohio, USA 20 D3

Clipperton Island *External territory* France, Pacific Ocean 123 F3

Cloncurry Australia 126 B5 130 A1

Clovis New Mexico, USA 27 E2

Cluj-Napoca Romania 88 B3

Coast Mountains *Mountain range* Canada 14 C2

Coast Ranges *Mountain range* W USA 24 A3

Coats Island *Island* Canada 18 C1

Coatzacoalcos Mexico 31 G4

Cobán Guatemala 32 B2

Cochabamba Bolivia 40 C4

Cochin India 116 D3

Cochrane Canada 18 C4

Cochrane Chile 45 B6

Coco *River* Honduras/Nicaragua 32 D2

Cocos (Keeling) Islands *External territory* Australia, Indian Ocean 112 D4

Cod, Cape *Coastal feature* NE USA 15 F3 21 G3

Coeur d'Alene Idaho, USA 24 C2

Coffs Harbour Australia 130 C2

Coihaique Chile 45 B6

Coimbatore India 116 D3

Coimbra Portugal 72 C3

Colbeck, Cape *Coastal feature* Antarctica 132 C4

Colchester England, UK 69 E6

Colhué Huapi, Lago *Lake* Argentina 45 B6

Colima *Peak* Mexico 15 E5

Colmar France 70 E4

Cologne *see* Köln

Colombia *Country* N South America 38-39

Colombian Basin *Undersea feature* Caribbean Sea 34 D5

Colombo *Capital of* Sri Lanka 117 E3

Colón, Archipiélago de *see* Galapagos Islands

Colorado *State* USA 22 C5

Colorado *River* USA 14 D3

Colorado *River* Argentina 45 C5

Colorado Plateau *Upland region* S USA 26 B1

Colorado Springs Colorado, USA 22 D4

Columbia South Carolina, USA 29 F2

Columbia *River* NW USA 24 C1

Columbus Georgia, USA 28 D3

Columbus Mississippi, USA 28 C2

Columbus Nebraska, USA 23 E4

Columbus Ohio, USA 20 D4

Comayagua Honduras 32 C2

Comilla Bangladesh 115 G4

Communism Peak *Peak* Tajikistan *Rus.* Pik Kommunizma, *prev.* Stalin Peak, Garmo Peak 92 C4

Como, Lago di *Lake* Italy 76 B2

Comodoro Rivadavia Argentina 45 C6

Comoros *Country* Indian Ocean 59

Conakry *Capital of* Guinea 52 C4

Concepción Chile 45 B5

Concepción Paraguay 42 B2

Conchos *River* Mexico 30 C2

Concord California, USA 25 B6

Concord New Hampshire, USA 20 G2

Concordia E Argentina 44 D3

Congo *Country* C Africa 57

Congo *River* C Africa *var.* Zaire 49 C5

Congo Basin *Drainage basin* C Africa 49 C5

Congo (Zaire) *Country* C Africa 57

Connecticut *State* USA 21 G3

Constance, Lake *River* C Europe 75 B7

Constantine Algeria 51 E1

Constantinople *see* Istanbul

Constanța Romania 88 D5

Coober Pedy Australia 129 E5

Cook, Mount *Peak* New Zealand *prev.* Aorangi 125 E5

Cook Islands *External territory* New Zealand, Pacific Ocean 122 D4

Cook Strait *Sea feature* New Zealand 131 G3

Cooktown Australia 126 B4

Coos Bay Oregon, USA 24 A

Copenhagen *Capital of* Denm 65 B7

Copiapó Chile 44 B3

Coppermine Canada 17 E3

Coquimbo Chile 44 B3

Corabia Romania 88 B5

Coral Sea Pacific Ocean 122 C3

Coral Sea Islands *External territory* Australia, Coral Se 126 C4

Corantijn *River* Guyana/Suriname *var.* Courantyne 39 C3

Cordillera Cantábrica *Mount range* Spain 72 D1

Córdoba Argentina 44 C3

Córdoba Spain 72 D4

Cordova Alaska, USA 16 D3

Corfu *see* Kérkyra

Corinth *see* Kórinthos

Corinth, Gulf of *see* Korinthiakós Kólpos

Corinto Nicaragua 32 C3

Cork Ireland 69 A6

Corner Brook Canada 19 G4

Coro Venezuela 38 D3

Coromandel New Zealand 131 G2

Coronel Oviedo Paraguay 42 C2

Corpus Christi Texas, USA 27 G4

Corrib, Lough *Lake* Ireland 69 A5

Corrientes Argentina 44 D3

Corse *Island* France *Eng.* Corsica 71 E7 82 D2

Corsica *see* Corse

Çorum Turkey 96 D2

Corvallis Oregon, USA 24 A3

Cosenza Italy 77 D6

Costa Blanca *Coastal region* Spain 73 F4

Costa Brava *Coastal region* Spa 73 H2

Costa Rica *Country* Central America 32-33

Côte d'Ivoire *see* Ivory Coast

Cotonou Benin 53 F5

Cotopaxi *Peak* Ecuador 36 B2

Cottbus Germany 74 D4

Council Bluffs Iowa, USA 23

Delft Netherlands 66 B4

Delfzijl Netherlands 66 E1

Delhi India 114 D3

Del Rio Texas, USA 27 F4

Demchok *Disputed region* China/India *var.* Dêmqog 106 A4 115 D2

Dêmqog *see* Demchok

Denali *Peak* Alaska, USA *prev.* Mount McKinley 14 C2

Den Helder Netherlands 66 C2

Denizli Turkey 96 B4

Denmark *Country* NW Europe 65

Denmark Strait *Sea feature* Greenland/Iceland *var.* Danmarksstraedet 63 D3

Denpasar Indonesia 120 D5

Denton Texas, USA 27 G2

Denver Colorado, USA 22 D4

Dera Ghāzi Khān Pakistan 114 C2

Dera Ismāīl Khān Pakistan 114 C2

Derby England, UK 69 D6

Derg, Lough *Lake* Ireland 69 B6

Desē Ethiopia 54 C4

Deseado *River* Argentina 45 C6

Des Moines Iowa, USA 23 F3

Despoto Planina *see* Rhodope Mountains

Dessau Germany 74 C4

Desventurados, Islas de los *Islands* Chile 37 A5 123 G4

Detroit Michigan, USA 20 D3

Deutschendorf *see* Poprad

Deva Romania 88 B4

Deventer Netherlands 66 D3

Devollit, Lumi i *River* Albania 81 D6

Devon Island *Island* Canada 17 G2

Devonport Tasmania, Australia 130 B5

Dezfūl Iran 100 C3

Dhaka *Capital of* Bangladesh *var.* Dacca 115 G4

Dhanbād India 115 F4

Dhanushkodi India 116 D3

Dhrepanon, Ákra *Coastal feature* Greece 84 C4

Diamantina *River* Australia 130 B1

Dickinson North Dakota, USA 22 D2

Diekirch Luxembourg 67 D7

Dieppe France 70 C3

Diffa Niger 53 H3

Digul *River* Indonesia 121 H5

Dijon France 70 D4

Dila Ethiopia 55 C5

Dili Indonesia 121 F5

Dilling Sudan 54 B4

Dilolo Congo (Zaire) 57 D8

Dimashq *see* Damascus

Dimitrovo *see* Pernik

Dinant Belgium 67 C7

Dinara *Mountains* Bosnia & Herzegovina/Croatia 80 B4

Dingle Bay *Sea feature* Ireland 69 A5

Diourbel Senegal 52 B3

Dirē Dawa Ethiopia 55 D5

Dirk Hartog Island *Island* Australia 129 A5

Disappointment, Lake *Salt lake* Australia 118 C4

Dispur India 115 G3

Divinópolis Brazil 43 F1

Diyarbakır Turkey 97 E4

Djambala Congo 57 B6

Djibouti *Country* E Africa 54

Djibouti *Capital of* Djibouti *var.* Jibuti 54 D4

Djúpivogur Iceland 63 E4

Dnieper *River* E Europe 51 F4

Dniester *River* Moldova/Ukraine 88 D3

Dnipropetrovs'k Ukraine 89 F3

Dobele Latvia *Ger.* Doblen 86 B3

Doblen *see* Dobele

Doboj Bosnia & Herzegovina 80 C3

Dobrich Bulgaria 84 E1

Dodecanese *see* Dodekánisos

Dodekánisos *Islands* Greece *Eng.* Dodecanese 85 E6

Dodge City Kansas, USA 23 E5

Dodoma *Capital of* Tanzania 55 C7

Doğu Karadeniz Dağları *Mountains* Turkey *var.* Anadolu Dağları 97 E2

Doha *Capital of* Qatar *Ar.* Ad Dawḥah 101 C5

Dolomites *see* Dolomiti

Dolomiti *Mountains* Italy *Eng.* Dolomites 76 C2

Dolores Argentina 44 D4

Dominica *Country* West Indies 35

Dominican Republic *Country* West Indies 35

Don *River* Russian Federation 94 A3

Donegal Bay *Sea feature* Ireland 69 A5

Donets *River* Russian Federation/Ukraine 88 G3 91 A6

Donets'k Ukraine 89 G3

Dongola Sudan 54 B3

Dongting Hu *Lake* China 109 C6

Donostia *see* San Sebastián

Dordogne *River* France 71 B5

Dordrecht Netherlands 66 C4

Dornbirn Austria 75 B7

Dorpat *see* Tartu

Dortmund Germany 74 A4

Dosso Niger 53 F3

Dothan Alabama, USA 28 D3

Douai France 70 C2

Douala Cameroon 57 A5

Douglas UK 69 C5

Douglas Arizona, USA 26 C3

Dourados Brazil 42 C2

Douro *River* Portugal/Spain *Sp.* Duero 72 C2

Dover England, UK 69 E7

Dover Delaware, USA 21 F4

Dözen *Island* Japan 111 B5

Drakensberg *Mountain range* Lesotho/South Africa 58 D5

Drake Passage *Sea feature* Atlantic Ocean/Pacific Ocean 37 C8

Dráma Greece 84 C3

Drammen Norway 65 B6

Drau *River* C Europe *var.* Drava 75 D7 80 C3

Drava *River* C Europe *var.* Drau 79 C7

Dresden Germany 74 D4

Drina *River* Bosnia & Herzegovina/Yugoslavia 80 D4

Galapagos Islands *Islands*
Ecuador, Pacific Ocean
var. Tortoise Islands, *Sp.*
Archipiélago de Colón 36 A2

Galați Romania 88 D4

Galesburg Illinois, USA 20 B4

Galicia Spain 72 C1

Galilee, Sea of *see* Tiberias, Lake

Galle Sri Lanka 117 E4

Gallipoli Italy 77 E5

Gällivare Sweden 64 D3

Gallup New Mexico, USA 26 C2

Galveston Texas, USA 27 G4

Galway Ireland 69 A5

Gambia *Country* W Africa 52

Gäncä Azerbaijan
Rus. Gyandzha, *prev.*
Kirovabad, Yelisavetpol 97 G2

Gand *see* Gent

Gander Canada 19 H3

Gandía Spain 73 F3

Ganges *River* S Asia 114 D3

Ganges Delta *Wetlands*
Bangladesh/India 115 G4

Ganges Plain *Region* S Asia
104 C3

Gangtok India 115 G3

Ganzhou China 109 C6

Gao Mali 53 E3

Gar China 106 A4

Garagum *see* Karakumy

Garagum Kanaly *see*
Karakumskiy Kanal

Garda, Lago di *Lake* Italy 76 C2

Gardēz Afghanistan 103 E4

Garissa Kenya 55 C6

Garmo Peak *see* Communism
Peak

Garonne *River* France 71 B5

Garoowe Somalia 55 E5

Garoua Cameroon 56 B4

Gary Indiana, USA 20 B3

Gaspé Canada 19 F4

Gastonia North Carolina, USA
29 E2

Gävle Sweden 65 C6

Gaya India 115 F4

Gaza Gaza Strip 99 A6

Gazandzhyk Turkmenistan
var. Kazandzhik, *Turkm.*
Gazanjyk 102 B2

Gazanjyk *see* Gazandzhyk

Gaza Strip *Disputed territory*
SW Asia 99 A6

Gaziantep Turkey *prev.* Aintab
96 D4

Gazimağusa Cyprus
var. Famagusta
Gk. Ammochostos 96 C5

Gdańsk Poland *Ger.* Danzig
78 C2

Gdingen *see* Gdynia

Gdynia Poland *Ger.* Gdingen
78 C2

Gedaref Sudan 54 C4

Geelong Australia 130 B4

Gëkdepe Turkmenistan
prev. Geok-Tepe, *Turkm.*
Gökdepe 102 B3

Gelsenkirchen Germany 74 A4

Gemena Congo (Zaire) 57 C5

Geneina Sudan 54 A4

General Eugenio A. Garay
Paraguay 42 A1

General Santos Philippines
121 F3

Geneva *see* Genève

Geneva, Lake *Lake*
France/Switzerland *Fr.* Lac
Léman, *var.* Le Léman,
Ger. Genfer See 71 D5 75 A8

Genève Switzerland
Eng. Geneva 75 A5

Genfer See *see* Geneva, Lake

Genk Belgium 67 D6

Genoa *see* Genova

Genova Italy *Eng.* Genoa 76 B3

Genova, Golfo di *Sea feature*
Italy 76 B3

Gent Belgium *Fr.* Gand,
Eng. Ghent 67 B5

Geok-Tepe *see* Gëkdepe

Georgenburg *see* Jurbarkas

Georges Bank *Undersea feature*
Atlantic Ocean 21 H2

George Town *Capital of* Cayman
Islands 34 B3

Georgetown Gambia 52 B3

Georgetown *Capital of* Guyana
39 G2

George Town Malaysia 120 B3

Georgia *Country* SW Asia 97 F2

Georgia *State* USA 29 E3

Gera Germany 75 C5

Geraldton Australia 102 D5

Gereshk Afghanistan 102 D5

Germany *Country* W Europe
74-75

Getafe Spain 73 E3

Gettysburg Pennsylvania, USA
21 E4

Gevgelija Macedonia 81 E6

Ghadāmis Libya 51 E3

Ghana *Country* W Africa 53

Ghanzi Botswana 58 C3

Ghardaïa Algeria 50 D2

Gharyān Libya 51 F2

Ghāt Libya 51 F4

Ghaznī Afghanistan 103 E4

Ghent *see* Gent

Gibraltar *External territory* UK,
SW Europe 72 D5

Gibraltar, Strait of *Sea feature*
Atlantic Ocean/Mediterranean
Sea 72 D5

Gibson Desert *Desert region*
Australia 129 C5

Gijón Spain 72 D1

Gilbert Islands *Islands* Kiribati
127 E2

Gillette Wyoming, USA 22 C3

Girne Cyprus *var.* Kyrenia
96 C5

Girona Spain 73 G2

Gisborne New Zealand 131 H2

Giurgiu Romania 88 C5

Gjirokastër Albania 81 D6

Gjøvik Norway 65 B5

Glasgow Scotland, UK 68 C4

Glasgow Montana, USA 22 C1

Gleiwitz *see* Gliwice

Glendale Arizona, USA 26 B2

Glendive Montana, USA 22 D1

Gliwice Poland *Ger.* Gleiwitz
79 C5

Gloucester England, UK 69 D6

Glubokoye *see* Hlybokaye

Goa *State* India 116 C2

Gobi *Desert* China/Mongolia
106 D3

Godāveri *River* India 104 B3

Godoy Cruz Argentina 44 B4

Godthåb *see* Nuuk

Godwin Austin, Mount *see* K2

Goiânia Brazil 41 F4

Gökdepe *see* Gëkdepe

Golan Heights *Disputed territory*
SW Asia 98 B4

Guadalquivir *River* Spain 72 D4

Guadeloupe *External territory* France, West Indies 35 G4

Guadiana *River* Portugal/Spain 72 C4

Gualeguaychú Argentina 44 D4

Guallatiri *Peak* Chile 36 B4

Guam *External territory* USA, Pacific Ocean 122 C3

Guanare Venezuela 38 D2

Guanare *River* Venezuela 38 D2

Guangxi *Autonomous region* China *var.* Kwangsi 109 B6

Guangzhou China *Eng.* Canton 109 C7

Guantánamo Cuba 34 D3

Guantánamo Bay *External territory* USA, Cuba 34 D3

Guatemala *Country* Central America 32

Guatemala City *Capital of* Guatemala 32 B2

Guaviare *River* Colombia 38 D3

Guayaquil Ecuador 38 A4

Guayaquil, Gulf of *Sea feature* Ecuador/Peru 38 A5

Guerguerat Western Sahara 50 A4

Guernsey *Island* Channel Islands 69 D8

Guiana Basin *Undersea feature* Atlantic Ocean 47 B4

Guiana Highlands *Upland* N South America 36 C2

Guider Cameroon 56 B4

Guimarães Portugal 72 C2

Guinea *Country* W Africa 52

Guinea, Gulf of *Sea feature* Atlantic Ocean 47 D5

Guinea-Bissau *Country* W Africa 52

Guiyang China 109 B6

Gujarāt *State* India 114 C4

Gujrānwāla Pakistan 114 C2

Gujrāt Pakistan 114 C2

Gulf, The *see* Persian Gulf

Gulfport Mississippi, USA 28 C3

Gulu Uganda 55 B6

Gumbinnen *see* Gusev

Guri, Embalse de *Reservoir* Venezuela 39 E2

Gusau Nigeria 53 G4

Gusev Kaliningrad, Russian Federation *prev.* Gumbinnen 86 B4

Gushgy Turkmenistan

Guwāhāti India 115 G3

Guyana *Country* NE South America 39

Gwalior India 114 D3

Gyandzha *see* Gäncä

Győr Hungary *Ger.* Raab 79 C6

Gyumri Armenia *Rus.* Kumayri, *prev.* Leninakan, Aleksandropol' 97 F2

Gyzylarbat Turkmenistan *prev.* Kizyl-Arvat 102 B2

H

Ha'apai Group *Islands* Tonga 127 F5

Haapsalu Estonia *Ger.* Hapsal 86 C2

Haarlem Netherlands 66 C3

Habomai Islands *Islands* Japan/Russian Federation (disputed) 110 E2

Hachijō-jima *Island* Japan 111 D5

Hachinohe Japan 110 D3

Hadejia *River* Nigeria 53 G3

Haeju North Korea 108 E4

Hafnarfjördhur Iceland 62 D4

Hagen Germany 74 A4

Hague, The *see* 's-Gravenhage

Haifa Israel *Heb.* Hefa 83 G4

Haikou China 109 C7

Hā'il Saudi Arabia 100 B4

Hainan *Island* China *var.* Hainan Dao 109 C8

Hainan Dao *see* Hainan Dao

Hai Phong Vietnam 118 D3

Haiti *Country* West Indies 34

Hajdarken *see* Khaydarkan

Hakodate Japan 110 D3

Ḥalab Syria 98 B2

Halden Norway 65 B6

Halifax Canada 19 F4

Halle Germany 74 C4

Hallein Austria 75 D7

Halls Creek Australia 128 C3

Halmahera *Island* Indonesia 121 F3

Halmstad Sweden 65 B7

Hamada Japan 111 B5

Ḥamāh Syria 98 B3

Hamamatsu Japan 111 C5

Hamar Norway 65 B5

Hamburg Germany 74 B3

Hämeenlinna Finland 65 D5

HaMelah, Yam *see* Dead Sea

Hamhŭng North Korea 108 E4

Hami China 106 C3

Hamilton Canada 18 D5

Hamilton New Zealand 131 C

Hamm Germany 74 B4

Hammerfest Norway 64 D2

Hampden New Zealand 131 B

Handan China 108 C4

HaNegev *Desert region* Israel *Eng.* Negev 99 A6

Hangayn Nuruu *Mountain rang* Mongolia 106 D2

Hangzhou China 109 D5

Hannover Germany *Eng.* Hanover 74 B4

Hanoi Vietnam 118 D3

Hanover *see* Hannover

Happy Valley-Goose Bay Canada 19 F2

Hapsal *see* Haapsalu

Ḥaraḍ Yemen 101 C5

Harare *Capital of* Zimbabwe 59 E3

Harbin China 108 E3

Hargeysa Somalia 55 D5

Hari *River* Indonesia 120 B4

Harirūd *River* C Asia 102 D4

Harper Liberia 52 D5

Harrisburg Pennsylvania, USA 21 E4

Harris Ridge *see* Lomonosov Ridge

Harstad Norway 64 C3

Hartford Connecticut, USA 21 G3

Hasselt Belgium 67 C6

Hastings New Zealand 131 H

Hastings Nebraska, USA 22 E

Hatay *see* Antakya

Hatteras, Cape *Coastal feature* North Carolina, USA 29 G1

attiesburg Mississippi, USA 28 C3

at Yai Thailand 119 C7

augesund Norway 65 A6

avana *Capital of Cuba* Sp. La Habana 34 B2

avre Montana, USA 22 C1

avre-Saint-Pierre Canada 19 F3

awaii *State* USA 123 E2

awaiian Islands *Islands* USA 93 H4

awlēr *see* Arbīl

awthorne Nevada, USA 25 C6

ay River Canada 17 E4

ays Kansas, USA 23 E4

eard Island *Island* Indian Ocean 113 C7

eerenveen Netherlands 66 D2

eerlen Netherlands 67 D6

efa Israel *prev.* Haifa 99 A5

efei China 109 D5

eidelberg Germany 75 B6

eilbronn Germany 75 B6

elena Montana, USA 22 B2

elmand *River* Afghanistan 102 C5

elmond Netherlands 67 D5

elsingborg Sweden 65 B7

elsingør Denmark 65 B7

elsinki *Capital of* Finland 65 D6

elwân Egypt 54 B1

engelo Netherlands 66 E3

enzada Myanmar 118 A4

erāt Afghanistan 102 C4

ermansverk Norway 65 A5

ermosillo Mexico 30 B2

erning Denmark 65 A7

ialeah Florida, USA 29 F5

iiumaa *Island* Estonia *Ger.* Dagden, *Swed.* Dagö 86 C2

ildesheim Germany 74 B4

illa *see* Al Ḥillah

ilversum Netherlands 66 C3

imalayas *Mountain range* S Asia 104 B2

imora Ethiopia 54 C4

ims Syria 98 B3

indu Kush *Mountain range* C Asia 103 E4

Hiroshima Japan 111 B5

Hitachi Japan 110 D4

Hjørring Denmark 65 A7

Hlybokaye Belarus *Rus.* Glubokoye 87 D5

Hobart Tasmania 130 B5

Hobbs New Mexico, USA 5627 E3

Hô Chi Minh Vietnam *var.* Ho Chi Minh City, *prev.* Saigon 119 E6

Ho Chi Minh City *see* Hô Chi Minh

Hodeida *see* Al Ḥudaydah

Hoek van Holland Netherlands 66 B4

Hoggar *see* Ahaggar

Hohhot China 107 F3

Hokkaidō *Island* Japan 110 D2

Holguín Cuba 34 C2

Hollywood Florida, USA 29 F5

Holland *see* Netherlands

Holon Israel 99 A5

Holyhead Wales, UK 69 C5

Homyel' Belarus *Rus.* Gomel' 87 D7

Honduras *Country* Central America 32-33

Honduras, Gulf of *Sea feature* Caribbean Sea 32 C2

Honefoss Norway 65 B6

Hông Gai Vietnam 118 E3

Hong Kong China *var.* Xianggang 109 C7

Hongze Hu *Lake* China 109 D5

Honiara *Capital of* Solomon Islands 126 C3

Honolulu Hawaii, USA 123 E2

Honshū *Island* Japan 110 D3

Honshu Ridge *Undersea feature* Pacific Ocean 105 F2

Hoorn Netherlands 66 C2

Hopa Turkey 97 F2

Hopedale Canada 19 F2

Hopkinsville Kentucky, USA 20 B5

Horki Belarus *Rus.* Gorki 87 E6

Horlivka Ukraine *Rus.* Gorlovka 88 G3

Horn, Cape *Coastal feature* Chile 45 C8

Horog *see* Khorog

Horsens Denmark 65 A7

Hotan China 106 B4

Hot Springs Arkansas, USA 28 B2

Hotspur Seamount *Undersea feature* Atlantic Ocean 41 H5 43 H1

Hô Thac Ba *Lake* Vietnam 118 D3

Houston Texas, USA 27 G4

Hovd Mongolia 106 C2

Hövsgöl Nuur *Lake* Mongolia 106 D1

Howe, Cape *Coastal feature* Australia 124 D4 130 C4

Hradec Králové Czech Republic *Ger.* Königgrätz 79 B5

Hrodna Belarus *Rus.* Grodno 87 B5

Huacho Peru 40 A3

Huainan China 109 D5

Huambo Angola 58 B2

Huancayo Peru 40 B4

Huang He *River* China *Eng.* Yellow River 104 D2 107 F4 108 C4

Huánuco Peru 40 B4

Huaraz Peru 40 B3

Huascarán *Peak* Peru 36 B3

Hubli India 116 C2

Hudson *River* NE USA 21 F3

Hudson Bay *Sea feature* Canada 15 E2

Hudson Strait *Sea feature* Canada 15 F2

Huê Vietnam 118 E4

Huehuetenango Guatemala 32 B2

Huelva Spain 72 C4

Huesca Spain 73 F2

Hughenden Australia 130 B1

Hull *see* Kingston upon Hull

Hulun Nur *Lake* China 107 F1

Humboldt *River* W USA 25 C5

Hungarian Plain *Plain* C Europe 83 E1

Hungary *Country* C Europe 79

Huntington West Virginia, USA 20 D5

Huntsville Alabama, USA 28 D2

Hurghada Egypt 54 B2

Huron, Lake *Lake* Canada/USA 15 F3

Húsavík Iceland 63 E4
Huvadhu Atoll *Island* Maldives 116 C5
Hvar *Island* Croatia 80 B4
Hyargas Nuur *Lake* Mongolia 106 C2
Hyderābād India 114 B3 116 D3
Hyères, Îles d' *Islands* France 71 D6

I

Iași Romania 88 D3
Ibadan Nigeria 53 F5
Ibagué Colombia 38 B3
Ibarra Ecuador 38 A4
Iberian Peninsula *Peninsula* SW Europe 46 D3 82 D3
Ibiza *see* Eivissa
Ica Peru 40 B4
İçel *see* Mersin
Iceland *Country* Atlantic Ocean 63 E4
Idaho *State* USA 24
Idaho Falls Idaho, USA 24 E3
Idfu Egypt 52 B2
Idlib Syria 98 B2
Ieper Belgium *Fr.* Ypres 67 A6
Ifôghas, Adrar des *Upland* Mali *var.* Adrar des Iforas 53 F2
Iforas, Adrar des *see* Ifôghas, Adrar des
Iglau *see* Jihlava
Iglesias Italy 77 A5
Ihosy Madagascar 59 G3
Iisalmi Finland 64 E4
Ijebu-Ode Nigeria 53 F5
IJssel *River* Netherlands 66 D3
IJsselmeer *Lake* Netherlands *prev.* Zuider Zee 66 D2
Ikaría *Island* Greece 85 D5
Iki *Island* Japan 111 A6
Ilagan Philippines 121 E1
Ilebo Congo (Zaire) 57 C6
Iligan Philippines 121 E2
Illapel Chile 44 B3
Illinois *State* USA 20 B4
Iloilo Philippines 121 E2
Ilorin Nigeria 53 F4
İluh *see* Batman
Ilulissat Greenland 62 B3

Imatra Finland 65 E5
Imperatriz Brazil 41 F2
Impfondo Congo 57 C5
Imphāl India 115 H4
Independence Missouri, USA 23 F4
Independence Fjord *Inlet* Greenland 62 D1
India *Country* S Asia 114-115 116-117
Indian Ocean 112-113
Indiana *State* USA 20 C4
Indianapolis Indiana, USA 20 C4
Indonesia *Country* SE Asia 120-121
Indore India 114 D4
Indus *River* S Asia 114 C1
Indus Delta *Wetlands* Pakistan 114 B4
Inglefield Land *Region* Greenland 62 A2
Ingolstadt Germany 75 E6
Inguri *see* Enguri
Inhambane Mozambique 59 E3
Inn *River* C Europe 75 D6
Inner Islands *Islands* Seychelles 59 H1
Inner Mongolia *Autonomous region* China 107 F3
Innsbruck Austria 75 C7
In Salah Algeria 50 D3
Insein Myanmar 118 B4
Interlaken Switzerland 75 B7
Inukjuak Canada 18 D2
Inuvik Canada 17 E3
Invercargill New Zealand 131 F5
Inverness Scotland, UK 68 C3
Ioánnina Greece 84 A4
Ionian Islands *see* Iónioi Nísoi
Ionian Sea Mediterranean Sea 83 E3
Iónioi Nísoi *Island group* Greece *Eng.* Ionian Islands 85 A5
Íos *Island* Greece 85 D6
Iowa *State* USA 23 F3
Ipoh Malaysia 120 B3
Ipswich Australia 130 C2
Ipswich England, UK 69 E6
Iqaluit Canada 17 H3
Iquique Chile 44 B1

Iquitos Peru 40 B2
Irákleio Greece 85 D7
Iran *Country* SW Asia 100-101
Iranian Plateau *Upland* Iran 100 D3
Irānshahr Iran 100 E4
Irapuato Mexico 31 E4
Iraq *Country* SW Asia 100 B3
Irbid Jordan 99 B5
Ireland *Country* W Europe 68-69
Irian Jaya *Province* Indonesia 121 H4
Iringa Tanzania 55 C7
Irish Sea British Isles 69 C5
Irkutsk Russian Federation 95 E4
Irrawaddy *River* Myanmar 118 B2
Irrawaddy Delta *Wetlands* Myanmar 118 A4
Ísafjörðhur Iceland 62 D4
Ischia, Isola d' *Island* Italy 77 C5
Ishikari *River* Japan 110 D2
Isiro Congo (Zaire) 57 E5
İskenderun Turkey *Eng.* Alexandretta 96 D4
Iskŭr *River* Bulgaria 84 C1
Iskŭr, Yazovir *Reservoir* Bulgaria 84 C2
Islay *Island* Scotland, UK 68 B4
Islāmābād *Capital of* Pakistan 114 C1
Ismaila *see* Ismâ'ilîya
Ismâ'ilîya Egypt *Eng.* Ismaila 54 B1
Isna Egypt 54 B2
Isparta Turkey 96 B4
Israel *Country* SW Asia 98-99
Issyk-Kul' Kyrgyzstan *prev.* Rybach'ye, *Kir.* Ysyk-Köl 103 G2
Issyk-Kul, Ozero *Lake* Kyrgyzstan 103 G2
İstanbul Turkey *var.* Stambul, *prev.* Constantinople, Byzantium, *Bul.* Tsarigrad 96 B2
İstanbul Boğazı *see* Bosporus
Itabuna Brazil 41 G4
Itagüí Colombia 38 B2
Italy *Country* S Europe 76-77

Kabale Uganda 55 B6

Kabalebo Reservoir *Reservoir* Suriname 39 G3

Kabinda Congo (Zaire) 57 D7

Kåbol *see* Kåbul

Kåbul *Capital of* Afghanistan *Per.* Kåbol 103 E4

Kachch, Gulf of *Sea feature* Arabian Sea 114 B4

Kachch, Rann of *Wetland* India/Pakistan *var.* Rann of Kutch 114 B4

Kadugli Sudan 54 B4

Kaduna Nigeria 53 G4

Kaédi Mauritania 52 C3

Kâğıthane Turkey 96 B2

Kagoshima Japan 111 A6

Kahramanmaraş Turkey *var.* Marash, Maraş 96 D4

Kai, Kepulauan *Island group* Indonesia 120 A3

Kaikoura New Zealand 131 G3

Kainji Reservoir *Reservoir* Nigeria 53 F4

Kairouan Tunisia 51 E1

Kaitaia New Zealand 131 G1

Kajaani Finland 64 E4

Kaka Turkmenistan *prev.* Kaakhka, *var.* Kaachka 102 C3

Kakhovs'ke Vodoskhovyshche *Reservoir* Ukraine 89 F3

Kalahari Desert *Desert* southern Africa 58 C3

Kalamariá Greece 84 B3

Kalámata Greece 85 B6

Kalât Afghanistan 102 D5

Kalemie Congo (Zaire) 57 E7

Kalgoorlie Australia 129 C6

Kaliningrad *External territory* Russian Federation 86 A4 94 A2

Kaliningrad Kaliningrad, Russian Federation *prev.* Königsberg 86 A4

Kalinkavichy Belarus *Rus.* Kalinkovichi 87 D7

Kalinkovichi *see* Kalinkavichy

Kalisch *see* Kalisz

Kalispell Montana, USA 22 B1

Kalisz Poland *Ger.* Kalisch 78 C4

Kalmar Sweden 65 C7

Kalpeni Island *Island* India 116 C3

Kama *River* Russian Federation 90 D4

Kamchatka *Peninsula* Russian Federation 95 A3

Kamchiya *River* Bulgaria 84 E2

Kamina Congo (Zaire) 57 D7

Kamishli *see* Al Qâmishlî

Kamloops Canada 17 E5

Kampala *Capital of* Uganda 55 B6

Kâmpóng Cham Cambodia 119 D6

Kâmpóng Chhnăng Cambodia 119 D5

Kâmpóng Saôm Cambodia 119 D6

Kâmpôt Cambodia 119 D6

Kampuchea *see* Cambodia

Kam''yanets'-Podil's'kyy Ukraine 88 C3

Kananga Congo (Zaire) 57 D7

Kanazawa Japan 110 C4

Kandahâr Afghanistan *var.* Qandahâr 102 D5

Kandi Benin 53 F4

Kandla India 114 C4

Kandy Sri Lanka 117 E3

Kanestron, Ákra *Coastal feature* Greece 84 C4

Kangaatsiaq Greenland 62 B4

Kangaroo Island *Island* Australia 124 C4

Kangerlussuaq Greenland 62 B4

Kangertittivaq *Region* Greenland 62 D3

Kanggye North Korea 108 E4

Kanjiža Yugoslavia 80 D2

Kankan Guinea 52 D4

Kano Nigeria 53 G4

Kânpur India *prev.* Cawnpore 115 E3

Kansas *State* USA 22-23

Kansas City Kansas, USA 23 F4

Kansas City Missouri, USA 23 F4

Kansk Russian Federation 95 A3

Kao-hsiung Taiwan 109 D7

Kaolack Senegal 52 B3

Kapchagay Kazakhstan 94 C5

Kapfenberg Austria 75 E7

Kaposvár Hungary 79 C7

Kapsukas *see* Marijampolė

Kapuas *River* Indonesia 120 C...

Kara-Balta Kyrgyzstan 103 F2...

Kara-Bogaz-Gol, Zaliv *Sea feature* Caspian Sea 102 A2

Karabük Turkey 96 C2

Karâchi Pakistan 114 B4

Karaganda Kazakhstan 94 C4

Karaj Iran 100 C3

Karakol Kyrgyzstan *prev.* Przheval'sk 103 G2

Kara Kum *Desert* Turkmenista... *see* Karakumy 92 C4

Karakumskiy Kanal *Canal* Turkmenistan *Turkm.* Garagum Kanaly 102 C3

Karakumy *Desert* Turkmenistan *Turkm.* Garagum, *var.* Qara Qum *Eng.* Kara Kum 102 C...

Karamay China 106 B2

Karasburg Namibia 58 C4

Kara Sea *see* Karskoye More

Karbalâ' Iraq *var.* Kerbala 100 B3

Kardítsa Greece 84 B4

Kariba, Lake *Lake* Zambia/Zimbabwe 58 D2

Karkinits'ka Zatoka *Sea featur...* Black Sea 89 F4

Karl-Marx-Stadt *see* Chemnitz

Karlovac Croatia 80 B3

Karlovy Vary Czech Republic *Ger.* Karlsbad 79 A5

Karlsbad *see* Karlovy Vary

Karlskrona Sweden 65 C7

Karlsruhe Germany 75 B6

Karlstad Sweden 65 B6

Karnâtaka *State* India 116 D1

Kárpathos *Island* Greece 85 E...

Kars Turkey 97 F2

Karshi Uzbekistan *prev.* Bek-Budi, *Uzb.* Qarshi 102 D3

Karskoye More Arctic Ocean *Eng.* Kara Sea 13 E6 90 E2 94 D2

Kasai *River* Congo (Zaire) 57 ...

Kasama Zambia 59 E1

Kaschau *see* Košice

Kâshân Iran 100 C3

Kashi China 106 A3

Kashmir *Disputed region* India/Pakistan 114 D1

Kasongo Congo (Zaire) 57 E6

ethbridge Canada 17 F5

eti, Kepulauan *Island group* Indonesia 121 F5

euven Belgium 67 C6

everkusen Germany 75 A5

evkás *see* Lefkáda

ewis *Island* Scotland, UK 68 B2

ewiston Idaho, USA 24 C2

ewiston Maine, USA 21 G2

exington Kentucky, USA 20 C5

eyte *Island* Philippines 121 F2

ezhë Albania 81 D5

.hasa China 106 C5

.iangyungang China 109 D5

.iaoyuan China 108 D3

.ibau *see* Liepája

.iberec Czech Republic *Ger.* Reichenberg 78 B4

.iberia *Country* W Africa 52

.iberia Costa Rica 32 D4

.ibreville *Capital of* Gabon 57 A5

.ibya *Country* N Africa 51

.ibyan Desert *Desert* N Africa 48 C3

.iechtenstein *Country* C Europe 75 B7

.iège Belgium 67 D6

.iegnitz *see* Legnica

.ienz Austria 75 D7

.iepája Latvia *Ger.* Libau 86 B3

.iffey *River* Ireland 69 B5

.iguria Italy 76 B3

.igurian Sea *Mediterranean Sea* 71 E6

.ikasi Congo (Zaire) 57 E8

.ille France 70 C2

.illehammer Norway 65 B5

.ilongwe *Capital of* Malawi 59 E2

.ima *Capital of* Peru 40 B4

.ima Ohio, USA 20 C4

.imassol Cyprus *var.* Lemesos 96 C5

.imerick Ireland 69 A6

.ímnos *Island* Greece *var.* Lemnos 84 C4

.imoges France 70 C5

.imón Costa Rica 33 E4

.impopo *River* southern Africa 58 D3

.inares Chile 44 B4

.inares Spain 73 E4

Lincoln England, UK 69 D5

Lincoln Nebraska, USA 23 F4

Lincoln Sea *Arctic Ocean* 62 B1

Linden Guyana 39 G2

Lindi *River* Congo (Zaire) 55 C8

Line Islands *Island group* Kiribati 127 H3

Lingga, Kepulauan *Island group* Indonesia 120 B4

Linköping Sweden 65 C6

Linosa *Island* Italy 77 C8

Linz Austria 75 D6

Lion, Golfe du *Sea feature* Mediterranean Sea 71 D6

Lipari *Island* Italy 77 D6

Lipari Islands *see* Isole Eolie

Lira Uganda 55 B6

Lisbon *Capital of* Portugal *Port.* Lisboa 72 B4

Litang China 109 A5

Litani *River* SW Asia 89 B4

Lithuania *Country* E Europe 86-87

Little Andaman *Island* India 117 G2

Little Minch *Sea feature* Scotland, UK 68 B3

Little Rock Arkansas, USA 28 B2

Liuzhou China 109 B7

Liverpool England, UK 69 D5

Livingston, Lake *Lake* Texas, USA 27 H3

Livingstone Zambia 58 D3

Livno Bosnia & Herzegovina 80 B4

Livorno Italy 76 B3

Ljubljana *Capital of* Slovenia 80 A2

Ljusnan *River* Sweden 65 B5

Llanos *Region* Colombia/Venezuela 39 E2

Lleida Spain *Cast.* Lérida 73 F2

Lobatse Botswana 58 C4

Lobito Angola 58 B2

Locarno Switzerland 75 B8

Lodja Congo (Zaire) 57 D6

Łódź Poland *Rus.* Lodz 78 D4

Lofoten *Island group* Norway 64 B3

Logan, Mount *Peak* Canada 14 C2

Logroño Spain 73 E2

Loire *River* France 70 B4

Loja Ecuador 38 A5

Lokitaung Kenya 55 C5

Loksa Estonia *Ger.* Loxa 86 D2

Lombok *Island* Indonesia 120 D5

Lomé *Capital of* Togo 53 F5

Lomond, Loch *Lake* Scotland, UK 68 C4

Lomonosov Ridge *Undersea feature* Arctic Ocean *var.* Harris Ridge 12 B4

London Canada 18 C5

London *Capital of* UK 69 E6

Londonderry Northern Ireland, UK 68 B4

Londonderry, Cape *Coastal feature* Australia 124 B2 128 C2

Londrina Brazil 42 D2

Long Beach California, USA 25 C8

Long Island *Island* Bahamas 34 D2

Long Island *Island* NE USA 21 G3

Longreach Australia 126 B5

Longview Texas, USA 27 G3

Longview Washington, USA 24 B2

Longyearbyen Svalbard 63 G2

Lop Nur *Lake* China 106 C3

Lorca Spain 73 F4

Lord Howe Rise *Undersea feature* Pacific Ocean 122 C4

Lorient France 70 A3

Los Alamos New Mexico, USA 26 D2

Los Angeles California, USA 25 C8

Loslau *see* Wodzisław Śląski

Los Mochis Mexico 30 C3

Losonc *see* Lučenec

Losontz *see* Lučenec

Lot *River* France 71 B5

Louangphrabang Laos 118 C3

Loubomo Congo 57 B6

Louisiana *State* USA 28 B3

Louisville Kentucky, USA 20 C5

Lovech Bulgaria 84 C2

Lower California *see* Baja California

Loxa *see* Loksa

Loyauté, Îles *Island group* New Caledonia 126 D5

Loznica Yugoslavia 80 C3

Luanda *Capital of* Angola 58 B1

Luanshya Zambia 58 D2

Lubānas Ezers *Lake* Latvia 86 D4

Lubango Angola 58 B2

Lubbock Texas, USA 27 E2

Lübeck Germany 74 C3

Lublin Poland *Rus.* Lyublin 78 E4

Lubny Ukraine 89 F2

Lubumbashi Congo (Zaire) 57 E8

Lucapa Angola 58 C1

Lucena Philippines 120 E1

Lučenec Slovakia *Hung.* Losonc, *Ger.* Losontz 79 D6

Lucerne *see* Luzern

Lucknow India 115 E3

Lüderitz Namibia 58 B4

Ludhiāna India 114 D2

Lugano Switzerland 75 B8

Lugo Spain 72 C1

Luhans'k Ukraine 89 H3

Luleå Sweden 64 D4

Lumsden New Zealand 131 F5

Luninyets Belarus 97 C6

Lusaka *Capital of* Zambia 58 D2

Lushnjë Albania 81 D6

Lüt, Baḥrat *see* Dead Sea

Luts'k Ukraine 88 C1

Lutzow-Holm Bay *Sea feature* Antarctica 133 F1

Luxembourg *Country* W Europe 67 D8

Luxembourg *Capital of* Luxembourg 67 D8

Luxor Egypt 54 B2

Luzern Switzerland *Fr.* Lucerne 75 B7

Luzon *Island* Philippines 121 E1

Luzon Strait *Sea feature* Philippines/Taiwan 105 E3

L'viv Ukraine *Rus.* L'vov 88 B2

L'vov *see* L'viv

Lyepyel' Belarus *Rus.* Lepel' 87 D5

Lyon France 71 D5

Lyublin *see* Lublin

M

Ma‘ān Jordan 99 B6

Maas *River* W Europe *var.* Meuse 66 D4

Maastricht Netherlands 67 D6

Macao *External territory* Portugal, E Asia *var.* Macau 109 C7

Macapá Brazil 41 F1

Macau *see* Macao

Macdonald Islands *Islands* Indian Ocean 113 B7

Macdonnell Ranges *Mountains* Australia 128 D4

Macedonia *Country* SE Europe officially Former Yugoslav Republic of Macedonia, *abbrev.* FYR Macedonia 81

Maceió Brazil 41 H3

Machakos Kenya 55 C6

Machala Ecuador 38 A5

Mackay Australia 126 B5 130 C1

Mackay, Lake *Lake* Australia 128 D4

Mackenzie *River* Canada 17 E4

Mackenzie Bay *Sea feature* Atlantic Ocean 133 G2

Mâcon France 70 D5

Macon Georgia, USA 29 E2

Madagascar *Country* Indian Ocean 59

Madagascar Basin *Undersea feature* Indian Ocean 113 B5

Madagascar Ridge *Undersea feature* Indian Ocean 113 A5

Madang Papua New Guinea 126 B3

Madeira *River* Bolivia/Brazil 40 D2

Madeira *Island group* Portugal 50 A2

Madhya Pradesh *State* India 115 E4

Madison Wisconsin, USA 20 B3

Madona Latvia *Ger.* Modohn 86 D3

Madras India 117 E2

Madre de Dios *River* Bolivia/Peru 40 C3

Madrid *Capital of* Spain 73 E3

Madurai India 116 D3

Magadan Russian Federation 95 G3

Magallanes *see* Punta Arenas

Magallanes, Estrecho de *see* Magellan, Strait of

Magdalena *River* Colombia 38 B2

Magdeburg Germany 74 C4

Magellan, Strait of *Sea feature* S South America *Sp.* Estrecho de Magallanes 37 B7

Maggiore, Lake *Lake* Italy/Switzerland 75 B8

Mahajanga Madagascar 59 G2

Mahalapye Botswana 58 D3

Mahanādi *River* India 115 F5

Mahārashtra *State* India 114 D5

Mahé *Island* Seychelles 59 H1

Mahilyow Belarus *Rus.* Mogilëv 87 E6

Mährisch-Ostrau *see* Ostrava

Maicao Colombia 38 C1

Maiduguri Nigeria 53 H4

Maimana *see* Meymaneh

Maine *State* USA 21 G1

Mainz Germany 75 B5

Maiquetía Venezuela 38 D1

Maíz, Islas del *Islands* Nicaragua 33 E3 34 B5

Majorca *see* Mallorca

Majuro *Island* Marshall Islands 126 D1

Makarska Croatia 80 B4

Makeni Sierra Leone 52 C4

Makeyevka *see* Makiyivka

Makgadikgadi *Salt pan* Botswana 58 D3

Makhachkala Russian Federation 91 B7 94 A4

Makiyivka Ukraine *Rus.* Makeyevka 89 G5

Makkah Saudi Arabia *Eng.* Mecca 101 A5

Makkovik Canada 19 G2

Makurdi Nigeria 53 G4

Malabo *Capital of* Equatorial Guinea 57 A5

Malacca *see* Melaka

Malacca, Strait of *Sea feature* Indonesia/Malaysia 104 C4 119 C8

Mary Turkmenistan *prev.* Merv 102 C3

Maryland *State* USA 21 F4

Mascarene Islands *Island group* Indian Ocean 59 H3

Mascarene Plateau *Undersea feature* Indian Ocean 113 B5

Maseru *Capital* of Lesotho 58 D4

Mashhad Iran *var.* Meshed 100 E3

Masindi Uganda 55 B6

Mason City Iowa, USA 23 F3

Masqaṭ *see* Muscat

Massachusetts *State* USA 21 G3

Massawa Eritrea 54 C4

Massif Central *Upland* France 71 C5

Massoukou Gabon 57 B6

Masterton New Zealand 131 G3

Matadi Congo (Zaire) 57 B7

Matagalpa Nicaragua 32 D3

Matamoros Mexico 31 E2

Matanzas Cuba 34 B2

Matara Sri Lanka 117 E4

Mataró Spain 73 G2

Mato Grosso, Planalto de *Upland* Brazil 41 E3

Matosinhos Portugal 72 C2

Matrûh Egypt 54 B1

Matsue Japan 111 B5

Matsuyama Japan 111 B5

Maturín Venezuela 39 E1

Maun Botswana 58 D3

Mauritania *Country* W Africa 52

Mauritius *Country* Indian Ocean 59 H3

Mayaguana *Island* Bahamas 34 D2

Mayotte *External territory* France, Indian Ocean 59 G2

Mayyit, Al Baḥr al *see* Dead Sea

Mazār-e Sharīf Afghanistan 102 D3

Mazatenango Guatemala 32 B2

Mazatlán Mexico 30 C3

Mažeikiai Lithuania 86 B3

Mazury *Region* Poland 78 D3

Mazyr Belarus *Rus.* Mozyr' 87 D7

Mbabane *Capital* of Swaziland 59 E4

Mbala Zambia 59 E1

Mbale Uganda 55 C6

Mbandaka Congo (Zaire) 57 C5

Mbeya Tanzania 55 B8

Mbuji-Mayi Congo (Zaire) 57 D7

McKinley, Mount *see* Denali

McMurdo Sound *Sea feature* Antarctica 133 E5

Mead, Lake Lake SW USA 25 D7 26 A1

Mecca *see* Makkah

Mechelen Belgium 67 C5

Medan Indonesia 120 A3

Medellín Colombia 38 B2

Médenine Tunisia 51 F2

Medford Oregon, USA 24 B4

Medina *see* Al Madinah

Mediterranean Sea Atlantic Ocean 82-83

Meekatharra Australia 129 B5

Meerut India 114 D3

Mek'elē Ethiopia 54 C4

Meknès Morocco 50 C2

Mekong *River* SE Asia 104 D3

Mekong Delta *Wetlands* Vietnam 119 E6

Melaka Malaysia *prev.* Malacca 120 B3

Melanesia *Region* Pacific Ocean 124-125 126-127

Melbourne Australia 130 B4

Melbourne Florida, USA 29 F4

Melilla *External territory* Spain, N Africa 50 C1

Melitopol' Ukraine 89 F4

Melo Uruguay 42 E4

Melville Island *Island* Australia 128 D2

Melville Island *Island* Canada 17 E2

Memel *see* Klaipėda

Memel *see* Neman

Memphis Tennessee, USA 28 C2

Mende France 71 C6

Mendi Papua New Guinea 126 B3

Mendoza Argentina 44 B4

Menongue Angola 58 C2

Menorca *Island* Spain *Eng.* Minorca 73 H3

Mentawai, Kepulauan *Island group* Indonesia 120 A4

Meppel Netherlands 66 D2

Merced California, USA 25 B6

Mercedario *Peak* Argentina 37 B5

Mercedes Argentina 44 C4

Mercedes Uruguay 42 B5

Mergui Myanmar 119 B5

Mergui Archipelago *Island chain* Myanmar 119 B6

Mérida Mexico 31 H3

Mérida Spain 72 D4

Mérida Venezuela 38 C2

Meridian Mississippi, USA 28 C3

Merredin Australia 129 B6

Mersin Turkey *var.* İçel 96 C4

Meru Kenya 55 C6

Merv *see* Mary

Mesa Arizona, USA 26 B2

Meshed *see* Mashhad

Messina Italy 77 D6

Messina, Stretto di *Sea feature* Ionian Sea/Tyrrhenian Sea 77 D7

Mesters Vig Greenland 62 D3

Mestre Italy 76 C2

Meta *River* Colombia/Venezuela 38 C2

Metković Croatia 80 C4

Metz France 70 D3

Meuse *River* W Europe *var.* Maas 70 D3

Mexicali Mexico 30 A1

Mexicana, Altiplanicie *see* Mexico, Plateau of

Mexico *Country* North America 30-31

México, Golfo de *see* Mexico, Gulf of

Mexico, Gulf of *Sea feature* Atlantic Ocean/Caribbean Sea 46 A4

Mexico, Plateau of *Upland* Mexico *Sp.* Altiplanicie Mexicana 14 D4

Mexico City *Capital* of Mexico *Sp.* Ciudad de México 31 E4

Meymaneh Afghanistan *var.* Maimana 102 D4

Mezen' *River* Russian Federation 90 D3

Miami Florida, USA 29 F5

Michigan *State* USA 20 C2

Montréal Canada 19 E4

Montreux Switzerland 75 A5

Montserrat *External territory* UK, West Indies 35

Monument Valley *Valley* SW USA 26 C1

Monywa Myanmar 118 A3

Monza Italy 76 B2

Moora Australia 129 B6

Moorhead Minnesota, USA 23 E2

Moosonee Canada 18 C3

Mopti Mali 53 E3

Morava *River* C Europe 79 B6 80 E4

Moravská Ostrava *see* Ostrava

Morawhanna Guyana 39 F2

Moray Firth *Inlet* Scotland, UK 68 C3

Moree Australia 130 C2

Morehead City North Carolina, USA 29 C2

Morelia Mexico 31 E4

Morena, Sierra *Mountain range* Spain 72 D4

Morghāb *River* Afghanistan/Turkmenistan 102 D4

Morioka Japan 110 D3

Morocco *Country* N Africa 50

Morogoro Tanzania 55 C7

Morondava Madagascar 59 F3

Moroni *Capital of* Comoros 59 F2

Morotai, Pulau *Island* Indonesia 121 F3

Moscow *Capital of* Russian Federation *Rus.* Moskva 90 B4 94 B2

Mosel *River* W Europe *Fr.* Moselle 75 A5

Moselle *River* W Europe *Ger.* Mosel 67 E8 70 E4

Moshi Tanzania 55 C7

Moskva *see* Moscow

Mosquito Coast *Coastal region* Nicaragua 33 E3

Moss Norway 65 B6

Mossendjo Congo 57 B6

Mossoró Brazil 41 H2

Most Czech Republic *Ger.* Brüx 78 A4

Mostaganem Algeria 50 D1

Mostar Bosnia & Herzegovina 80 C4

Mosul *see* Al Mawşil

Motril Spain 73 E5

Moulins France 70 C4

Moulmein Myanmar 118 B4

Moundou Chad 56 C4

Mount Gambier Australia 130 A4

Mount Isa Australia 126 A5 130 A1

Mount Vernon Illinois, USA 20 B5

Mouscron Belgium 67 A6

Moyale Kenya 55 C5

Moyobamba Peru 40 B2

Mozambique *Country* SE Africa 59

Mozambique Channel *Sea Feature* Indian Ocean 59 F3

Mozambique Ridge *Undersea feature* Indian Ocean 49 D8

Mozyr' *see* Mazyr

Mpika Zambia 59 E2

Mtwara Tanzania 55 C8

Muang Khammouan Laos 118 D4

Muang Không Laos 119 D5

Muang Xaignabouri Laos 118 D3

Mufulira Zambia 58 D2

Mugla Turkey 96 A4

Mukacheve Ukraine 88 B2

Mulhacen *Peak* Spain 60 C5

Mulhouse France 70 E4

Mull *Island* Scotland, UK 68 B3

Muller, Pegunungan *Mountains* Indonesia 120 D4

Multān Pakistan 114 C2

Mumbai *see* Bombay

Muna, Pulau *Island* Indonesia 121 E4

München Germany *Eng.* Munich 75 C6

Muncie Indiana, USA 20 C4

Munich *see* München

Münster Germany 74 A4

Muonio *River* Finland/Sweden 64 D3

Muqdisho *see* Mogadishu

Mur *River* C Europe 75 D7

Murcia *Region* Spain 73 F4

Mures *River* Hungary/Roma 79 D7

Murfreesboro Tennessee, USA 28 D1

Murgab Tajikistan 103 F3

Murgab *River* Turkmenistan *var.* Murghab 102 C3

Murghab *see* Murgab

Müritz *Lake* Germany 74 D3

Murmansk Russian Federation 90 C2 94 C1

Murray *River* Australia 130 A3

Murrumbidgee *River* Australia 130 B3

Murska Sobota Slovenia 80 E1

Murzuq Libya 51 F3

Muş Turkey 97 F3

Muscat *Capital of* Oman *Ar.* Masqaţ 101 E5

Musgrave Ranges *Mountain range* Australia 129 D5

Mwanza Tanzania 55 B6

Mwene-Ditu Congo (Zaire) 57

Mweru, Lake *Lake* Congo (Zaire)/Zambia 57 D7

Myanmar *Country* SE Asia *var.* Burma 118-119

Mykolayiv Ukraine *Rus.* Nikolayev 89 E4

Mysore India 116 D2

Mzuzu Malawi 59 E2

N

Naberezhnyye Chelny Russia Federation *prev.* Brezhnev 91 C5

Nacala Mozambique 59 F2

Næstved Denmark 65 D8

Naga Philippines 120 E1

Nagano Japan 110 C4

Nagasaki Japan 111 A6

Nāgercoil India 116 D3

Nagorno-Karabakh *Region* Azerbaijan 97 G2

Nagoya Japan 111 C5

Nāgpur India 114 D4

Nagqu China 106 C5

Nagykanizsa Hungary *Ger.* Grosskanizsa 79 C7

Nagyszombat *see* Trnava

Naha Japan 111 A8

kin Canada 19 N2
krobi *Capital of* Kenya 55 C6
jaf *see* An Najaf
jrān Saudi Arabia 101 B6
kamura Japan 111 B6
khichevan' *see* Naxçıvan
khodka Russian Federation 94 C3
khon Ratchasima Thailand 119 C5
khon Sawan Thailand 119 C5
khon Si Thammarat Thailand 119 C6
kina Canada 18 B3
kskov Denmark 65 D8
kuru Kenya 55 C6
l'chik Russian Federation 91 A7 94 A4
mangan Uzbekistan 103 E2
m Đinh Vietnam 118 D3
mib Desert *Desert* Namibia 58 B3
mibe Angola 58 A2
mibia *Country* southern Africa 58
mpa Idaho, USA 24 D3
mp'o North Korea 108 E4
mpula Mozambique 59 F2
mur Belgium 67 C6
nchang China 109 C6
ncy France 70 D3
ndad India 114 D5 116 D1
njing China 109 D5
nning China 109 B7
nortalik Greenland 62 C4
ntes France 70 B4
pier New Zealand 131 H2
ples *see* Napoli
po *River* Ecuador/Peru 40 B2
poli Italy *Eng.* Naples 77 D5
rbonne France 71 C6
rva Estonia 86 E2
rva *River* Estonia/Russian Federation 86 E2

Narva Bay *Sea feature* Gulf of Finland *Est.* Narva Laht, *Rus.* Narvskiy Zaliv 86 E2
Narva Laht *see* Narva Bay
Narvik Norway 64 C3
Narvskiy Zaliv *see* Narva Bay
Naryn Kyrgyzstan 103 G2
Naryn *River* Kyrgyzstan/Uzbekistan 103 F2
Nāshik India 114 C5
Nashville Tennessee, USA 28 D1
Nāsir, Buheiret *Reservoir* Egypt 55 B2
Nasiriya *see* An Nāşiriyah
Nassau *Capital of* Bahamas 34 C1
Natal Brazil 41 H3
Natitingou Benin 53 F4
Natuna, Kepulauan *Island group* Indonesia 122 C5
Nauru *Country* Pacific Ocean 126 D3
Navapolatsk Belarus *Rus.* Novopolotsk 87 D5
Navassa Island *External territory* USA, West Indies 34 D3
Navoi Uzbekistan *Uzb.* Nawoiy 102 D2
Nawābshāh Pakistan 114 B3
Nawoiy *see* Navoi
Naxçıvan Azerbaijan *Rus.* Nakhichevan' 97 G3
Náxos *Island* Greece 85 D6
Nazareth *see* Nazaret
Nazca Peru 40 B4
Nazaret Israel *Eng.* Nazareth 99 A5
Nazrēt Ethiopia 55 C5
Nazwá Oman 101 E5
N'Dalatando Angola 58 B1
Ndélé Central African Republic 56 C4
N'Djamena *Capital of* Chad 56 B3
Ndola Zambia 58 D2
Nebitdag Turkmenistan 102 B2
Nebraska *State* USA 22-23 E3
Neches *River* S USA 27 H3
Necochea Argentina 45 D5
Neftezavodsk *see* Seydi

Negēlē Ethiopia 55 C5
Negev *see* HaNegev
Negro, Río *River* Argentina 45 C5
Negro, Rio *River* Brazil/Uruguay 40 D2
Negro, Rio *River* N South America 38 D3
Negros *Island* Philippines 121 E2
Neiva Colombia 38 B3
Nellore India 114 D2
Nelson New Zealand 131 G3
Neman *River* NE Europe *Bel.* Nyoman, *Lith.* Nemunas, *Ger.* Memel, *Pol.* Niemen 86 B4
Nemunas *see* Neman
Nemuro Japan 110 E2
Nepal *Country* S Asia 115
Nepalganj Nepal 115 E3
Neretva *River* Bosnia & Herzegovina 80 C4
Neris *River* Belarus/Lithuania *Bel.* Viliya, *Pol.* Wilja 86 C4
Ness, Loch *Lake* Scotland, UK 68 C3
Netherlands *Country* W Europe *var.* Holland 66-67
Netherlands Antilles *External territory* Netherlands, West Indies *prev.* Dutch West Indies 36 C1
Netze *see* Noteć
Neubrandenburg Germany 74 D3
Neuchâtel, Lac de *Lake* Switzerland 75 A7
Neuhäusl *see* Nové Zámky
Neumünster Germany 74 B2
Neuquén Argentina 45 C5
Neusiedler See *Lake* Austria/Hungary 75 E7
Neusohl *see* Banská Bystrica
Neutra *see* Nitra
Nevada *State* USA 24-25
Nevel' Russian Federation 90 A4
Nevers France 70 C4
Nevşehir Turkey 96 D3
New Amsterdam Guyana 39 G2
Newark New Jersey, USA 21 F3
New Britain *Island* Papua New Guinea 126 C3

Oka *River* Russian Federation 95 E4

Okahandja Namibia 58 C3

Okavango *River var.* Cubango southern Africa 58 C2

Okavango Delta *Wetland* Botswana 58 C3

Okayama Japan 111 B5

Okazaki Japan 111 C5

Okeechobee, Lake *Lake* Florida, USA 29 F4

Okhotsk Russian Federation 95 G3

Okhotsk, Sea of *Pacific Ocean* 122 C1

Okinawa *Island* Japan 111 A8

Oki-shotō *Island group* Japan 111 B5

Oklahoma *State* USA 27 F1

Oklahoma City Oklahoma, USA 27 F2

Okushiri-tō *Island* Japan 110 C2

Okāra Pakistan 114 C2

Öland *Island* Sweden 65 C7

Olavarría Argentina 44 D4

Olbia Italy 77 A5

Oldenburg Germany 74 B3

Oleksandriya Ukraine *Rus.* Aleksandriya 89 E3

Olenëk Russian Federation 95 E3

Olhão Portugal 72 C5

Olita *see* Alytus

Olmaliq *see* Almalyk

Olmütz *see* Olomouc

Olomouc Czech Republic *Ger.* Olmütz 79 C5

Olsztyn Poland *Ger.* Allenstein 78 D2

Olt *River* Romania 88 B5

Olten Switzerland 75 B7

Olympia Washington, USA 24 B2

Omaha Nebraska, USA 23 F4

Oman *Country* SW Asia 101 D6

Oman, Gulf of *Sea feature* Indian Ocean 112 B2

Omdurman Sudan 54 B4

Omsk Russian Federation 94 C4

Ondangwa Namibia 58 C3

Onega *River* Russian Federation 90 B4

Onega, Lake *see* Onezhskoye Ozero

Onezhskoye Ozero *Lake* Russian Federation *Eng.* Lake Onega 90 B3

Ongole India 117 E2

Onitsha Nigeria 53 G5

Ontario *Province* Canada 18 B3

Ontario, Lake *Lake* Canada/USA 15 F3

Oostende Belgium *Eng.* Ostend 67 A5

Oosterschelde *Inlet* Netherlands 66 B4

Opole Poland *Ger.* Oppeln 78 C4

Oporto *see* Porto

Oppeln *see* Opole

Oradea Romania 88 B3

Oran Algeria 50 D1

Orange Australia 130 C3

Orange River *River* southern Africa 58 C4

Oranjestad Netherlands Antilles 35 E5

Ord *River* Australia 128 D3

Ordu Turkey 96 D2

Ordzhonikidze *see* Vladikavkaz

Örebro Sweden 65 C6

Oregon *State* USA 24

Orël Russian Federation 81 A5

Orem Utah, USA 22 B4

Orenburg Russian Federation 91 C6 94 B4

Orense *see* Ourense

Orestiáda Greece 84 D3

Orhon *River* Mongolia 107 E2

Orinoco *River* Colombia/Venezuela 39 E3

Orissa *State* India 115 E5

Oristano Italy 77 A5

Orizaba, Pico de *see* Citlaltépetl

Orkney *Islands* Scotland, UK 68 C2

Orlando Florida, USA 29 E4

Orléans France 70 C4

Ormsö *see* Vormsi

Örnsköldsvik Sweden 65 C5

Orontes *River* SW Asia 98 B3

Orosirá Rodópis *see* Rhodope Mountains

Orsha Belarus 87 E5

Orsk Russian Federation 91 D[94 B4

Oruro Bolivia 40 C4

Ōsaka Japan 111 C5

Ösel *see* Saaremaa

Osh Kyrgyzstan 103 F2

Oshawa Canada 18 D5

Oshkosh Wisconsin, USA 20 [

Osijek Croatia 80 C3

Oslo *Capital* of Norway 65 B6

Osmaniye Turkey 96 D4

Osnabrück Germany 74 B4

Osorno Chile 45 B5

Oss Netherlands 66 D4

Ossora Russian Federation 95 H2

Ostend *see* Oostende

Östersund Sweden 65 C5

Ostfriesische Inseln *Islands* Germany *Eng.* East Frisian Islands 74 A3

Ostrava Czech Republic *Ger.* Mährisch-Ostrau, *prev.* Moravská Ostrava 79 C

Ostrołęka Poland 78 D3

Ostrowiec Świętokrzyski Poland 78 D4

Ōsumi-shotō *Island group* Japa 111 A7

Otaru Japan 110 D2

Otra *River* Norway 65 A6

Otranto Italy 77 E5

Otranto, Strait of *Sea feature* Albania/Italy 81 C6

Ottawa *Capital* of Canada 18

Ottawa *River* Canada 18 D4

Ou *River* Laos 118 C3

Ouachita *River* SE USA 28 B2

Ouagadougou *Capital* of Burk 53 E4

Ouahigouya Burkina 53 E3

Ouargla Algeria 51 E2

Oudtshoorn South Africa 58 [

Ouémé *River* Benin 53 F4

Ouessant, Île d' *Island* France 70 A3

Ouésso Congo 57 C5

Oujda Morocco 50 D2

Oulu Finland 64 D4

Oulu *River* Finland 64 D4

Oulujärvi *Lake* Finland 64 E4

Ounas *River* Finland 64 D3

Pechora *River* Russian Federation 90 D3

Pecos Texas, USA 27 E3

Pecos *River* SW USA 26 D2

Pécs Hungary *Ger.* Fünfkirchen 79 C7

Pegu Myanmar 118 B4

Peipsi Järv *see* Peipus, Lake

Peipus, Lake *Lake* Estonia/Russian Federation *Est.* Peipsi Järv, *Rus.* Chudskoye Ozero 86 D2

Peiraías Greece *var.* Piraiévs, *Eng.* Piraeus 83 F3 85 C5

Peking *see* Beijing

Pelagie, Isola *Island* Italy 77 B8

Peloponnese *see* Pelopónnisos

Pelopónnisos *Peninsula* Greece *Eng.* Peloponnese 85 B6

Pelotas Brazil 42 C4

Pelotas *River* Brazil 42 D3

Pematangsiantar Indonesia 120 A3

Pemba *Island* Tanzania 49 E5

Pendleton Oregon, USA 24 C2

Pennines *Hills* England, UK 68 D4

Pennsylvania *State* USA 20-21

Penong Australia 129 D6

Penonomé Panama 33 F5

Pensacola Florida, USA 28 D3

Penza Russian Federation 91 B5

Penzance England, UK 69 C7

Peoria Illinois, USA 20 B4

Pereira Colombia 38 B3

Périgueux France 71 B5

Perm' Russian Federation *prev.* Molotov 91 D5 94 B3

Pernau *see* Pärnu

Pernik Bulgaria *prev.* Dimitrovo 84 B2

Pernov *see* Pärnu

Perpignan France 71 C6

Persian Gulf *Sea feature* Arabian Sea *var.* The Gulf 112 B2

Perth Australia 129 B6

Perth Scotland, UK 68 C3

Perth Basin *Undersea feature* Indian Ocean 124 A3

Peru C South America 40

Peru Basin *Undersea feature* Pacific Ocean 123 G4

Peru-Chile Trench *Undersea feature* Pacific Ocean 123 G4

Perugia Italy 76 C4

Pescara Italy 76 D4

Peshāwar Pakistan 114 C1

Petah Tiqwa Israel 99 A5

Peterborough England, UK 69 E6

Peterborough Canada 18 D5

Peter the First Island *Island* Antarctica 132 A4

Petra Jordan 99 B6

Petrich Bulgaria 84 B3

Petroaleksandrovsk *see* Turtkul'

Petrograd *see* St Petersburg

Petropavlovsk Russian Federation 94 C4

Petropavlovsk-Kamchatskiy Russian Federation 95 H3

Petrozavodsk Russian Federation 90 B3

Pevek Russian Federation 95 G1

Pforzheim Germany 75 B6

Phangan, Ko *Island* Thailand 119 C6

Philadelphia Pennsylvania, USA 21 F4

Philippines *Country* Asia 121

Philippine Sea Pacific Ocean 121 F1

Philippopolis *see* Plovdiv

Phnom Penh *Capital of* Cambodia 119 D6

Phoenix Arizona, USA 26 B2

Phoenix Islands *Island group* Kiribati 127 F3

Phôngsali Laos 118 C3

Phuket Thailand 119 B7

Phuket, Ko *Island* Thailand 119 B7

Phumĭ Sâmraông Cambodia 119 D5

Piacenza Italy 76 B2

Pianosa *Island* Italy 76 D4

Piatra-Neamţ Romania 88 C3

Piave *River* Italy 76 C2

Pielinen *Lake* Finland 64 E4

Pierre South Dakota, USA 23 E3

Piešťany Slovakia *Ger.* Pistyan, *Hung.* Pöstyén 79 C6

Pietermaritzburg South Africa 58 D4

Pihkva Järv *see* Pskov, Lake

Piła Poland *Ger.* Schneidemühl 78 C3

Pilar Paraguay 42 B3

Pilchilemu Chile 44 B4

Pilcomayo *River* C South America 42 B2 44 D2

Pillau *see* Baltiysk

Pilsen *see* Plzeň

Pinang, Pulau *Island* Malaysia 120 B3

Pinar del Río Cuba 34 A2

Píndos *Mountain range* Greece *Eng.* Pindus Mountains 61 E 84 A4

Pindus Mountains *see* Pindos

Pine Bluff Arkansas, USA 28

Pinega *River* Russian Federati 90 C3

Pineiós *River* Greece 84 B4

Pine Island Bay *Sea feature* Antarctica 132 B3

Ping, Mae Nam *River* Thailan 118 C4

Pingxiang China 109 B7

Pínnes, Ákra *Coastal feature* Greece 84 C4

Pinsk Belarus *Pol.* Pińsk 87 B4

Piraeus *see* Peiraías

Piraiévs *see* Peiraías

Pisa Italy 76 B3

Pisco Peru 40 B4

Pishpek *see* Bishkek

Pistyan *see* Piešťany

Pitcairn Islands *External territ* UK, Pacific Ocean 123 E4

Piteå Sweden 64 D4

Piteşti Romania 88 C4

Pittsburgh Pennsylvania, USA 21 E4

Pituffik Greenland 62 A2

Piura Peru 40 A2

Pivdennyy Bug *River* Ukraine 89 E3

Plasencia Spain 72 D3

Plate *River* Argentina/Urugua 42 B5 44 D4

Platte *River* C USA 23 E4

Plattensee *see* Balaton

Plenty, Bay of *Sea feature* New Zealand 131 H2

Pleven Bulgaria 84 C1

Płock Poland 78 D3

Prome Myanmar 118 A4

Prossnitz *see* Prostějov

Prostějov Czech Republic *Ger.* Prossnitz 79 C5

Provence *Region* France 71 D6

Providencia, Isla de *Island* Colombia 33 E3 34 B4

Provo Utah, USA 22 B4

Prudhoe Bay Alaska, USA 16 D2

Prydz Bay *Sea feature* Antarctica 133 G2

Przheval'sk *see* Karakol

Pskov Russian Federation 90 A4

Pskov, Lake *Lake* Estonia/Russian Federation *Est.* Pihkva Järv, *Rus.* Pskovskoye Ozero 86 D3

Pskovskoye Ozero *see* Pskov, Lake

Ptich' *see* Ptsich

Ptsich *River* Belarus *Rus.* Ptich' 87 D6

Pucallpa Peru 40 B3

Puebla Mexico 31 F4

Puerto Aisén Chile 45 B6

Puerto Bahía Negra Paraguay 42 E1

Puerto Barrios Guatemala 32 C2

Puerto Busch Bolivia 40 D5

Puerto Carreño Colombia 38 D2

Puerto Cortés Honduras 32 C2

Puerto Deseado Argentina 45 C7

Puerto Maldonado Peru 40 C4

Puerto Montt Chile 45 B5

Puerto Natales Chile 45 B7

Puerto Plata Dominican Republic 35 E3

Puerto Princesa Philippines 120 E2

Puerto Rico *External territory* USA, West Indies 35 F3

Puerto Rico Trench *Undersea feature* Caribbean Sea 35 F3

Puerto Santa Cruz Argentina 45 C7

Puerto Suárez Bolivia 40 D5

Puerto Vallarta Mexico 30 D4

Puerto Williams Chile 45 C8

Pula Croatia 80 B2

Punakha Bhutan 115 G3

Punata Bolivia 40 C4

Pune India *prev.* Poona 114 C5 116 C1

Punjab *State* India 114 C2

Puno Peru 40 C4

Punta Arenas Chile *prev.* Magallanes 45 B8

Puntarenas Costa Rica 32 D4

Purmerend Netherlands 66 C3

Purus *River* Brazil/Peru 40 C3

Pusan South Korea 108 E4

Putumayo *River* NW South America 38 C4

Pyandzh *see* Panj

Pyapon Myanmar 118 B4

Pyarnu *see* Pärnu

Pyinmana Myanmar 118 B3

Pyongyang *Capital of* North Korea 108 E4

Pyramiden Svalbard 63 G2

Pyramid Lake *Lake* Nevada, USA 25 C5

Pyrenees *Mountain range* SW Europe 60 C5

Q

Qaanaaq Greenland *var.* Thule 62 A2

Qal'eh-ye Now Afghanistan 102 D4

Qamdo China 106 D5

Qandahār *see* Kandahār

Qaqortoq Greenland 62 C4

Qara Qum *see* Karakumy

Qarshi *see* Karshi

Qasigiannguit Greenland 62 B3

Qatar *Country* SW Asia 101 D5

Qattara Depression *see* Qaṭṭâra, Monkhafad el

Qaṭṭâra, Monkhafad el *Desert basin* Egypt *Eng.* Qattara Depression 48 C2 54 A1

Qena Egypt 54 B2

Qeqertarsuaq Greenland 62 B3

Qeqertarsuaq *Island* Greenland 62 B3

Qeqertarsuatsiaat Greenland 62 B4

Qilian Shan *Mountain range* China 106 D4

Qingdao China 108 D4

Qinghai Hu *Lake* China *var.* Koko Nor 106 D4

Qing-Zang Gaoyuan *Plateau* China *Eng.* Plateau of Tibet 104 C2 106 B4

Qin Ling *Mountains* China 109 B5

Qiqihar China 108 D3

Qizilqum *see* Kyzyl Kum

Qom Iran *var.* Kum 100 C3

Qondūz *River* Afghanistan 103 E4

Qondūz *see* Kunduz

Quba Azerbaijan *Rus.* Kuba 97 H2

Québec Canada 19 E4

Québec *Province* Canada 18 D0

Queen Charlotte Islands *Island* Canada 16 D5

Queen Charlotte Sound *Sea feature* Canada 16 D5

Queen Elizabeth Islands *Island* Canada 17 F1

Queen Maud Land *Region* Antarctica 133 E1

Queensland *State* Australia 12 B5 130 B1

Queenstown New Zealand 131 F4

Quelimane Mozambique 59 E3

Querétaro Mexico 31 E4

Quetta Pakistan 114 B2

Quezaltenango Guatemala 32 B2

Quibdó Colombia 38 B2

Quimper France 70 A3

Qui Nhon Vietnam 119 E5

Quito *Capital of* Ecuador 38 A4

Qüqon *see* Kokand

Qyteti Stalin *see* Kuçovë

R

Raab *see* Győr

Raab *see* Rába

Rába *River* Austria/Hungary *Ger.* Raab 79 C7

Rabat *Capital of* Morocco 50 C2

Race, Cape *Coastal feature* Canada 15 G3 19 H4

Rach Gia Vietnam 119 D6

Ródos Greece *Eng.* Rhodes 85 E6

Rodosto *see* Tekirdağ

Roeselare Belgium 67 A6

Roma Australia 130 C6

Roma *see* Rome

Romania *Country* SE Europe 88

Romanovka Russian Federation 95 F4

Rome *Capital of* Italy *It.* Roma 76 C4

Rome Georgia, USA 28 D2

Rønne Denmark 65 D8

Ronne Ice Shelf *Ice feature* Antarctica 132 C2

Roosendaal Netherlands 66 C4

Rosario Argentina 44 D4

Roseau *Capital of* Dominica 35 G4

Rosenau *see* Rožňava

Rositten *see* Rēzekne

Ross Dependency *Territory* New Zealand, Antarctica 132-133

Ross Ice Shelf *Ice feature* Antarctica 132 D4

Rosso Mauritania 52 B3

Ross Sea Antarctica 132 D5

Rostak *see* Ar Rustāq

Rostock Germany 74 C2

Rostov-na-Donu Russian Federation 91 A6 94 A3

Roswell New Mexico, USA 26 D2

Rotorua New Zealand 131 G2

Rotterdam Netherlands 66 C4

Rouen France 70 C3

Rovaniemi Finland 64 D3

Rovno *see* Rivne

Rovuma *River* Mozambique/ Tanzania 55 B7 59 F2

Rožňava Slovakia *Ger.* Rosenau, *Hung.* Rozsnyó 79 D6

Rozsnyó *see* Rožňava

Rub' al Khali *Desert* SW Asia *Eng.* Great Sandy Desert, Empty Quarter 101 D6

Rudnyy Kazakhstan 94 B4

Rudolf, Lake *Lake* Ethiopia/ Kenya *var.* Lake Turkana 48 D4 55 C5

Ruiz *Peak* Colombia 36 B2

Rumbek Sudan 55 B5

Rundu Namibia 58 C3

Ruse Bulgaria 84 D1

Russian Federation *Country* Europe/Asia 90-91 94-95

Rust'avi Georgia 97 G2

Rutland Vermont, USA 21 F2

Rwanda *Country* C Africa 55

Ryazan' Russian Federation 91 B5 94 B3

Rybach'ye *see* Issyk-Kul'

Rybinskoye Vodokhranilishche *Reservoir* Russian Federation *Eng.* Rybinsk Reservoir 90 B4

Rybnik Poland 79 C5

Ryūkyū-rettō *Island group* Japan 111 A8

Rzeszów Poland 79 E5

S

Saale *River* Germany 74 C4

Saarbrücken Germany 75 A6

Saare *see* Saaremaa

Saaremaa *Island* Estonia *var.* Saare, Sarema, *Ger.* Ösel, *var.* Oesel 86 C2

Sabadell Spain 73 G2

Sabhā Libya 51 F2

Sable, Cape *Coastal feature* Canada 19 F5

Sabzevār Iran 100 D3

Sacramento California, USA 25 B6

Ṣa'dah Yemen 101 B6

Sado *Island* Japan 110 C4

Safi Morocco 50 B2

Saginaw Michigan, USA 20 C3

Sahara *Desert* N Africa 48 B3

Sahel *Region* W Africa 48 B3 53 F3

Saïda Lebanon *anc.* Sidon 98 B4

Saidpur Bangladesh 115 G3

Saigon *see* Hồ Chi Minh

Saimaa *Lake* Finland 65 E5

Saint-Brieuc France 70 A3

Saint Catherines Canada 18 D5

Saint-Chamond France 71 D5

St Christopher & Nevis *see* St Kitts & Nevis

St Cloud Minnesota, USA 23 F2

St-Denis *Capital of* Réunion 59 H3

Saintes France 70 B5

Saint-Étienne France 71 D5

St. George's *Capital of* Grenada 35 G5

St Helena *External territory* UK, Atlantic Ocean 47 D5

St Helens, Mount *Peak* USA 14 D3

St Helier *Capital* Jersey 69 D8

Saint-Jean, Lake *Lake* Canada 19 E4

Saint John Canada 19 F4

St John's Canada 19 H3

St Joseph Missouri, USA 23 F4

St Kitts & Nevis *Country* West Indies *var.* St Christopher & Nevis 35

St.-Laurent-du-Maroni French Guiana 39 H2

Saint Lawrence *River* Canada 19 E4

Saint Lawrence, Gulf of *Sea feature* Canada 19 G4

St. Lawrence Island *Island* Alaska, USA 16 B2

Saint-Lô France 71 B3

Saint-Louis Senegal 52 B3

St Louis Missouri, USA 23 G4

St Lucia *Country* West Indies 35

Saint-Malo France 70 B3

Saint-Nazaire France 70 A4

St Paul Minnesota, USA 23 F2

St Peter Port *Capital of* Guernsey 69 D8

St Petersburg Russian Federation *Rus.* Sankt-Peterburg, *prev.* Leningrad, Petrograd 90 B3 94 B2

St Petersburg Florida, USA 29 E4

St Pierre Canada 19 H4

Saint Pierre Saint Pierre & Miquelon 19 H4

Saint Pierre & Miquelon *External territory* France, Atlantic Ocean 19 H4

St Vincent, Cape *see* São Vicent Cabo de

St Vincent & The Grenadines *Country* West Indies 35

Sajama *Peak* Bolivia 36 B4

Sakākah Saudi Arabia 100 B4

Sakakawea, Lake *Lake* North Dakota, USA 22 D2

Santa Rosa Argentina 45 C4

Santa Rosa California, USA 25 A6

Santa Rosa de Copán Honduras 32 C2

Santa Rosa Island Island W USA 25 B8

Santee River SE USA 29 F2

Santiago Capital of Chile 44 B4

Santiago Dominican Republic 35 E3

Santiago Panama 33 F5

Santiago Spain 72 C1

Santiago de Cuba Cuba 34 C3

Santiago del Estero Argentina 44 C3

Santo Domingo Capital of Dominican Republic 35 E3

Santo Domingo de los Colorados Ecuador 38 A4

Santos Brazil 43 E2

Santos Plateau Undersea feature Atlantic Ocean 43 E3

Sanya China 109 B8

São Borja Brazil 42 C3

São Francisco River Brazil 41 G3

São José do Rio Preto Brazil 43 E2

São Luís Brazil 41 G2

Saône River France 70 D4

São Paulo Brazil 41 F5 43 E2

São Roque, Cabo de Coastal feature Brazil 36 E3

São Tomé Capital of Sao Tome & Principe 57 A5

São Tomé Island Sao Tome & Principe 57 A6

Sao Tome & Principe Country W Africa 57

São Vicente, Cabo de Coastal feature Portugal Eng. Cape St Vincent 60 B5 72 B5

Sapporo Japan 110 D2

Saragossa see Zaragoza

Sarajevo Capital of Bosnia & Herzegovina 80 C4

Sarandë Albania 81 D7

Saransk Russian Federation 91 B5

Saratov Russian Federation 91 B6

Sarawak State Malaysia 120 D3

Sardegna Island Italy Eng. Sardinia 77 B5 83 D3

Sardinia see Sardegna

Sarema see Saaremaa

Sargasso Sea Atlantic Ocean 46 B4

Sargodha Pakistan 114 C2

Sarh Chad 56 C4

Saruhan see Manisa

Sasebo Japan 111 A6

Saskatchewan Province Canada 17 F5

Saskatchewan River Canada 17 F5

Saskatoon Canada 17 F5

Sassari Italy 77 A5

Satu Mare Romania 88 B3

Saudi Arabia Country SW Asia 100-101

Sault Sainte Marie Canada 18 C4

Sault Sainte Marie Michigan, USA 20 C1

Saurimo Angola 58 C1

Sava River SE Europe 80 D3

Savannah Georgia, USA 29 F3

Savannah River SE USA 29 F3

Savannakhét Laos 118 D4

Savissivik Greenland 62 A2

Savona Italy 76 A3

Savonlinna Finland 65 E5

Şawqirah Oman 101 D6

Sayat Turkmenistan 102 D3

Sayhut Yemen 101 D7

Saynshand Mongolia 107 E2

Say 'ün Yemen 101 C6

Schaffhausen Switzerland 75 B7

Schaulen see Šiauliai

Schefferville Canada 19 E2

Scheldt River W Europe 67 B5

Schiermonnikoog Island Netherlands 66 D1

Schneidemühl see Piła

Schwäbische Alb Mountains Germany 75 B6

Schwarzwald Forested mountain region Germany Eng. Black Forest 75 B6

Schwerin Germany 74 C3

Schweriner See Lake Germany 74 C3

Scilly, Isles of Islands UK 69 B8

Scotia Ridge Undersea feature Atlantic Ocean 47 B7

Scotia Sea Atlantic Ocean 47 B7

Scotland National region UK 68

Scottsbluff Nebraska, USA 22 D3

Scottsdale Arizona, USA 26 B2

Scranton Pennsylvania, USA 21 F3

Scutari, Lake Lake Albania/Yugoslavia 81 C5

Seattle Washington, USA 24 B2

Ségou Mali 52 D3

Segovia Spain 73 E2

Segura River Spain 73 E4

Seikan Tunnel Tunnel Japan 110 D3

Seinäjoki Finland 65 D5

Seine River France 70 C3

Sekondi-Takoradi Ghana 53 E5

Selfoss Iceland 63 E4

Selma Alabama, USA 28 D3

Semara Western Sahara 50 B3

Semarang Indonesia 120 C5

Semipalatinsk Kazakhstan 94 D4

Sên River Cambodia 118-119 D5

Sendai Japan 110 D4

Senegal Country W Africa 52

Senegal River Africa 52 B3

Seoul Capital of South Korea Kor. Sŏul 108 E4

Sept-Îles Canada 19 F3

Seraing Belgium 67 D6

Seram Island Indonesia 121 F4

Serbia Republic Yugoslavia 80 D3

Seremban Malaysia 120 B3

Sermersuaq Region Greenland 62 B2

Serov Russian Federation 94 C3

Serpent's Mouth, The Sea feature Trinidad & Tobago/Venezuela Sp. Boca de la Serpiente 39 F1

Serra do Mar Mountains Brazil 42 D3

Sérres Greece 84 C3

Sétif Algeria 51 E1

Setúbal Portugal 72 C4

Seul, Lake Lake Canada 18 A3

Sevana Lich Lake Armenia 97 G2

Sevastopol' Ukraine 89 C5

ingfield Illinois, USA
0 B4

ingfield Massachusetts, USA
1 G3

ingfield Missouri, USA
3 F5

ingfield Oregon, USA 24 B3

brenica Bosnia &
Herzegovina 80 C4

Lanka Country S Asia
rev. Ceylon 117

nagar India 114 D1

nagarind Reservoir Reservoir
Thailand 119 C5

inabad see Dushanbe

ingrad see Volgograd

lin Peak see Communism
Peak

linsk see Novokuznetsk

mbul see İstanbul

nleyville see Kisangani

novoy Range Mountain range
Russian Federation 93 F3

ra Planina see Balkan
Mountains

ra Zagora Bulgaria 84 D2

anger Norway 65 A6

vropol' Russian Federation
1 A7 94 A3

inamanger see Szombathely

inkjer Norway 64 B4

panakert see Xankändi

ttin see Szczecin

wart Island Island New
Zealand 131 F5

o Macedonia 81 E5

ling Scotland, UK 68 C4

ckerau Austria 75 E6

ckholm Capital of Sweden
65 C6

ckton California, USA 25 B6

eng Treng Cambodia 119 D5

ke-on-Trent England, UK
59 D6

lp see Słupsk

rnoway Scotland, UK 68 B2

alsund Germany 74 D2

anraer Scotland, UK 68 C4

asbourg France
Ger. Strassburg 70 E4

atford-upon-Avon England,
UK 69 D6

Strimon see Struma

Stromboli Island Italy 77 D6

Struma prev. Ceylon
Bulgaria/Greece Gk. Strimon,
var. Strymon 84 C3

Strumica Macedonia 81 E5

Strymon see Struma

Stuhlweissenburg see
Székesfehérvár

Stuttgart Germany 75 B6

Subotica Yugoslavia 80 D2

Suceava Romania 88 C3

Sucre Capital of Bolivia 40 C5

Sudan Country NE Africa 54-55

Sudbury Canada 18 C4

Sudd Region Sudan 55 B5

Sudeten Mountains Central
Europe var. Sudetes, Sudetic
Mountains, Cz./Pol. Sudety
79 B5

Sudetes see Sudeten

Sudetic Mountains see Sudeten

Sudety see Sudeten

Suez Egypt 54 B1

Suez, Gulf of Sea feature Red Sea
99 A8

Suez Canal Canal Egypt
Ar. Qanāt as Suways 48 D2

Şuhār Oman 101 D5

Sühbaatar Mongolia 107 E1

Sukhumi see Sokhumi

Sukkur Pakistan 114 B3

Sula, Kepulauan Island group
Indonesia 121 F4

Sulawesi Island Indonesia
Eng. Celebes 121 E4

Sulu Archipelago Island group
Philippines 121 E3

Sülüktü see Sulyukta

Sulu Sea Pacific Ocean 121 E2

Sulyukta Kyrgyzstan
Kir. Sülüktü 103 E2

Sumatra Island Indonesia 121 B4

Sumba Island Indonesia 121 E5

Sumbawanga Tanzania 55 B7

Sumbe Angola 58 B2

Sumgait see Sumqayıt

Sumqayıt Azerbaijan
Rus. Sumgait 97 H2

Sumy Ukraine 89 F2

Sunderland England, UK 68 D4

Sundsvall Sweden 65 C5

Suntar Russian Federation 94 F3

Sunyani Ghana 53 E4

Superior Wisconsin, USA 20 A1

Superior, Lake Lake
Canada/USA 18 C3

Suqutrá Island Yemen
var. Socotra 101 D7 112 B3

Şūr Oman 101 E5

Surabaya Indonesia 120 D5

Sūrat India 114 C5

Surat Thani Thailand 119 C6

Sûre River W Europe 67 D7

Surigao Philippines 120 F2

Surinam see Suriname

Suriname Country NE South
America var. Surinam 39

Surkhob River Tajikistan 103 E3

Surt Libya var. Sidra 51 G2

Surt, Khalīj Sea feature
Mediterranean Sea Eng. Gulf
of Sirte, Gulf of Sidra 51 G2
83 E4

Susanville California, USA
25 B5

Suva Capital of Fiji 127 E4

Svalbard External territory
Norway, Arctic Ocean 63 G2

Svay Riêng Cambodia 119 D6

Sverdlovsk see Yekaterinburg

Svetlogorsk see Svyetlahorsk

Svyetlahorsk Belarus
Rus. Svetlogorsk 87 D7

Swakopmund Namibia 58 B3

Swansea Wales, UK 69 C6

Swaziland Country southern
Africa 58-59

Sweden Country N Europe
64-65

Sweetwater Texas, USA 27 F3

Swindon England, UK 69 D6

Switzerland Country
C Europe 75

Sydney Australia 130 C3

Sydney Canada 19 G4

Syktyvkar Russian Federation
90 D4 94 C3

Sylhet Bangladesh 115 G4

Syracuse see Siracusa

Syracuse New York, USA 21 F3

Syr Darya River C Asia 102

Syria Country SW Asia 98-99

Syrian Desert Desert SW Asia
Ar. Bādiyat ash Shām 100 A3

myr, Ozero *Lake* Russian
Federation 95 E2

myr, Poluostrov *Peninsula*
Russian Federation *Eng.*
Taymyr Peninsula 93 I1 95 E2

myr Peninsula *see* Taymyr,
Poluostrov

ilisi *Capital of Georgia*
Geor. T'bilisi, *prev.* Tiflis 97 F2

dzhen Turkmenistan
Turkm. Tejen 102 C3

gucigalpa *Capital of Honduras*
32 C2

heran *see* Tehrān

hrān *Capital of Iran*
prev. Teheran 100 C3

huantepec, Golfo de *Sea*
feature Mexico 31 G5

jen *see* Tedzhen

jo *see* Tagus

kirdağ Turkey *It.* Rodosto
96 A2

el Aviv-Yafo Israel 99 A5

eles Piras *River* Brazil 41 E3

ell Atlas *Plateau* Africa 82 C3

el'man *see* Tel'mansk

el'mansk Turkmenistan
Turkm. Tel'man 102 C2

elšiai Lithuania *Ger.* Telschen
86 B3

emuco Chile 45 B5

enerife *Island* Spain 50 A3

ennant Creek Australia 126 A5
128 E3

ennessee *State* USA 28 D1

ennessee *River* SE USA 29 C1

epelenë Albania 81 D6

epic Mexico 30 D4

eplice Czech Republic *Ger.*
Teplitz, *prev.* Teplice-Šanov,
Ger. Teplitz-Schönau 78 A4

eplice-Šanov *see* Teplice

eplitz *see* Teplice

eplitz-Schönau *see* Teplice

eraina *Island* Kiribati 127 G2

eresina Brazil 41 G2

ermez Uzbekistan 103 E3

erneuzen Netherlands 67 B5

erni Italy 76 C4

ernopil' Ukraine
Rus. Ternopol' 88 C2

errassa Spain 73 G2

Terschelling *Island* Netherlands
66 C1

Teruel Spain 73 F3

Teseney Eritrea 54 C4

Tete Mozambique 59 E2

Tétouan Morocco 50 C1

Tetovo Macedonia 81 D5

Tetschen *see* Děčín

Tevere *River* Italy 76 C4

Texas *State* USA 26-27

Texas City Texas, USA 27 G4

Texel *Island* Netherlands 66 C2

Thailand *Country* SE Asia
118-119

Thailand, Gulf of *Sea feature*
South China Sea 119 C6

Thames *River* England, UK
69 D6

Thâne India 115 C5 116 C1

Thar Desert *Desert*
India/Pakistan 114 C3

Thásos *Island* Greece 84 C3

Thaton Myanmar 118 B4

Theiss *see* Tisza

Thermaic Gulf *see* Thermaïkós
Kólpos

Thermaïkós Kólpos *Sea feature*
Greece *Eng.* Thermaic Gulf
84 B4

Thessaloníki Greece
var. Salonica 84 B3

Thiès Senegal 52 B3

Thiladunmathi Atoll *Island*
Maldives 116 C4

Thimphu *Capital of Bhutan*
115 G3

Thionville France 70 D3

Thíra *Island* Greece 85 D6

Thompson Canada 17 G4

Thon Buri Thailand 119 C5

Thorn *see* Toruń

Thorshavn *see* Tórshavn

Thracian Sea Greece
Gk. Thrakikó Pelagos 84 D3

Thrakikó Pélagos *see* Thracian
Sea

Thule *see* Qaanaaq

Thun Switzerland 75 A7

Thunder Bay Canada 18 B4

Thüringer Wald *Forested moun-*
tains Germany 75 C5

Thurso Scotland, UK 68 C2

Tianjin China *var.* Tientsin
108 D4

Tiaret Algeria 50 D1

Tiberias, Lake *Lake* Israel
var. Sea of Galilee, *Heb.* Yam
Kinneret, *Ar.* Bahrat Tabariya
99 B5

Tibesti *Mountains* Chad/Libya
48 C3

Tibet *Autonomous region* China
Chin. Xizang 106 C5

Tibet, Plateau of *see* Qing-Zang
Gaoyuan

Tienen Belgium 67 C6

Tien Shan *Mountain range*
C Asia 92 D4

Tientsin *see* Tianjin

Tierra del Fuego *Island*
Argentina/Chile 45 C8

Tiflis *see* Tbilisi

Tighina Moldova *prev.* Bendery
88 D2

Tigris *River* SW Asia 92 B4

Tijuana Mexico 30 A1

Tiksi Russian Federation 95 F2

Tilburg Netherlands 66 C4

Tillabéri Niger 53 F3

Tilsit *see* Sovetsk

Timaru New Zealand 131 F4

Timişoara Romania 88 A4

Timmins Canada 18 C4

Timor *Island* Indonesia 121 F5

Timor Sea Indian Ocean
112 E4

Timor Trough *Undersea feature*
Indian Ocean 128 C1

Tindouf Algeria 50 B3

Tínos *Island* Greece 85 D5

Tirana *Capital of Albania* 81 D6

Tiraspol Moldova 88 A4

Tîrgovişte *see* Târgovişte

Tîrgu Mureş *see* Târgu Mureş

Tirol *Region* Austria *var.* Tyrol
75 C7

Tirso *River* Italy 77 A5

Tiruchchirāppalli India 116 C3

Tisa *see* Tisza

Tisza *River* E Europe *Ger.*
Theiss, *Cz./Rom./SCr.* Tisa
79 D6

Titicaca, Lake *Lake* Bolivia/Peru
40 C4

Titov Veles Macedonia 81 E5

Tlemcen Algeria 50 D2

Toamasina Madagascar 59 G3

Ushak *see* Uşak

Ushuaia Argentina 45 C8

Ust'-Chaun Russian Federation 95 G1

Ustica, Isola de *Island* Italy 77 C6

Ústí nad Labem *Czech Republic Ger.* Aussig 78 A4

Ust'-Kamchatsk Russian Federation 95 H2

Ust'-Kamenogorsk Kazakhstan 94 D5

Ustyurt Plateau *Upland* Kazakhstan/Uzbekistan 102 B1

Usumacinta *River* Guatemala/Mexico 32 B1

Usumbura *see* Bujumbura

Utah *State* USA 22 B4

Utena Lithuania 86 C4

Utica New York, USA 21 F2

Utrecht Netherlands 66 C3

Uttar Pradesh *State* India 115 E3

Uummannarsuaq *Coastal feature* Greenland *Dan.* Cap Farvel, *Eng.* Cape Farewell 62 C5

Uvs Nuur *Lake* Mongolia 106 C2

Uyo Nigeria 53 G5

Uyuni Bolivia 41 C5

Uzbekistan *Country* C Asia 102-103

Uzhhorod Ukraine *Rus.* Uzhgorod 88 B2

V

Vaal *River* South Africa 58 D4

Vaasa Finland 65 D5

Vadodara India 114 C4

Vaduz *Capital of* Liechtenstein 75 B7

Vág *see* Váh

Váh *River* Slovakia *Ger.* Waag, *Hung.* Vág 79 C6

Valdés, Península *Peninsula* Argentina 45 C6

Valdez Alaska, USA 16 D3

Valdivia Chile 45 B5

Valdosta Georgia, USA 29 E3

Valence France 71 D5

Valencia Spain 73 F3

Valencia Venezuela 38 D1

Valencia *Region* Spain 73 F3

Valentine Nebraska, USA 23 E3

Valera Venezuela 38 C1

Valga Estonia *Ger.* Walk 86 D3

Valladolid Spain 72 D2

Valledupar Colombia 38 C1

Vallenar Chile 44 B3

Valletta *Capital of* Malta 77 C8

Valley, The *Capital of* Anguilla 35 G3

Valmiera Latvia *Ger.* Wolmar 86 C3

Valparaíso Chile 44 B4

Van Turkey 97 F3

Van, Lake *see* Van Gölü

Vanadzor Armenia *prev.* Kirovakan 97 F2

Vancouver Canada 17 E5

Vancouver Washington, USA 24 B2

Vancouver Island *Island* Canada 16 D5

Vänern *Lake* Sweden 65 B6

Vangaindrano Madagascar 59 G4

Van Gölü *Lake* Turkey *Eng.* Lake Van 97 F3

Vantaa Finland 65 D5

Vanua Levu *Island* Fiji 127 E4

Vanuatu *Country* Pacific Ocean 122

Vārānasi India 115 E3

Varaždin Croatia 80 B2

Vardar *River* Greece/Macedonia *prev.* Axios 81 E6 84 B3

Vardø Norway 64 E2

Varkaus Finland 65 E5

Varna Bulgaria 84 E1

Västerås Sweden 65 C6

Västervik Sweden 65 C7

Vatican City *Country* S Europe 76 C4

Vava'u Group *Island group* Tonga 127 F4

Vawkavysk Belarus *Rus.* Volkovysk, *Pol.* Wołkowysk 87 B6

Växjö Sweden 65 B7

Vaygach, Ostrov *Island* Russian Federation 90 E3

Vejle Denmark 65 A7

Velenje Slovenia 80 A2

Velika Plana Yugoslavia 80 D□

Velingrad Bulgaria 84 C2

Vellore India 116 D2

Venezia Italy *Eng.* Venice 76 □

Venezuela *Country* N South America 38-39

Venezuela, Gulf of *Sea feature* Caribbean Sea 38 C1

Venezuelan Basin *Undersea feature* Caribbean Sea 35 F4

Venice *see* Venezia

Venice, Gulf of *Sea feature* Adriatic Sea 76 C2

Venlo Netherlands 67 D5

Venta *River* Latvia/Lithuania 86 B3

Ventspils Latvia *Ger.* Windau 86 B3

Vera Argentina 44 D3

Veracruz Mexico 31 F4

Verkhoyansk Khrebet *Mountain range* Russian Federation 93 F2 95 F3 Verkhoyansk Range 93 F2 95 F3

Verkhoyansk Range *see* Verkhoyanskiy Khrebet

Vermont *State* USA 21 G2

Vernon Texas, USA 27 F2

Véroia Greece 84 B3

Verona Italy 76 B3

Versailles France 70 C3

Verviers Belgium 67 D6

Vesoul France 70 D4

Veszprém Hungary *Ger.* Veszprim 79 C7

Veszprim *see* Veszprém

Viana do Castelo Portugal 72 C2

Vianden Luxembourg 67 D7

Viareggio Italy 76 B3

Vicenza Italy 76 B2

Vichy France 71 C5

Victoria *State* Australia 128 D2 130 B4

Victoria Canada 16 D5

Victoria *Capital of* Seychelles 59 H1

Victoria Texas, USA 27 G4

Victoria *River* Australia 124 B2

Victoria, Lake *Lake* E Africa *var.* Victoria Nyanza 55 B6

Victoria Falls *Waterfall* Zambia/Zimbabwe 49 C6

W

Warangal India 115 E5 117 E1

Warsaw *Capital of* Poland *Pol.* Warszawa, *Ger.* Warschau 78 D3

Warschau *see* Warsaw

Warszawa *see* Warsaw

Warta *River* Poland *Ger.* Warthe 78 C4

Warthe *see* Warta

Wash, The *Inlet* England, UK 69 E5

Washington *State* USA 24

Washington DC *Capital of* USA 21 E4

Washington Land *Region* Greenland 62 A2

Waterford Ireland 69 B6

Watertown New York, USA 21 F2

Watertown South Dakota, USA 23 E2

Watson Lake Canada 17 E4

Wau Sudan 55 B5

Wawa Canada 18 C4

Weddell Sea Antarctica 132 C2

Weed California, USA 24 B4

Weichsel *see* Wisła

Weissenstein *see* Paide

Wellington *Capital of* New Zealand 131 G3

Wellington, Isla *Island* Chile 45 B7

Wels Austria 75 D6

Wenden *see* Cēsis

Werder *see* Virtsu

Werro *see* Võru

Wesenberg *see* Rakvere

Weser *River* Germany 74 B3

West Australian Basin *Undersea feature* Indian Ocean 113 D5

West Bank *Disputed territory* SW Asia 99 A5

West Bengal *State* India 115 F4

Western Australia *State* Australia 128 C4

Western Dvina *River* E Europe *Bel.* Dzvina, *Ger.* Düna, *Latv.* Daugava, *Rus.* Zapadnaya Dvina 86 D4

Western Ghats *Mountain range* India 104 B3

Western Isles *see* Outer Hebrides

Western Sahara *Region occupied by Morocco* N Africa 50 A3

Western Sierra Madre *see* Sierra Madre Occidental

Westerschelde *Inlet* Netherlands 67 B5

West European Basin *Undersea feature* Atlantic Ocean 46 C3

West Falkland *Island* Falkland Islands 45 C7

West Frisian Islands *see* Waddeneilanden

West Indies *Island group* North America 46 A4

West Palm Beach Florida, USA 29 F5

Westport New Zealand 131 F3

West Siberian Plain *Region* Russian Federation 92 C2 94 D3

West Virginia *State* USA 20-21 D5

Wetar, Pulau *Island* Indonesia 121 F5

Wexford Ireland 69 B6

Whangarei New Zealand 131 G1

Wheeling Ohio, USA 20 D4

Whitehorse Canada 16 D4

White Nile *River* Sudan 55 B5

White River *River* S USA 28 B1

White Sea *see* Beloye More

White Volta *River* Burkina/Ghana 53 E4

Whitney, Mount *Peak* W USA 14 D4

Whyalla Australia 129 E6 130 A3

Wichita Kansas, USA 23 E5

Wichita Falls Texas, USA 27 F2

Wicklow Mountains *Mountains* Ireland 69 B6

Wien *see* Vienna

Wiener Neustadt Austria 75 E7

Wiesbaden Germany 75 B5

Wight, Isle of *Island* England, UK 69 D7

Wilcannia Australia 130 B3

Wilhelm, Mount *Peak* Papua New Guinea 124 C1

Wilja *see* Neris

Wilkes Land *Region* Antarctica 133 G5

Willemstad Netherlands Antilles 35 E5

Williamsport Pennsylvania, USA 21 E3

Williston North Dakota, USA 22 D1

Wilmington Delaware, USA 21 F4

Wilmington North Carolina, USA 29 G2

Wilna *see* Vilnius

Wilno *see* Vilnius

Wilson North Carolina, USA 29 F1

Windau *see* Ventspils

Windhoek *Capital of* Namibia 58 C3

Windsor Canada 18 C5

Windward Islands *Islands* West Indies 35 G4

Winisk Canada 18 C2

Winisk *River* Canada 18 B3

Winnemucca Nevada, USA 25 C5

Winnipeg Canada 17 G5

Winnipeg, Lake *Lake* Canada 17 G5

Winnipegosis, Lake *Lake* Canada 17 G5

Winston-Salem North Carolina, USA 29 F1

Winterthur Switzerland 75 B7

Wisconsin *State* USA 20 B2

Wismar Germany 74 C3

Wisła *River* Poland *Ger.* Weichsel, *Eng.* Vistula 61 E3 78 D4

W.J. van Blommesteinmeer *Reservoir* Suriname 39 H3

Włocławek Poland 78 C3

Wodzisław Śląski Poland *Ger.* Loslau 79 C5

Wolfsburg Germany 74 C4

Wollongong Australia 130 C3

Wolmar *see* Valmiera

Wönsan North Korea 108 E4

Woods, Lake of the *Lake* Canada/USA 18 A4

Worcester England, UK 69 D6

Worcester Massachusetts, USA 21 G3

Worms *see* Vormsi

Wołkowysk *see* Vawkavysk

ULTIMATE POCKET
BOOK OF THE
WORLD
FACTFILE

A DORLING KINDERSLEY BOOK

Project Editor Debra Clapson
Project Cartographer Julia Lunn
Project Art Editor Yahya El-Droubie

Designer Katy Wall
Cartographic Research Michael Martin
Database Editor Ruth Duxbury

Art Director Chez Picthall
Editorial Direction Andrew Heritage, Louise Cavanagh
Production Controller David Proffit

Editorial Contributors
Kevin McRae, Melanie McRae, Louisa Somerville, Sean Connolly

Dorling Kindersley would like to thank
The Flag Institute, Chester for providing the national flags

Produced by Dorling Kindersley Cartography

First American Edition, 1996
2 4 6 8 10 9 7 5 3

Published in the United States by Dorling Kindersley Publishing Inc.,
95 Madison Avenue, New York, New York 10016
First published in this version 1998

Copyright © 1996, 1998 Dorling Kindersley Limited, London
Visit us on the World Wide Web at http://www.dk.com

ISBN 07894-3623-X

Film output in England by Euroscan
Printed and bound in Italy by L.E.G.O

ULTIMATE POCKET
BOOK OF THE
WORLD

FACTFILE

CONTENTS

AFRICA 58-59

ASIA

AUSTRALASIA & OCEANIA

PHYSICAL WORLD

POLITICAL WORLD

ARCTIC OCEAN

Queen Elizabeth Is

Greenland
(Denmark)

Victoria I.   Baffin I.

ALASKA
(USA)

Aleutian Is. (USA)

C A N A D A

ATLANTIC
OCEAN

PACIFIC
OCEAN

UNITED STATES
OF AMERICA

Bermuda
(UK)

Hawaii
(USA)

MARSHALL IS.

MEXICO   BELIZE

GUATEMALA   HONDURAS
EL SALVADOR   NICARAGUA
COSTA RICA
PANAMA

VEN.

Wallis & Futuna
(France)

NAURU

K I R I B A T I

TUVALU   Tokelau   Cook Is.
(NZ)   (NZ)
American
Samoa
(USA)
French Polynesia
FIJI   Niue   (France)
(NZ)
VANUATU   TONGA
SOLOMON IS.   SAMOA
ew Caledonia
(France)

Pitcairn Is.
(UK)

PACIFIC
OCEAN

NEW ZEALAND

DOMINICAN REP.

BAHAMAS   Turks &
Caicos Is.
(UK)
CUBA
Cayman Is.
(UK)
JAMAICA   HAITI

Puerto Rico
(USA)
Virgin Is.
(USA)
British Virgin Is.
(UK)
Anguilla
(UK)
ANTIGUA &
BARBUDA
Guadeloupe
(France)
DOMINICA
ST KITTS & NEVIS   Martinique
Montserrat (UK)   (France)
ST LUCIA
Aruba
(Neth.)   BARBADOS
Netherlands Antilles   GRENADA
(Neth.)   ST VINCENT
& THE GRENADINES
TRINIDAD & TOBAGO

COLOMBIA

ECUADOR   GUYANA   SURINAME
French
Guiana
(France)

PERU   B R A Z I L

BOLIVIA
PARAGUAY

CHILE   URUGUAY
ARGENTINA

ATLANTIC
OCEAN

Falkland Is.
(UK)

South Georgia
(UK)

South
Sandwich Is.
(UK)

South Shetland Is.   South Orkney Is
(UK)   (UK)

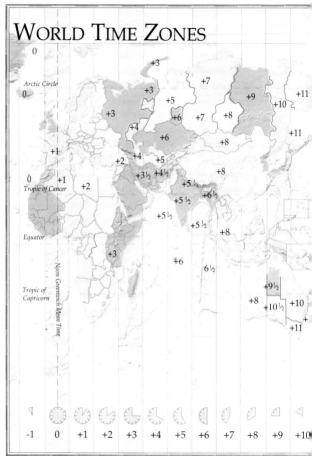

WORLD TIME ZONES

nbers on the map show the number of hours ahead of, or behind, GMT (Greenwich Mean Time).

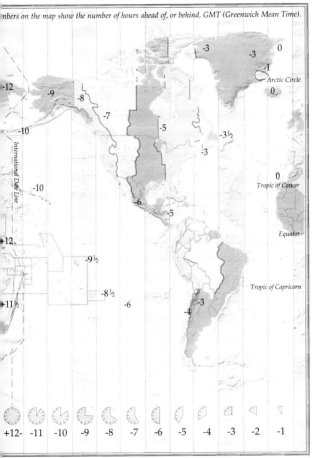

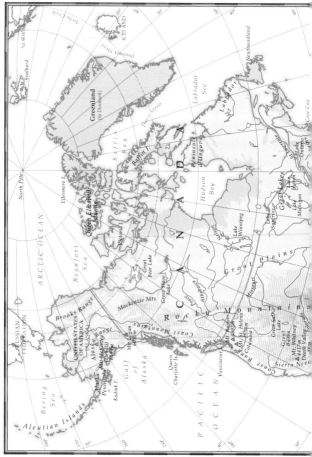

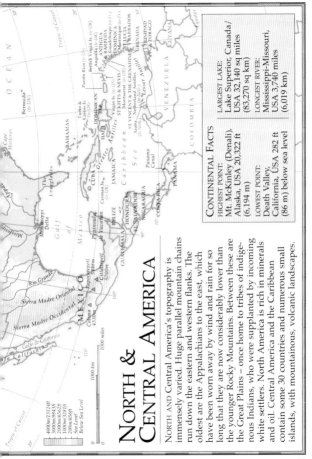

NORTH & CENTRAL AMERICA

NORTH AND CENTRAL America's topography is immensely varied. Huge parallel mountain chains run down the eastern and western flanks. The oldest are the Appalachians to the east, which have been worn away by wind and rain for so long that they are now considerably lower than the younger Rocky Mountains. Between these are the Great Plains – once home to tribes of indigenous Indians, who were supplanted by incoming white settlers. North America is rich in minerals and oil. Central America and the Caribbean contain some 30 countries and numerous small islands, with mountainous and volcanic landscapes.

CONTINENTAL FACTS

HIGHEST POINT:
Mt. McKinley (Denali),
Alaska, USA 20,322 ft
(6,194 m)

LOWEST POINT:
Death Valley,
California, USA 282 ft
(86 m) below sea level

LARGEST LAKE:
Lake Superior, Canada/
USA 32,140 sq miles
(83,270 sq km)

LONGEST RIVER:
Mississippi-Missouri,
USA 3,740 miles
(6,019 km)

15

CANADA

CANADA EXTENDS from its long border with the USA northward to the Arctic Ocean. In recent years, the continued political relationship of French-speaking Québec with the rest of the country has been the key constitutional issue.

GEOGRAPHY

Arctic tundra and islands give way southward to forests, interspersed with lakes and rivers, and then central plains, with vast prairies. Rocky Mountains lie in the west, beyond which are the Coast Mountains, islands and fjords. Fertile lowlands in the east.

CLIMATE

Ranges from polar and subpolar in the north to cool in the south. Winters in the interior are colder and longer than on the coasts, with temperatures well below freezing and deep snow; summers are hotter. The Pacific coast has the warmest winters.

PEOPLE AND SOCIETY

Most people live along narrow strip near the US border, fostering shared cultural values. Social differences, however, include wider welfare provision and Commonwealth membership. Government welcomes ethnic diversity among immigrants. Land claims by indigenous peoples settled in recent years.

THE ECONOMY

Wide-ranging resources, providing cheap energy and raw materials for manufacturing, underpin high standard of living. Better productivity and rise of high-tech industries have increased unemployment. Concern over primary export prices.

◆ INSIGHT: *The magnetic north pole, where the trembling needle of a compass stands still, is located just off Bathurst Island in northern Canada*

3000m/9843ft
2000m/6562ft
1000m/3281ft
500m/1640ft
200m/656ft
Sea Level

0   400 km
0   400 miles

Greenland

USA   CANADA   USA

ARCTIC OCEAN

Ellesmere I.

80°

Baffin
Bay

Queen Elizabeth
Islands

Parry Islands
Bathurst I.

Devon I.

Beaufort
Sea

Banks I.

UNITED STATES

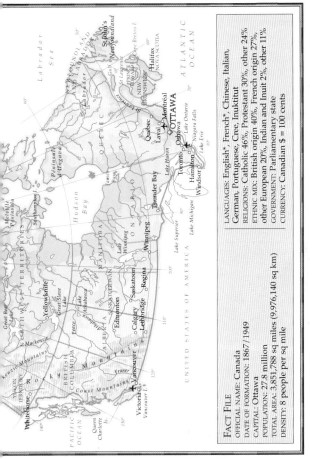

FACT FILE

OFFICIAL NAME: Canada
DATE OF FORMATION: 1867/1949
CAPITAL: Ottawa
POPULATION: 27.8 million
TOTAL AREA: 3,851,788 sq miles (9,976,140 sq km)
DENSITY: 8 people per sq mile

LANGUAGES: English*, French*, Chinese, Italian, German, Portuguese, Cree, Inuktitut
RELIGIONS: Catholic 46%, Protestant 30%, other 24%
ETHNIC MIX: British origin 40%, French origin 27%, other European 20%, Indian and Inuit 2%, other 11%
GOVERNMENT: Parliamentary state
CURRENCY: Canadian $ = 100 cents

UNITED STATES OF AMERICA

STRETCHING ACROSS the most temperate part of North America, and with many natural resources, the USA is the world's leading economic power.

GEOGRAPHY
Central plain, mountains in west, hills and low mountains in east. Forested north and east, south-western deserts. Volcanic islands in Hawaii. Forest, tundra in Alaska.

CLIMATE
Wide variety. Continental in north, hot summers and mild winters in southeast, desert climate in southwest. Arctic climate in Alaska; Florida and Hawaii tropical.

PEOPLE AND SOCIETY
Multiracial population, established through successive waves of immigration, initially from Europe and Africa, with more recent influxes from Latin America and Asia. Strong sense of nationhood, despite cultural diversity. Conservative, usually Christian consensus, is increasingly challenged by liberal, secular values of US popular culture.

FACT FILE
OFFICIAL NAME: United States of America
DATE OF FORMATION: 1787/1959
CAPITAL: Washington D.C.
POPULATION: 265.8 million
TOTAL AREA: 3,681,760 sq miles (9,372,610 sq km)

DENSITY: 72 people per sq mile
LANGUAGES: English*, Spanish, other
RELIGIONS: Protestant 56%, Catholic 28%, Muslim 3%, other 13%
ETHNIC MIX: White (inc. Hispanic) 83%, Black 13%, other 4%
GOVERNMENT: Multiparty republic
CURRENCY: US $ = 100 cents

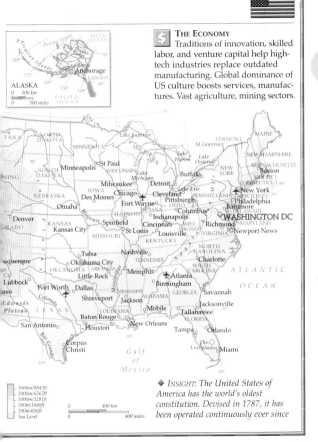

$ THE ECONOMY

Traditions of innovation, skilled labor, and venture capital help high-tech industries replace outdated manufacturing. Global dominance of US culture boosts services, manufactures. Vast agriculture, mining sectors.

ALASKA
0   500 km
0   500 miles

3000m/9843ft
2000m/6562ft
1000m/3281ft
500m/1640ft
200m/656ft
Sea Level

0   400 km
0   400 miles

◆ INSIGHT: *The United States of America has the world's oldest constitution. Devised in 1787, it has been operated continuously ever since*

19

MEXICO

LOCATED BETWEEN the southern end of North America and the Central American states, Mexico was a Spanish colony for 300 years, until 1836.

 GEOGRAPHY
Coastal plains along Pacific and Atlantic seaboards rise to a high arid central plateau. To the east and west are Sierra Madre mountain ranges. Limestone lowlands in the Yucatan peninsula.

CLIMATE
Plateau and high mountains are warm for much of year. Pacific coast is tropical: storms occur mostly March–December. Northwest is dry.

THE ECONOMY
One of the world's largest oil producers, with large reserves. Tropical fruits, vegetables grown as cash crops. Population growth outstripping job creation. North American Free Trade Agreement, signed with USA and Canada, came into force in 1994. US companies poised to move into Mexico and enter competition with Mexican industry.

3000m/9843ft	
2000m/6562ft	
1000m/3281ft	
500m/1640ft	
200m/656ft	
Sea Level	

0   200 km

0   200 miles

FACT FILE

OFFICIAL NAME: United Mexican State
DATE OF FORMATION: 1836/1867
CAPITAL: Mexico City
POPULATION: 95.5 million
TOTAL AREA: 756,061 sq miles (1,958,200 sq km)

DENSITY: 126 people per sq mile
LANGUAGES: Spanish*, Mayan dialects
RELIGIONS: Roman Catholic 89%, Protestant 6%, other 5%
ETHNIC MIX: *mestizo* 55%, Indian 30%, White 6%, other 9%
GOVERNMENT: Multiparty republic
CURRENCY: Peso = 100 centavos

◆ INSIGHT: *More people emigrate from Mexico than any other state in the world. Hundreds of thousands of Mexicans cross into the US each year, many of them staying as illegal immigrants*

PEOPLE AND SOCIETY

Most Mexicans are *mestizos* of mixed Spanish and Indian descent. Rural Indians are largely segregated from Hispanic society and most live in poverty. The situation leads to intermittent rebellion by land-less Indians. Men remain dominant in business and few women take part in the political process. Mexico is a multiparty democracy in name; in practice, the PRI (Institutional Revolutionary Party) has retained power since 1929. Rural depopulation and high unemployment are major problems. Mexico has a faster-growing population than any other large country. Between 1960 and 1980, its population doubled.

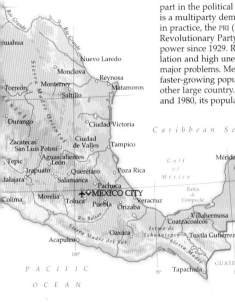

RICA

Rio Grande

Rio Grande

Sierra Madre Oriental

huahua

Nuevo Laredo

Monclova

Reynosa

Torreón   Monterrey
          Saltillo   Matamoros

Durango   Ciudad Victoria

Zacatecas   Ciudad
San Luis Potosí   de Valles   Tampico

Tepic   Aguascalientes
        León

Irapuato

dalajara   Salamanca   Querétaro   Poza Rica

              Pachuca

Colima   Morelia   ✛◇MEXICO CITY
         Toluca   Puebla   Veracruz
                  Orizaba

Acapulco   Oaxaca

PACIFIC

OCEAN

Caribbean Sea

Yucatán Channel

Gulf
of
Mexico

Mérida

Península
de
Yucatán

Bahía
de
Campeche

Chetumal

BELIZE

Villahermosa
Coatzacoalcos
Istmo de
Tehuantepec   Tuxtla Gutiérrez
              Sierra Madre

GUATEMALA

Tapachula

Rio Balsas

Sierra Madre del Sur

100°

95°

90°

GUATEMALA

THE LARGEST state on the Central American isthmus, Guatemala returned to civilian rule in 1986, after 32 years of repressive military rule.

 GEOGRAPHY
Narrow Pacific coastal plain. Central highlands with volcanoes. Short, swampy Caribbean coast. Tropical rain forests in the north.

 CLIMATE
Tropical, hot, and humid in coastal regions and north. More temperate in central highlands.

PEOPLE AND SOCIETY
Indians form a majority, but power, wealth, and land controlled by *Ladino* elite. Highland Indians were main victims of the military's indiscriminate campaign against guerrilla groups 1978–1984. Since civilian rule, the level of violence has diminished, but extreme poverty is still widespread.

THE ECONOMY
Agriculture is key sector. Sugar, coffee, beef, bananas, and cardamom top exports. Political stability has revived tourism.

◆ *INSIGHT: Guatemala, which means "land of trees," was the center of the ancient Maya civilization*

FACT FILE

OFFICIAL NAME: Republic of Guatemala
DATE OF FORMATION: 1838
CAPITAL: Guatemala City
POPULATION: 10 million
TOTAL AREA: 42,043 sq miles (108,890 sq km)

DENSITY: 231 people per sq mile
LANGUAGES: Spanish*, Quiché, Mam, Kekchí, Cakchiquel
RELIGIONS: Christian 99%, other 1%
ETHNIC MIX: Maya Indian 55%, *Ladino* (Euro-Indian, White) 45%
GOVERNMENT: Multiparty republic
CURRENCY: Quetzal = 100 centavos

BELIZE

BELIZE LIES on the eastern shore of the Yucatan Peninsula in Central America. A former British colony, it became fully independent in 1981.

 GEOGRAPHY
Almost half the land area is forested. Low mountains in southeast. Flat swampy coastal plains.

 CLIMATE
Tropical. Very hot and humid, with May–December rainy season.

 PEOPLE AND SOCIETY
Spanish-speaking *mestizos* now outnumber black Creoles for the first time. The huge influx of migrants from other countries in the region in the past decade has caused some tension. Newcomers have provided labor for agriculture, but have put pressure on social services. Traditional Creole dominance has been weakened by emigration to the United States.

THE ECONOMY
Agriculture, tourism, and remittances from Belizeans living abroad are economic mainstays. Citrus fruit concentrates, lobsters, shrimp, and textiles are exported.

◆ INSIGHT: *Belize's barrier reef is the second largest in the world*

	1000m/3281ft
	500m/1640ft
	200m/656ft
	Sea Level

0   50 km
0   50 miles

FACT FILE	
OFFICIAL NAME: Belize	LANGUAGES: English*, English Creole, Spanish, Maya, Garifuna
DATE OF FORMATION: 1981	RELIGIONS: Christian 87%, other 13%
CAPITAL: Belmopan	ETHNIC MIX: *mestizo* 44%, Creole 30%, Indian 11%, Garifuna 8%, other 7%
POPULATION: 200,000	GOVERNMENT: Parliamentary democracy
TOTAL AREA: 8,865 sq miles (22,960 sq km)	
DENSITY: 23 people per sq mile	CURRENCY: Belizean $ =100 cents

23

EL SALVADOR

EL SALVADOR IS Central America's smallest state. A 12-year war between US-backed government troops and left-wing guerrillas ended in 1992.

 GEOGRAPHY
Narrow coastal belt backed by mountain ranges with over 20 volcanic peaks. Central plateau.

CLIMATE
Tropical coastal belt is very hot, with seasonal rains. Cooler, temperate climate in highlands.

 PEOPLE AND SOCIETY
Population is largely *mestizo*; ethnic tensions are few. The civil war was fought over economic disparities, which still exist, despite some reform. 75,000 people died during the war, many were unarmed civilians. Around 500,000 more were displaced – mainly rural peasant families. In 1992, left-wing movement gave up its arms and joined formal political process.

THE ECONOMY
Civil war caused $2 billion-worth of damage. Huge amounts of foreign aid needed for survival. Overdependence on coffee, which accounts for 90% of exports.

◆ *INSIGHT: Named for the Savior, Jesus Christ, El Salvador is the most densely populated state in the region*

FACT FILE

OFFICIAL NAME: Republic of El Salvador
DATE OF FORMATION: 1856/1838
CAPITAL: San Salvador
POPULATION: 5.4 million
TOTAL AREA: 8,124 sq miles (21,040 sq km)

DENSITY: 679 people per sq mile
LANGUAGES: Spanish*, Nahua
RELIGIONS: Roman Catholic 75%, other (inc. Protestant) 25%
ETHNIC MIX: *mestizo* (Euro-Indian) 89%, Indian 10%, White 1%
GOVERNMENT: Multiparty republic
CURRENCY: Colón = 100 centavos

HONDURAS

STRADDLING THE Central American isthmus, Honduras returned to democratic civilian rule in 1981 after a succession of military regimes.

 GEOGRAPHY
Narrow plains along both coasts. Mountainous interior, cut by river valleys. Tropical forests, swamps, and lagoons in the east.

 CLIMATE
Tropical coastal lowlands are hot and humid, with May–October rains. Interior is cooler and drier.

PEOPLE AND SOCIETY
Majority of population is *mestizo*. Garifunas on Caribbean coast maintain their own language and culture. Indians inhabit the east, and remote mountain areas; their land rights are often violated. Most of the rural population live in poverty. Land reform and high unemployment are main issues facing the government.

THE ECONOMY
Second poorest country in the region. Bananas are the traditional cash crop – production is dominated by two US companies. Coffee, timber, livestock are also exported.

◆ *INSIGHT: Honduran currency is named after a Lenca Indian chief who was the main leader of resistance to the Spanish conquest in the 16th century*

FACT FILE

OFFICIAL NAME: Republic of Honduras
DATE OF FORMATION: 1838
CAPITAL: Tegucigalpa
POPULATION: 5.6 million
TOTAL AREA: 43,278 sq miles (112,090 sq km)

DENSITY: 127 people per sq mile
LANGUAGES: Spanish*, English Creole, Garifuna, Indian languages
RELIGIONS: Catholic 97%, other 3%
ETHNIC MIX: *mestizo* 90%, Indian 7%, Garifuna (Black Carib) 2%, White 1%
GOVERNMENT: Multiparty republic
CURRENCY: Lempira = 100 centavos

NICARAGUA

NICARAGUA LIES at the heart of Central America. An 11-year war between left-wing Sandinistas and right-wing US-backed Contras ended in 1989.

GEOGRAPHY
Extensive forested plains in the east. Central mountain region with many active volcanoes. Pacific coastlands are dominated by lakes.

CLIMATE
Tropical. Hot all year round in the lowlands. Cooler in the mountains. Occasional hurricanes.

PEOPLE AND SOCIETY
The isolated Atlantic regions, populated by Miskito Indians and blacks, gained limited independence in 1987. Elections in 1990 brought a right-wing pro-US party to power, but the Sandinistas remain a major political force in a country where poverty and unrest are rising.

◆ INSIGHT: *Lake Nicaragua is the only freshwater lake to contain ocean animals*

THE ECONOMY
Coffee, sugar, and cotton exports are affected by low world prices. Economy is dependent on foreign aid; the United States is the largest donor.

FACT FILE

OFFICIAL NAME: Republic of Nicaragua
DATE OF FORMATION: 1838
CAPITAL: Managua
POPULATION: 4.1 million
TOTAL AREA: 50,193 sq miles (130,000 sq km)

DENSITY: 88 people per sq mile
LANGUAGES: Spanish*, English Creole, Miskito
RELIGIONS: Catholic 95%, other 5%
ETHNIC MIX: *mestizo* 69%, White 17%, Black 9%, Indian 5%
GOVERNMENT: Multiparty republic
CURRENCY: Córdoba = 100 pence

COSTA RICA

COSTA RICA is the most stable country in Central America. Its neutrality in foreign affairs is long-standing, but it has very strong US ties.

GEOGRAPHY
Coastal plains of swamp and savanna rise to a fertile central plateau, which leads to a mountain range with active volcanic peaks.

CLIMATE
Hot and humid in coastal regions. Temperate uplands. High annual rainfall.

PEOPLE AND SOCIETY
Population has a mixture of Spanish, African, and native Indian ancestry. Costa Rica's long democratic tradition, developed public health system, and high literacy rates are unrivaled in the region. Landowners and the United States influence politics.

◆ *INSIGHT: Costa Rica's constitution is the only one in the world to forbid national armies*

THE ECONOMY
Traditionally agricultural, but mining and manufacturing are developing rapidly. Bananas, beef, and coffee are the leading exports. Tourism and travel have increased considerably in recent years.

FACT FILE

OFFICIAL NAME: Republic of Costa Rica
DATE OF FORMATION: 1821/1838
CAPITAL: San José
POPULATION: 3.3 million
TOTAL AREA: 19,730 sq miles (51,100 sq km)

DENSITY: 166 people per sq mile
LANGUAGES: Spanish*, English Creole, Bribri, Cabecar
RELIGIONS: Catholic 95%, other 5%
ETHNIC MIX: White/mestizo (Euro-Indian) 96%, Black 2%, Indian 2%
GOVERNMENT: Multiparty republic
CURRENCY: Colón = 100 centimos

PANAMA

PANAMA IS the southernmost country in Central America. The Panama Canal (under US-control until 2000) links the Pacific and Atlantic oceans.

 GEOGRAPHY
Lowlands along both coasts, with savanna-covered plains and rolling hills. Mountainous interior. Swamps and rain forests in the east.

 CLIMATE
Hot and humid, with heavy rainfall in May–December wet season. Cooler at high altitudes.

PEOPLE AND SOCIETY
Multiethnic society, dominated by people of Spanish origin. Indians live in remote areas. The Canal and US military bases have given society a cosmo-politan outlook, but the Catholic extended family remains strong. In 1989, US troops invaded to arrest its dictator General Noriega on drug charges and to restore civilian rule.

THE ECONOMY
Important banking sector, plus related financial and insurance services. Earnings from merchant ships sailing under Panamanian flag. Banana and shrimp exports.

◆ *INSIGHT: The Panama Canal extends for 50 miles (80 km). Around 12,000 ships pass through it each year*

FACT FILE

OFFICIAL NAME: Republic of Panama
DATE OF FORMATION: 1903/1914
CAPITAL: Panama City
POPULATION: 2.6 million
TOTAL AREA: 29,761 sq miles (77,080 sq km)

DENSITY: 87 people per sq mile
LANGUAGES: Spanish*, English Creole, Indian languages
RELIGIONS: Catholic 93%, other 7%
ETHNIC MIX: *mestizo* 70%, Black 14%, White 10%, Indian 6%
GOVERNMENT: Multiparty republic
CURRENCY: Balboa = 100 centesimos

JAMAICA

FIRST COLONIZED by the Spanish and then, from 1655, by the English, the Caribbean island of Jamaica achieved independence in 1962.

 GEOGRAPHY
Mainly mountainous, with lush tropical vegetation. Inaccessible limestone area in the northwest. Low, irregular coastal plains are broken by hills and plateaus.

CLIMATE
Tropical. Hot and humid, with temperate interior. Hurricanes are likely June–November.

 PEOPLE AND SOCIETY
Ethnically diverse, but tensions result from the gulf between rich and poor, rather than race. Economic and political life dominated by a few wealthy, long-established families. Armed crime, much of it drug-related, is a problem. Large areas of Kingston are ruled by *Dons*, gang leaders who administer their own violent justice.

 THE ECONOMY
Major producer of bauxite (aluminum ore). Tourism well developed. Light industry and data processing for US companies. Sugar, coffee, and rum are exported.

◆ *INSIGHT: Jamaica's Rastafarians look to the late emperor of Ethiopia, Haile Selassie, as their spiritual leader, and Africa as their spiritual home*

	2000m/6562ft	
	1000m/3281ft	
	500m/1640ft	
	200m/656ft	
	Sea Level	

0   40 km
0   40 miles

FACT FILE

OFFICIAL NAME: Jamaica
DATE OF FORMATION: 1962
CAPITAL: Kingston
POPULATION: 2.5 million
TOTAL AREA: 4,243 sq miles (10,990 sq km)
DENSITY: 590 people per sq mile

LANGUAGES: English*, English Creole, Hindi, Spanish, Chinese
RELIGIONS: Christian 60%, other 40%
ETHNIC MIX: Black 75%, mixed 15%, South Asian 5%, other 5%
GOVERNMENT: Parliamentary democracy
CURRENCY: Jamaican $ = 100 cents

CUBA

CUBA IS the largest island in the Caribbean and the only Communist country in the Americas. It has been led by Fidel Castro since 1959.

 GEOGRAPHY
Mostly fertile plains and basins. Three mountainous areas. Forests of pine and mahogany cover one quarter of the country.

CLIMATE
Subtropical. Hot all year round, and very hot in summer. Heaviest rainfall in the mountains. Hurricanes can strike in autumn.

PEOPLE AND SOCIETY
Castro's regime has reduced once extreme wealth disparities, given education a high priority, and established an efficient health service. Political dissent, however, is not tolerated. Recent fall in living standards has led 30,000 Cubans to flee by boat, to seek asylum in the United States.

THE ECONOMY
Main product is sugar. Cuba's economy is in crisis following the loss of its patron and supplier, the former USSR. Recent reforms have allowed small-scale enterprise and use of US dollar. The 30-year-old US trade embargo continues.

◆ *INSIGHT: To combat fuel shortages, over half a million traditional black bicycles have been imported from China*

FACT FILE	
OFFICIAL NAME: Republic of Cuba	LANGUAGES: Spanish*, English, French, Chinese
DATE OF FORMATION: 1902	RELIGIONS: Roman Catholic 40%, other 60% (inc. unaffiliated)
CAPITAL: Havana	ETHNIC MIX: White 66%, Afro-European 22%, other 12%
POPULATION: 10.9 million	GOVERNMENT: Socialist republic
TOTAL AREA: 42,803 sq miles (110,860 sq km)	CURRENCY: Peso = 100 centavos
DENSITY: 255 people per sq mile	

BAHAMAS

LOCATED IN the western Atlantic, off the Florida coast, the Bahamas comprises some 700 islands and 2,400 keys, 30 of which are inhabited.

GEOGRAPHY
Long, mainly flat coral formations with a few low hills. Some islands have pine forests, lagoons, and mangrove swamps.

CLIMATE
Subtropical. Hot summers and mild winters. Heavy rainfall, especially in summer. Hurricanes can strike July–December.

PEOPLE AND SOCIETY

Over half the population live on New Providence. Tourist industry employs 40% of the work force. Remainder are engaged in traditional fishing and agriculture, or in administration. Close US ties were strained in 1980s, with senior government members implicated in narcotics corruption. In 1993, tough policies instituted to deter settling of Haitian refugees.

THE ECONOMY
Tourism accounts for half of all revenues. Major international financial services sector, including banking and insurance.

◆ INSIGHT: Six tourists per inhabitant visit the Bahamas every year

Strait of Florida
Grand Bahama I.
Freeport
26°
Great Abaco
Berry Is.
New Providence
Nicholls Town
NASSAU
Andros Town
Andros I.
Eleuthera I.
ATLANTIC
OCEAN
Cat I.
74°
San Salvador
24°
Exuma Cays
Rum Cay
78°
Long I.
Crooked I.
Mayaguana
Acklins I.
22°
Caicos Passage
Sea Level
Great Inagua
0   100 km
0   100 miles

FACT FILE

OFFICIAL NAME: The Commonwealth of the Bahamas
DATE OF FORMATION: 1973
CAPITAL: Nassau
POPULATION: 300,000
TOTAL AREA: 5,359 sq miles (13,880 sq km)

DENSITY: 55 people per sq mile
LANGUAGES: English*, English Creole
RELIGIONS: Protestant 76%, Roman Catholic 19%, other 5%
ETHNIC MIX: Black 85%, White 15%
GOVERNMENT: Parliamentary democracy
CURRENCY: Bahamian $ = 100 cents

HAITI

SHARES THE Caribbean island of Hispaniola with the Dominican Republic. At independence in 1804, it became the world's first black republic.

 GEOGRAPHY
Predominantly mountainous, with forests and fertile plains.

CLIMATE
Tropical, with rain throughout the year. Humid in coastal areas, much cooler in the mountains.

PEOPLE AND SOCIETY
Majority of population is of African descent. A few have European roots, primarily French. Rigid class structure maintains vast disparities of wealth. Most Haitians live in extreme poverty. In recent years, political oppression and a collapsing economy led thousands to seek US asylum. In 1994, US-led troops reinstated the elected president, who was ousted by the military in 1991.

THE ECONOMY
Few natural resources. In 1994, after three years of UN sanctions, the country's economic links were restored and foreign aid resumed.

◆ INSIGHT: *Haiti's independence was achieved after Toussaint l'Ouverture led a slave rebellion in 1791*

▨	1000m/3281ft
▨	500m/1640ft
▨	200m/656ft
	Sea Level

0   50 km
0   50 miles

FACT FILE

OFFICIAL NAME: Republic of Haiti
DATE OF FORMATION: 1804
CAPITAL: Port-au-Prince
POPULATION: 6.9 million
TOTAL AREA: 10,714 sq miles (27,750 sq km)
DENSITY: 644 people per sq mile

LANGUAGES: French*, French Creole*, English
RELIGIONS: Roman Catholic 80%, Protestant 16%, Voodoo 4%
ETHNIC MIX: Black 95%, Afro-European 5%
GOVERNMENT: Multiparty republic
CURRENCY: Gourde = 100 centimes

DOMINICAN REPUBLIC

OCCUPIES THE eastern two thirds of the island of Hispaniola in the Caribbean. Frequent coups and a strong US influence mark its recent past.

GEOGRAPHY
Highlands and rainforested mountains – including highest peak in Caribbean, Pico Duarte – interspersed with fertile valleys. Extensive coastal plain in the east.

CLIMATE
Hot and humid close to sea level, cooler at altitude. Heavy rainfall, especially in the northeast.

PEOPLE AND SOCIETY
White landowners and the military hold political power. Mixed-race majority control commerce and form bulk of middle classes. Many of the poor are black. White and mixed-race women are starting to enter the professions. Poverty and unemployment have led some Dominicans to emigrate to the United States, or become drug-traffickers.

THE ECONOMY
Mining – mainly of nickel and gold – and sugar are major sectors. Hidden economy based on trans-shipment of narcotics to the United States. Recent growth in tourism.

◆ INSIGHT: Santo Domingo is the oldest city in the Americas. It was founded in 1496 by the brother of Christopher Columbus

FACT FILE

OFFICIAL NAME: Dominican Republic
DATE OF FORMATION: 1865
CAPITAL: Santo Domingo
POPULATION: 7.6 million
TOTAL AREA: 18,815 sq miles (48,730 sq km)

DENSITY: 403 people per sq mile
LANGUAGES: Spanish*, French Creole
RELIGIONS: Roman Catholic 95%, other (Protestant, Jewish) 5%
ETHNIC MIX: Afro-European 73%, White 16%, Black 11%
GOVERNMENT: Multiparty republic
CURRENCY: Peso = 100 centavos

ST. KITTS & NEVIS

ST. KITTS and Nevis lies in the northern part of the Leeward Islands chain in the Caribbean. Nevis is the less developed of the two islands.

 GEOGRAPHY
Volcanic in origin, with forested, mountainous interiors. Nevis has hot and cold springs.

CLIMATE
Tropical, tempered by trade winds. Little seasonal variation in temperature. Moderate rainfall.

PEOPLE AND SOCIETY
Majority of the population is of African descent. Intermarriage has blurred other racial lines and eliminated ethnic tensions. For most people, the extended family is the norm. Wealth disparities are not great, but urban professionals enjoy a higher standard of living than rural sugarcane farmers. Politics is based on the British system; funds are provided by professionals and the trade unions. The proposed Leeward Islands union is the main political issue.

THE ECONOMY
Sugar industry, currently UK-managed, has preferential access to EU and US markets. Successful and still expanding tourist industry.

◆ *INSIGHT: Nevis, renowned as a spa since the 18th century, is known as the "Queen of the Caribbean"*

FACT FILE
OFFICIAL NAME: Federation of Saint Christopher and Nevis
DATE OF FORMATION: 1983
CAPITAL: Basseterre
POPULATION: 44,000
TOTAL AREA: 139 sq miles (360 sq km)

DENSITY: 316 people per sq mile
LANGUAGES: English*, English Creole
RELIGIONS: Protestant 85%, Roman Catholic 10%, other Christian 5%
ETHNIC MIX: Black 95%, mixed 5%
GOVERNMENT: Parliamentary democracy
CURRENCY: E. Caribbean $ = 100 cents

ANTIGUA & BARBUDA

LYING AT the outer edge of the Leeward Islands group in the Caribbean, Antigua and Barbuda's area includes the uninhabited islet of Redonda.

 GEOGRAPHY
Mainly low-lying limestone and coral islands with some higher volcanic areas. Antigua's coast is indented with bays and harbors.

 CLIMATE
Tropical, moderated by trade winds and sea breezes. Humidity and rainfall are low for the region.

 PEOPLE AND SOCIETY
Population almost entirely of African origin, with small communities of Europeans and South Asians. Women's status has risen as a result of greater access to education. Wealth disparities are small and unemployment is low. Politics dominated for past 30 years by the Bird family.

◆ *INSIGHT: In 1865, Redonda was "claimed" by an eccentric Englishman as a kingdom for his son*

THE ECONOMY
Tourism is the main source of revenue and the biggest provider of jobs. Fishing and sea-island cotton industries are expanding.

FACT FILE

OFFICIAL NAME: Antigua and Barbuda
DATE OF FORMATION: 1981
CAPITAL: St. John's
POPULATION: 65,000
TOTAL AREA: 170 sq miles (440 sq km)

DENSITY: 385 people per sq mile
LANGUAGES: English*, English Creole
RELIGIONS: Protestant 87%, Roman Catholic 10%, other 3%
ETHNIC MIX: Black 98%, other 2%
GOVERNMENT: Parliamentary democracy
CURRENCY: E. Caribbean $ = 100 cents

DOMINICA

DOMINICA RESISTED European colonization until the 18th century, when it was controlled first by the French, and then, until 1978, by the British.

GEOGRAPHY
Mountainous and densely forested. Volcanic activity has given it very fertile soils, hot springs, geysers, and black sand beaches.

CLIMATE
Tropical, cooled by constant trade winds. Heavy annual rainfall. Tropical depressions and hurricanes are likely June–November.

PEOPLE AND SOCIETY
Population mainly of African origin. Small community of Carib Indians – the last remaining in the Caribbean – on the east coast. Most people live in extended families. Electoral system based on British model; politicians tend to come from professional classes, usually doctors or lawyers. For 15 years until 1995, Dominica was governed by Eugenia Charles, the first female prime minister in the Caribbean.

THE ECONOMY
Bananas and tourism are the economic mainstays. Current preferential access to EU and US markets now threatened by moves to deregulate the banana trade.

◆ INSIGHT: Dominica is known as the "Nature Island" due to its spectacular flora and fauna

	2000m/6562ft
	1000m/3281ft
	500m/1640ft
	200m/656ft
	Sea Level

FACT FILE

OFFICIAL NAME: Commonwealth of Dominica
DATE OF FORMATION: 1978
CAPITAL: Roseau
POPULATION: 72,000
TOTAL AREA: 290 sq miles (750 sq km)

DENSITY: 250 people per sq mile
LANGUAGES: English*, French Creole, Carib, Cocoy
RELIGIONS: Roman Catholic 77%, Protestant 15%, other 8%
ETHNIC MIX: Black 98%, Indian 2%
GOVERNMENT: Multiparty republic
CURRENCY: E. Caribbean $ = 100 cents

ST. LUCIA

AMONG THE most beautiful of the Caribbean Windward Islands, St. Lucia retains both French and British influences from its colonial history.

 GEOGRAPHY
Volcanic and mountainous, with some broad fertile valleys. The Pitons, ancient lava cones, rise from the sea on the forested west coast.

 CLIMATE
Tropical, moderated by trade winds. May–October wet season brings daily warm showers. Rainfall is highest in the mountains.

PEOPLE AND SOCIETY
Population is a tension-free mixture of descendants of Africans, Europeans, and South Asians. Family and religious life is important to most St. Lucians. In rural areas women often head the households, and run much of the farming. There is growing local resistance to overdevelopment of the island by tourism. A proposed union with the other Windward Islands is the main political issue.

THE ECONOMY
Mainly agricultural, with some light industry. Bananas are biggest export. Successful tourist industry, but most resorts are foreign-owned.

◆ *INSIGHT: St. Lucia has the most Nobel laureates per capita in the world*

FACT FILE

OFFICIAL NAME: Saint Lucia
DATE OF FORMATION: 1979
CAPITAL: Castries
POPULATION: 156,000
TOTAL AREA: 239 sq miles (620 sq km)
DENSITY: 653 people per sq mile

LANGUAGES: English*, French Creole, Hindi, Urdu
RELIGIONS: Catholic 90%, other 10%
ETHNIC MIX: Black 90%, Afro-European 6%, South Asian 4%
GOVERNMENT: Parliamentary democracy
CURRENCY: E. Caribbean $ = 100 cents

ST. VINCENT & THE GRENADINES

INDEPENDENT FROM Britain in 1979, the volcanic islands of St. Vincent and the Grenadines form part of the Windward group in the Caribbean.

GEOGRAPHY
St. Vincent is mountainous and forested, with one of two active volcanoes in the Caribbean, La Soufrière. The Grenadines are 32 islands and keys fringed by beaches.

CLIMATE
Tropical, with constant trade winds. Hurricanes are likely during July–November wet season.

PEOPLE AND SOCIETY
Population is racially diverse, but intermarriage has reduced tensions. Society is informal and relaxed, but family life is strongly influenced by the Anglican Church. Locals fear that their traditional lifestyle is being threatened by the expanding tourist industry.

◆ INSIGHT: The islands' precolonial inhabitants, the Carib Indians, named them "Harioun" – home of the blessed

THE ECONOMY
Dependent on agriculture and tourism. Bananas are the main cash crop. Tourism, targeted at the jet-set and cruise-ship markets, is concentrated on the Grenadines.

```
1000m/3281ft
500m/1640ft
200m/656ft
Sea Level

0      10 km
0      10 miles
```

Chateaubelair
La Sou
4,049
Georgetown
St. Vincent
KINGSTOW
Amos Vale
Airport
13°10′
Bequia
Caribbean
Sea
Isle
à Quatre
13°00′
Baliceaux
Mustique
12°50′
Canouan
61°10′
Mayreau
Union I.
12°40′
The Grenadines
ATLANTIC
OCEAN
61°20′

FACT FILE

OFFICIAL NAME: St. Vincent and the Grenadines
DATE OF FORMATION: 1979
CAPITAL: Kingstown
POPULATION: 109,000
TOTAL AREA: 131 sq miles (340 sq km)

DENSITY: 832 people per sq mile
LANGUAGES: English*, English Creole
RELIGIONS: Protestant 62% Roman Catholic 19%, other 19%
ETHNIC MIX: Black 82%, mixed 14%, White 3%, South Asian 1%
GOVERNMENT: Parliamentary democracy
CURRENCY: E. Caribbean $ = 100 cents

BARBADOS

BARBADOS IS the most easterly of the Caribbean Windward Islands. Under British rule for 339 years, it became fully independent in 1966.

GEOGRAPHY
Encircled by coral reefs. Fertile and predominantly flat, with a few gentle hills to the north.

CLIMATE
Moderate tropical climate. Sunnier and drier than its more mountainous neighbors.

PEOPLE AND SOCIETY
Some latent tension between white community, which controls politics and much of the economy, and majority black population, but violence is rare. Increasing social mobility has enabled black Bajans to enter the professions. Despite political stability and good social services, emigration is high, notably to the United States and the UK.

◆ INSIGHT: *Barbados retains a strong British influence and is referred to by its neighbors as "Little England"*

THE ECONOMY
Sugar is the traditional cash crop. Well-developed tourist industry employs almost 40% of the work force. Financial services and information processing are important new growth sectors.

FACT FILE
OFFICIAL NAME: Barbados
DATE OF FORMATION: 1966
CAPITAL: Bridgetown
POPULATION: 260,000
TOTAL AREA: 166 sq miles (430 sq km)
DENSITY: 1,566 people per sq mile

LANGUAGES: English*, English Creole
RELIGIONS: Protestant 94%, Roman Catholic 5%, other 1%
ETHNIC MIX: Black 80%, mixed 15%, White 4%, other 1%
GOVERNMENT: Parliamentary democracy
CURRENCY: Barbados $ = 100 cents

GRENADA

THE WINDWARD island of Grenada became a focus of attention in 1983, when a US-led invasion severed the growing links with Cuba.

 GEOGRAPHY
Volcanic in origin, with densely forested central mountains. Its territory includes the islands of Carriacou and Petite Martinique.

CLIMATE
Tropical, tempered by trade winds. Hurricanes are a hazard in the July–November wet season.

PEOPLE AND SOCIETY
Grenadians are mainly of African origin; their traditions remain strong, especially on Carriacou. Interethnic marriage has reduced tensions between the groups. Extended families, often headed by women, are the norm. The invasion ousted the Marxist regime and restored democracy.

◆ *INSIGHT: Known as "the spice island of the Caribbean," it is the world's second largest nutmeg producer*

THE ECONOMY
Nutmeg, the most important crop, is currently affected by low world prices. Mace, cocoa, saffron, and cloves are also grown. Tourism has developed in the past decade.

| 500m/1640ft |
| 200m/656ft |
| Sea Level |

0   8 km
0   8 miles

Petite Martinique
Hillsborough
Carriacou
12°25′   61°25′

12°20′   Diamond I.
Ronde I.
Caribbean Sea
12°15′   61°30′

Victoria
12°10′
Grand   Grenada
Roy   Grenville
12°05′   61°35′

ATLANTIC OCEAN

ST. GEORGE'S
12°00′   Point Salines Airport
61°45′   61°40′

FACT FILE

OFFICIAL NAME: Grenada
DATE OF FORMATION: 1974
CAPITAL: St. George's
POPULATION: 91,000
TOTAL AREA: 131 sq miles (340 sq km)
DENSITY: 695 people per sq mile

LANGUAGES: English*, English Creole
RELIGIONS: Roman Catholic 68%, Protestant 32%
ETHNIC MIX: Black 84%, Afro-European 13%, South Asian 3%
GOVERNMENT: Parliamentary democracy
CURRENCY: E. Caribbean $ = 100 cents

TRINIDAD & TOBAGO

THE FORMER British colony of Trinidad and Tobago is the most southerly of the West Indies, lying just 9 miles (15 km) off the coast of Venezuela.

 GEOGRAPHY
Both islands are hilly and wooded. Trinidad has a rugged mountain range in the north, and swamps on its east and west coasts.

 CLIMATE
Tropical, with July–December wet season. Escapes the region's hurricanes, which pass to the north.

PEOPLE AND SOCIETY
Blacks and South Asians are the biggest groups. Minorities of Chinese and Europeans. Politics has recently become fragmented, and dominated by the race issue. An attempted coup by a Muslim sect in 1990 strengthened black opposition to the possibility of a South Asian prime minister.

◆ INSIGHT: *Trinidad and Tobago is the birthplace of steel bands and Calypso*

THE ECONOMY
Oil accounts for 70% of export earnings. Gas is increasingly being exploited to support new industries. Tourism, particularly on Tobago, is being developed.

FACT FILE

OFFICIAL NAME: Republic of Trinidad and Tobago
DATE OF FORMATION: 1962
CAPITAL: Port-of-Spain
POPULATION: 1.3 million
TOTAL AREA: 1,981 sq miles (5,130 sq km)

DENSITY: 656 people per sq mile
LANGUAGES: English*, other
RELIGIONS: Christian 58%, Hindu 30%, Muslim 8%, other 4%
ETHNIC MIX: Black 43%, South Asian 40%, mixed 14%, other 3%
GOVERNMENT: Multiparty republic
CURRENCY: Trin. & Tob. $ = 100 cents

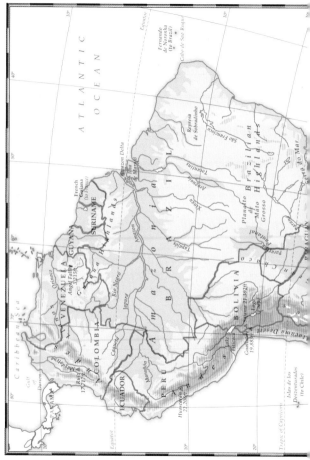

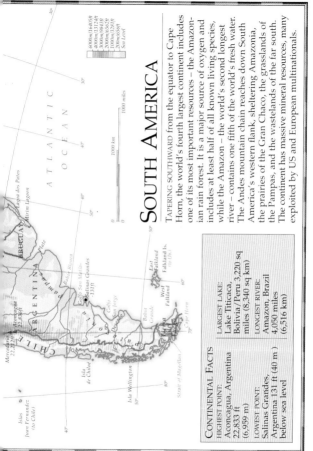

6000m/16405ft
4000m/13124ft
3000m/9843ft
2000m/6562ft
1000m/3281ft
200m/656ft
Sea Level

SOUTH AMERICA

TAPERING SOUTHWARD from the equator to Cape Horn, the world's fourth largest continent includes one of its most important resources – the Amazonian rain forest. It is a major source of oxygen and includes at least half of all known living species, while the Amazon – the world's second longest river – contains one fifth of the world's fresh water. The Andes mountain chain reaches down South America's western flank, sheltering Amazonia, the prairies of the Gran Chaco, the grasslands of the Pampas, and the wastelands of the far south. The continent has massive mineral resources, many exploited by US and European multinationals.

CONTINENTAL FACTS

HIGHEST POINT:
Aconcagua, Argentina
22,833 ft
(6,959 m)

LOWEST POINT:
Salinas Grandes,
Argentina 131 ft (40 m)
below sea level

LARGEST LAKE:
Lake Titicaca,
Bolivia/Peru 3,220 sq
miles (8,340 sq km)

LONGEST RIVER:
Amazon, Brazil
4,050 miles
(6,516 km)

COLOMBIA

LYING IN northwest South America, Colombia is one of the world's most violent countries, with powerful drugs cartels and guerrilla activity.

GEOGRAPHY
The densely forested and almost uninhabited east is separated from the western coastal plains by the Andes, which divide into three ranges with intervening valleys.

CLIMATE
Coastal plains are hot and wet. The highlands are cooler. The equatorial east has two wet seasons.

PEOPLE AND SOCIETY
Most Colombians are of mixed blood. Native Indians are concentrated in the southwest and Amazonia. Recent constitutional reform has given them a greater political voice. Blacks are the least represented group. The government, with US help, is engaged in an all-out war against the drug barons.

◆ INSIGHT: Colombia is the world's leading producer of emeralds

THE ECONOMY
Healthy and diversified export sector – especially coffee and coal. Considerable growth potential, but drug-related violence and corruption deter foreign investors.

FACT FILE

OFFICIAL NAME: Republic of Colombia
DATE OF FORMATION: 1819/1922
CAPITAL: Bogotá
POPULATION: 34 million
TOTAL AREA: 439,733 sq miles (1,138,910 sq km)

DENSITY: 78 people per sq mile
LANGUAGES: Spanish*, Indian languages, English Creole
RELIGIONS: Catholic 95%, other 5%
ETHNIC MIX: mestizo 58%, White 20%, mixed 14%, other 8%
GOVERNMENT: Multiparty republic
CURRENCY: Peso = 100 centavos

VENEZUELA

LOCATED ON the north coast of South America, Venezuela has the continent's most urbanized society. Most people live in the northern cities.

 GEOGRAPHY
Andes mountains and the Maracaibo lowlands in the north-west. Central grassy plains drained by Orinoco river system. Forested Guiana Highlands in the southeast.

 CLIMATE
Tropical. Hot and humid. Uplands are cooler. Orinoco plains are alternately parched or flooded.

 PEOPLE AND SOCIETY
Latin America's "melting pot" with immigrants from Europe and all over South America. The few indigenous Indians live in remote areas and maintain their traditional lifestyle. Oil wealth has brought prosperity, but many people still live in poverty. 1991 food riots forced government to initiate poverty programs. Corruption is a feature of Venezuelan political life.

THE ECONOMY
In addition to oil, Venezuela has vast reserves of coal, bauxite, iron, and gold. Government revenues dented by overstaffed and often inefficient state sector, plus widespread tax evasion.

◆ *INSIGHT: Venezuela's Angel Falls (3,212 ft) is the world's highest waterfall*

FACT FILE

OFFICIAL NAME: Republic of Venezuela
DATE OF FORMATION: 1830 / 1929
CAPITAL: Caracas
POPULATION: 20.6 million
TOTAL AREA: 352,143 sq miles (912,050 sq km)

DENSITY: 57 people per sq mile
LANGUAGES: Spanish*, Indian languages
RELIGIONS: Roman Catholic 96%, Protestant 2%, other 2%
ETHNIC MIX: *mestizo* 67%, White 21%, Black 10%, Indian 2%
GOVERNMENT: Multiparty republic
CURRENCY: Bolívar = 100 centimos

GUYANA

THE ONLY English-speaking country in South America, Guyana gained independence from Britain in 1966 and became a republic in 1970.

GEOGRAPHY
Mainly artificial coast, reclaimed by dikes and dams from swamps and tidal marshes. Forests cover 85% of the interior, rising to savanna uplands and mountains.

CLIMATE
Tropical. Coast cooled by sea breezes. Lowlands are hot, wet and humid. Highlands are a little cooler.

PEOPLE AND SOCIETY
Population largely descended from Africans brought over during slave trade or from South Asian laborers who arrived after slavery was abolished. Racial rivalry exists between the two groups. Small numbers of Chinese and native Indians. Government was once characterized by favoritism toward Afro-Guyanese. This was reversed with the election in 1992 of a South Asian-dominated party.

THE ECONOMY
Free-market economics have improved prospects. Bauxite, gold, rice, and diamonds are produced.

◆ INSIGHT: Guyana means "land of many waters" – it has 1,000 mi. of rivers

FACT FILE
OFFICIAL NAME: Republic of Guyana
DATE OF FORMATION: 1966
CAPITAL: Georgetown
POPULATION: 800,000
TOTAL AREA: 83,000 sq miles (214,970 sq km)
DENSITY: 10 people per sq mile

LANGUAGES: English*, English Creole, Hindi, Urdu, Indian languages
RELIGIONS: Christian 57%, Hindu 33%, Muslim 9%, other 1%
ETHNIC MIX: South Asian 51%, Black and mixed 43%, other 6%
GOVERNMENT: Multiparty republic
CURRENCY: Guyana $ =100 cents

SURINAME

A FORMER Dutch colony on the north coast of South America. Democracy was restored in 1991 after almost 11 years of military rule.

 GEOGRAPHY
Mostly covered by tropical rain forest. Coastal plain, central plateaus, and the Guiana Highlands.

 CLIMATE
Tropical. Hot and humid, cooled by trade winds. High rainfall, especially in the interior.

PEOPLE AND SOCIETY
About 200,000 people have emigrated to the Netherlands since independence. Of those left, 90% live near the coast, the rest live in scattered rain forest communities. Around 7,000 are indigenous Indians. Also *bosnegers* – descendants of runaway African slaves. They fought the Creole-dominated government in the 1980s. Many South Asians and Javanese work in farming. Since return to civilian rule, each group has a political party representing its interests.

THE ECONOMY
Aluminum and bauxite are the leading exports. Rice and fruit are main cash crops. Oil reserves.

◆ *INSIGHT: Suriname was ceded to Holland by the British, in exchange for New Amsterdam (New York), in 1667*

FACT FILE

OFFICIAL NAME: Republic of Suriname
DATE OF FORMATION: 1975
CAPITAL: Paramaribo
POPULATION: 400,000
TOTAL AREA: 63,039 sq miles (163,270 sq km)
DENSITY: 8 people per sq mile

LANGUAGES: Dutch*, Pidgin English (Taki-Taki), Hindi, Javanese, Carib
RELIGIONS: Christian 48%, Hindu 27%, Muslim 20%, other 5%
ETHNIC MIX: South Asian 37%, Creole 31%, Javanese 15%, other 17%
GOVERNMENT: Multiparty republic
CURRENCY: Guilder = 100 cents

47

ECUADOR

ECUADOR
Galápagos
Islands

ECUADOR SITS high on South America's western coast. Its territory includes the Galápagos Islands, 610 miles (970 km) to the west.

GEOGRAPHY
Broad coastal plain, inter-Andean central highlands, dense jungle in upper Amazon basin.

CLIMATE
Hot and moist on the coast, cool in the Andes, and hot equatorial in the Amazon basin.

PEOPLE AND SOCIETY
Most people live in coastal lowlands or Andean highlands. Many have migrated from over-farmed Andean valleys to main port and commercial center, Guayaquil. Strong and unified Indian movement backed by Catholic Church. Amazonian Indians are successfully pressing for recognition of land rights.

THE ECONOMY
World's biggest banana producer. Net oil exporter. Commercial agriculture is main employer. Fishing industry. Eco-tourism on Galápagos Islands.

4000m/13124ft
2000m/6562ft
500m/1640ft
Sea Level

0   100 km
0   100 miles

◆ INSIGHT: Darwin's study on the Galápagos Islands in 1856 played a major part in his theory of evolution

FACT FILE
OFFICIAL NAME: Republic of Ecuador
DATE OF FORMATION: 1830/1942
CAPITAL: Quito
POPULATION: 11.3 million
TOTAL AREA: 109,483 sq miles (283,560 sq km)
DENSITY: 104 people per sq mile

LANGUAGES: Spanish*, Quechua* and eight other Indian languages
RELIGIONS: Catholic 95%, other 5%
ETHNIC MIX: *mestizo* (Euro-Indian) 55%, Indian 25%, Black 10%, White 10%
GOVERNMENT: Multiparty republic
CURRENCY: Sucre = 100 centavos

PERU

ONCE THE heart of the Inca empire, before the Spanish conquest in the 16th century, Peru lies on the Pacific coast of South America.

 GEOGRAPHY
Coastal plain rises to Andes mountains. Uplands, dissected by fertile valleys, lie east of Andes. Tropical forest in extreme east.

CLIMATE
Coast is mainly arid. Middle slopes of Andes are temperate; higher peaks are snow-covered. East is hot, humid, and very wet.

PEOPLE AND SOCIETY
Populated mainly by Indians or mixed-race *mestizos*, but society is dominated by a small group of Spanish descendants. Indians, together with the small black community, suffer discrimination in the towns. In 1980, *Sendero Luminoso* (Shining Path) guerrillas began armed struggle against the government. Since then, over 25,000 people have died as a result of guerrilla, and army, violence.

THE ECONOMY
Abundant mineral resources. Rich fish stocks. Illegal export of coca leaves for cocaine production.

◆ INSIGHT: *Lake Titicaca is the world's highest navigable lake*

FACT FILE

OFFICIAL NAME: Republic of Peru
DATE OF FORMATION: 1824/1942
CAPITAL: Lima
POPULATION: 22.9 million
TOTAL AREA: 496,223 sq miles (1,285,220 sq km)
DENSITY: 47 people per sq mile

LANGUAGES: Spanish*, Quechua*, Aymará*, other Indian languages
RELIGIONS: Catholic 95%, other 5%
ETHNIC MIX: Indian 45%, *mestizo* 37%, White 15%, Black, Japanese, Chinese, and other 3%
GOVERNMENT: Multiparty republic
CURRENCY: New sol = 100 centimos

BRAZIL

COVERING ALMOST half of South America, Brazil is the site of the world's largest and ecologically most important rain forest. The country has immense natural and economic resources, but most of its people still live in poverty.

GEOGRAPHY

Vast, heavily wooded Amazon Basin covers northern half of the country. Semiarid scrubland in northeast. Grassy plains, fertile highlands in the south. Coastal plain with swampy areas in the southeast. Atlantic coastline is 1,240 miles (2,000 km) long.

CLIMATE

Constantly hot and humid in Amazon Basin. Frequent droughts in northeast. Greater range of temperature and rainfall on plateau. Hot summers and cool winters in south.

PEOPLE AND SOCIETY

Diverse population includes native Indians, blacks, and people of mixed race. Shanty towns in the cities attract poor migrants from the northeast. Urban crime, violent land disputes, and unchecked Amazonia development tarnish image as a modern nation. Catholicism and the family remain strong.

THE ECONOMY

Hyperinflation, poor planning, and corruption frustrate efforts to harness undoubted potential: vast mineral reserves, diverse industry and agriculture.

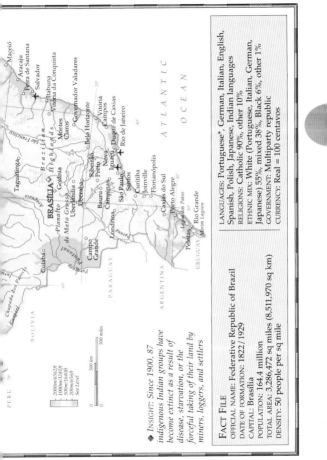

◆ INSIGHT: *Since 1900, 87 indigenous Indian groups have become extinct as a result of disease, starvation, or the forceful taking of their land by miners, loggers, and settlers*

FACT FILE

OFFICIAL NAME: Federative Republic of Brazil
DATE OF FORMATION: 1822/1929
CAPITAL: Brasília
POPULATION: 164.4 million
TOTAL AREA: 3,286,472 sq miles (8,511,970 sq km)
DENSITY: 50 people per sq mile

LANGUAGES: Portuguese*, German, Italian, English, Spanish, Polish, Japanese, Indian languages
RELIGIONS: Catholic 90%, other 10%
ETHNIC MIX: White (Portuguese, Italian, German, Japanese) 55%, mixed 38%, Black 6%, other 1%
GOVERNMENT: Multiparty republic
CURRENCY: Real = 100 centavos

CHILE

EXTENDS IN a ribbon down the west coast of South America. It returned to democracy in 1989 after a referendum rejected its military dictator.

GEOGRAPHY
Pampas (broad grassy plains) between coastal uplands and Andes. Atacama Desert in north. Deep sea channels, lakes, and fjords in south.

CLIMATE
Arid in the north. Hot, dry summers and mild winters in the center. Higher Andean peaks have glaciers and year round snow. Very wet and stormy in the south.

PEOPLE AND SOCIETY
Most people are of European descent, and are highly urbanized. Indigenous Indians live almost exclusively in the south. Poor housing, water and air pollution are problems in Santiago. General Pinochet's dictatorship was brutally repressive, but the business and middle classes prospered. Growth has continued under civilian rule, but many Chileans live in poverty.

THE ECONOMY
World's biggest copper producer. Growth in foreign investment due to political stability. Wine, fishmeal, fruit, and salmon are exported.

◆ INSIGHT: *Chile's Atacama Desert is the driest place on Earth*

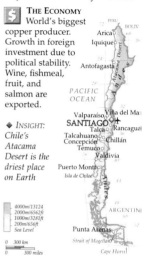

▩	4000m/13124
▩	2000m/6562ft
▩	1000m/3281ft
▩	200m/656ft
	Sea Level

0   300 km
0   300 miles

FACT FILE
OFFICIAL NAME: Republic of Chile
DATE OF FORMATION: 1818/1929
CAPITAL: Santiago
POPULATION: 13.8 million
TOTAL AREA: 292,258 sq miles (756,950 sq km)
DENSITY: 47 people per sq mile

LANGUAGES: Spanish*, Indian languages
RELIGIONS: Roman Catholic 89%, Protestant 11%
ETHNIC MIX: White and *mestizo* 92%, Indian 6%, other 2%
GOVERNMENT: Multiparty republic
CURRENCY: Peso = 100 centavos

BOLIVIA

BOLIVIA LIES landlocked high in central South America. Mineral riches once made it the region's wealthiest state. Today, it is the poorest.

 GEOGRAPHY
A high windswept plateau, the *altiplano*, lies between two Andean mountain ranges. Semi-arid grasslands to the southeast; dense tropical forests to the north.

CLIMATE
Altiplano has extreme tropical climate, with night frost in winter. North and east are hot and humid.

PEOPLE AND SOCIETY
Indigenous majority is discriminated against at most levels of society. Political process and economy remain under the control of a few wealthy families of Spanish descent. Most Bolivians are poor subsistence farmers or miners. Women have low status.

◆ INSIGHT: *La Paz is the world's highest capital city, at 13,385 feet (3,631 meters) above sea level*

THE ECONOMY
Gold, silver, zinc, and tin are mined. Recently discovered oil and natural gas deposits. Overseas investors remain deterred by social problems of extreme poverty, and the influence of cocaine barons.

```
3000m/9843ft
2000m/6562ft
1000m/3281ft
500m/1640ft
200m/656ft
Sea Level
```

FACT FILE

OFFICIAL NAME: Republic of Bolivia
DATE OF FORMATION: 1825 / 1938
CAPITAL: La Paz, Sucre
POPULATION: 7.8 million
TOTAL AREA: 424,162 sq miles (1,098,580 sq km)

DENSITY: 18 people per sq mile
LANGUAGES: Spanish*, Quechua*, Aymará*, Tupi-Guaraní
RELIGIONS: Catholic 95%, other 5%
ETHNIC MIX: Indian 55%, *mestizo* 27%, White 10%, other 8%
GOVERNMENT: Multiparty republic
CURRENCY: Boliviano = 100 centavos

PARAGUAY

LANDLOCKED in central South America. Its post-independence history has included periods of military rule. Free elections were held in 1993.

GEOGRAPHY
The River Paraguay divides hilly and forested east from a flat alluvial plain with marsh and semidesert scrubland in the west.

CLIMATE
Subtropical. Gran Chaco is generally hotter and drier. All areas experience floods and droughts.

PEOPLE AND SOCIETY
Population mainly of mixed Spanish and native Indian origin. Most are bilingual, but Guaraní is spoken by preference outside the capital. Gran Chaco is home to small groups of pure Guaraní Indians, cattle ranchers, and Mennonites, a sect of German origin, who live by a cooperative farming system.

◆ INSIGHT: *The joint Paraguay-Brazil hydroelectric power project at Itaipú is the largest in the world*

THE ECONOMY
Agriculture employs 45% of the work force. Soybeans and cotton are main exports. Electricity exporter – earnings cover oil imports. Growth is slow due to remote, landlocked position.

FACT FILE
OFFICIAL NAME: Republic of Paraguay
DATE OF FORMATION: 1811/1938
CAPITAL: Asunción
POPULATION: 4.5 million
TOTAL AREA: 157,046 sq miles (406,750 sq km)

DENSITY: 29 people per sq mile
LANGUAGES: Spanish*, Guaraní*, Plattdeutsch (Low German)
RELIGIONS: Catholic 90%, other 10%
ETHNIC MIX: *mestizo* (Euro-Indian) 95%, White 3%, Indian 2%
GOVERNMENT: Multiparty republic
CURRENCY: Guaraní = 100 centimos

URUGUAY

URUGUAY IS situated in southeastern South America. It returned to civilian government in 1985, after 12 years of military dictatorship.

GEOGRAPHY
Low, rolling grasslands cover 80% of the country. Narrow coastal plain. Alluvial flood plain in southwest. Five rivers flow westwards and drain into the River Uruguay.

CLIMATE
Temperate throughout the country. Warm summers, mild winters, and moderate rainfall.

PEOPLE AND SOCIETY
Uruguayans are largely second- or third-generation Italians or Spaniards. Wealth derived from cattle ranching enabled the country to become the first welfare state in South America. Economic decline since 1960s, but a large, if less prosperous, middle class remains. Although a Roman Catholic country, Uruguay is liberal in its attitude to religion and all forms are tolerated. Divorce is legal.

THE ECONOMY
Most land given over to crops and livestock. Wool, meat, and hides are exported. Earnings as offshore banking center. Buoyant tourism.

◆ INSIGHT: *Uruguay's literacy rates and life expectancy are the region's highest*

FACT FILE
OFFICIAL NAME: Republic of Uruguay
DATE OF FORMATION: 1828 / 1909
CAPITAL: Montevideo
POPULATION: 3.1 million
TOTAL AREA: 68,498 sq miles (177,410 sq km)

DENSITY: 45 people per sq mile
LANGUAGES: Spanish*, other
RELIGIONS: Roman Catholic 77%, Protestant 3%, Jewish 2%, other 18%
ETHNIC MIX: White 88%, *mestizo* (Euro-Indian) 8%, Black 4%
GOVERNMENT: Multiparty republic
CURRENCY: Peso = 100 centesimos

ARGENTINA

OCCUPYING MOST of the southern half of South America, Argentina extends 2,145 miles (3,460 km) from Bolivia to Tierra del Fuego. It is beginning to realize its potential after decades of political and economic instability.

GEOGRAPHY

Andes Mountains in the west run north–south, forming a natural border with Chile. East of the Andes are heavily wooded plains (Gran Chaco) in the north, treeless but fertile Pampas plains in the center. Bleak and arid Patagonia in the far south.

CLIMATE

Northeast is subtropical. Andes are semiarid in the north and snowy in the south. Western lowlands are arid. Pampas have a mild climate with summer rains.

THE ECONOMY

Harsh economic recovery program and new stable currency have offset worst excesses of hyperinflation and inefficient nationalized industries. Rich and varied agricultural base. Powerful agribusiness – Argentina is among the world's leading exporters of beef, wheat, and fruit. Important known oil and gas reserves are still underexploited. Skilled labor force.

56

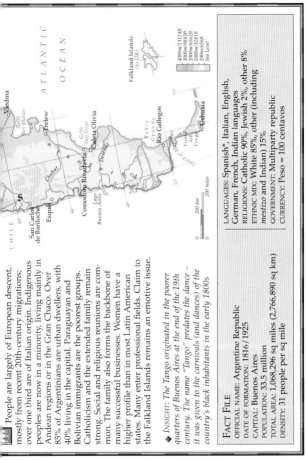

People are largely of European descent, mostly from recent 20th-century migrations; over one third are of Italian origin. Indigenous peoples are now in a minority, living mainly in Andean regions or in the Gran Chaco. Over 85% of Argentinians are urban dwellers, with 40% living in the capital. Paraguayan and Bolivian immigrants are the poorest groups. Catholicism and the extended family remain strong. Social and religious reunions are common. The family also forms the backbone of many successful businesses. Women have a higher profile than in most Latin American states. Many enter professional fields. Claim to the Falkland Islands remains an emotive issue.

◆ INSIGHT: *The Tango originated in the poorer quarters of Buenos Aires at the end of the 19th century. The name "Tango" predates the dance – it was given to the carnivals (and dances) of the country's black inhabitants in the early 1800s*

FACT FILE
OFFICIAL NAME: Argentine Republic
DATE OF FORMATION: 1816/1925
CAPITAL: Buenos Aires
POPULATION: 33.5 million
TOTAL AREA: 1,068,296 sq miles (2,766,890 sq km)
DENSITY: 31 people per sq mile

LANGUAGES: Spanish*, Italian, English, German, French, Indian languages
RELIGIONS: Catholic 90%, Jewish 2%, other 8%
ETHNIC MIX: White 85%, other (including mestizo and Indian) 15%
GOVERNMENT: Multiparty republic
CURRENCY: Peso = 100 centavos

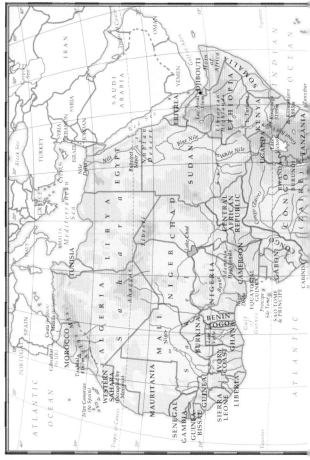

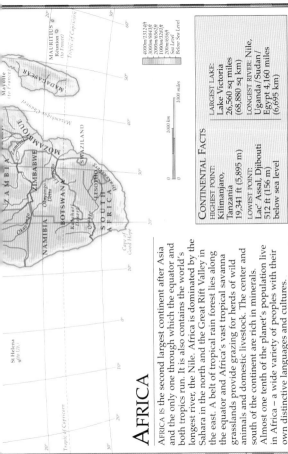

| 4000m/13124ft |
| 3000m/9843ft |
| 2000m/6562ft |
| 1000m/3281ft |
| 200m/656ft |
| Sea Level |
| Below Sea Level |

AFRICA

AFRICA is the second largest continent after Asia and the only one through which the equator and both tropics run. It is also contains the world's longest river, the Nile. Africa is dominated by the Sahara in the north and the Great Rift Valley in the east. A belt of tropical rain forest lies along the equator and Africa's vast tropical savanna grasslands provide grazing for herds of wild animals and domestic livestock. The center and south of the continent are rich in minerals. Almost one tenth of the planet's population live in Africa – a wide variety of peoples with their own distinctive languages and cultures.

CONTINENTAL FACTS

HIGHEST POINT:
Kilimanjaro,
Tanzania
19,341 ft (5,895 m)

LOWEST POINT:
Lac' Assal, Djibouti
512 ft (156 m)
below sea level

LARGEST LAKE:
Lake Victoria
26,560 sq miles
(68,880 sq km)

LONGEST RIVER: Nile,
Uganda/Sudan/
Egypt 4,160 miles
(6,695 km)

MOROCCO

A FORMER French colony in northwest Africa, independent in 1956. Morocco has occupied the disputed territory of Western Sahara since 1975.

 GEOGRAPHY
Fertile coastal plain is interrupted in the east by the Rif Mountains. Atlas Mountain ranges to the south. Beyond lies the outer fringe of the Sahara.

CLIMATE
Ranges from temperate and warm in the north, to semiarid in the south. Cooler in the mountains.

PEOPLE AND SOCIETY
About 35% are descendants of original Berber inhabitants of northwest Africa, and live mainly in mountain villages. Arab majority inhabit lowlands. Large rural-urban gap in wealth. High birth rate. King Hassan heads a powerful monarchy. Government threatened by Islamic militants who fear country is losing its Islamic, Arab identity and becoming too influenced by Europe.

THE ECONOMY
World's main exporter of phosphates. Tourism and agriculture have great potential. Production of cannabis complicates closer EU links.

◆ *INSIGHT: Fès's Karueein University, founded in A.D. 859, is the world's oldest existing educational institution*

FACT FILE

OFFICIAL NAME: Kingdom of Morocco
DATE OF FORMATION: 1956
CAPITAL: Rabat
POPULATION: 27 million
TOTAL AREA: 269,757 sq miles (698,670 sq km)

DENSITY: 101 people per sq mile
LANGUAGES: Arabic*, Berber, French
RELIGIONS: Muslim 99%, other 1%
ETHNIC MIX: Arab and Berber 99%, European 1%
GOVERNMENT: Constitutional monarchy
CURRENCY: Dirham = 100 centimes

ALGERIA

ALGERIA ACHIEVED independence from France in 1962. Today, its military-dominated government faces a severe challenge from Islamic extremists.

GEOGRAPHY
85% of the country lies within the Sahara. Fertile coastal region with plains and hills rises in the southeast to the Atlas Mountains.

CLIMATE
Coastal areas are warm and temperate, with most rainfall during the mild winters. The south is very hot, with negligible rainfall.

PEOPLE AND SOCIETY
Algerians are predominantly Arab, under 30 years of age, and urban. Most indigenous Berbers consider the mountainous Kabylia region in the northeast to be their homeland. The Sahara sustains just 500,000 people, mainly oil workers and Tuareg nomads with goat and camel herds, who move between the irrigated oases. In recent years, political violence has claimed the lives of 3,000 people.

THE ECONOMY
Oil and gas exports. Political turmoil has led to exodus of skilled foreign labor. Limited agriculture.

◆ INSIGHT: *The world's highest sand dunes are found in east central Algeria*

FACT FILE

OFFICIAL NAME: Democratic and Popular Republic of Algeria
DATE OF FORMATION: 1962
CAPITAL: Algiers
POPULATION: 200,000
TOTAL AREA: 919,590 sq miles (2,381,740 sq km)

DENSITY: 29 people per sq mile
LANGUAGES: Arabic*, Berber, French
RELIGIONS: Muslim 99%, Christian and Jewish 1%
ETHNIC MIX: Arab and Berber 99% European 1%
GOVERNMENT: Military regime
CURRENCY: Dinar = 100 centimes

TUNISIA

TUNISIA HAS traditionally been one of the more liberal Arab states, but its government is now facing a challenge from Islamic fundamentalists.

GEOGRAPHY
Mountains in the north are surrounded by plains. Vast, low-lying salt pans in the center. To the south lies the Sahara.

CLIMATE
Summer temperatures are high. The north is often wet and windy in winter. Far south is arid.

PEOPLE AND SOCIETY
Population almost entirely of Arab-Berber descent, with Jewish and Christian minorities. Many still live in extended families. Women have better rights than in any other Arab country and make up 25% of the total work force. Politics, however, remains a male preserve. Low birth rate is a result of a long-standing family planning policy.

◆ INSIGHT: Matmata – a Berber village – appeared in the movie "Star Wars"

THE ECONOMY
Well-diversified, despite limited resources. Oil and gas exports. Expanding manufacturing. Tourism. European investment.

FACT FILE

OFFICIAL NAME: Republic of Tunisia
DATE OF FORMATION: 1956
CAPITAL: Tunis
POPULATION: 8.6 million
TOTAL AREA: 63,170 sq miles (163,610 sq km)

DENSITY: 136 people per sq mile
LANGUAGES: Arabic*, French
RELIGIONS: Muslim 98%, Christian 1%, other 1%
ETHNIC MIX: Arab and Berber 98%, European 1%, other 1%
GOVERNMENT: Multiparty republic
CURRENCY: Dinar = 1,000 millimes

LIBYA

SITUATED ON the Mediterranean coast of North Africa, Libya is a Muslim dictatorship, politically marginalized by the West for its terrorist links.

GEOGRAPHY
Apart from the coastal strip and a mountain range in the south, Libya is desert or semidesert. Oases provide agricultural land.

CLIMATE
Hot and arid. Coastal area has temperate climate, with mild, wet winters and hot, dry summers.

PEOPLE AND SOCIETY
Most Libyans are of Arab and Berber origin. 1969 revolution brought Colonel Gadaffi to power. He represents independence, Islamic faith, belief in communal lifestyle, and hatred of urban rich. Revolution wiped out private enterprise and middle classes. Jews and European settlers were banished. Since then, Libya has changed from being largely a nation of nomads and livestock herders to 70% city-dwellers.

THE ECONOMY
90% of export earnings come from oil. Subject to fluctuating world prices. Dates, olives, peaches, and grapes are grown in the oases.

◆ INSIGHT: *Libya's sulfur-free oil yields little pollution when burned*

FACT FILE

OFFICIAL NAME: The Great Socialist People's Libyan Arab *Jamahiriya*
DATE OF FORMATION: 1951
CAPITAL: Tripoli
POPULATION: 5.5 million
TOTAL AREA: 679,358 sq miles (1,759,540 sq km)

DENSITY: 8 people per sq mile
LANGUAGES: Arabic*, Tuareg
RELIGIONS: Muslim 97%, other 3%
ETHNIC MIX: Arab and Berber 97%, other 3%
GOVERNMENT: Socialist *jamahiriya* (state of the masses)
CURRENCY: Dinar = 1,000 dirhams

EGYPT

EGYPT OCCUPIES the northeast corner of Africa. Its essentially pro-Western, military-backed regime is being challenged by Islamic fundamentalists.

 GEOGRAPHY
Fertile Nile valley separates arid Libyan Desert from smaller semiarid eastern desert. Sinai peninsula has mountains in south.

 CLIMATE
Summers are very hot, but winters are cooler. Rainfall is negligible, except on the coast.

PEOPLE AND SOCIETY
Continuously inhabited for over 8,000 years, with a tradition of religious and ethnic tolerance. Egyptians are mostly Arabs, Bedouins, and Nubians. Women play full part in education system, politics, and economy. Government is fighting Islamic terrorist groups, whose acts of violence have included attacks on politicians, police, and tourists.

◆ INSIGHT: *Egypt has been a major tourist destination since the 1880s*

THE ECONOMY
Oil and gas are main sources of revenue. Tolls from the Suez Canal. Successful tourist industry is threatened by security fears.

FACT FILE
OFFICIAL NAME: Arab Republic of Egypt
DATE OF FORMATION: 1936 / 1982
CAPITAL: Cairo
POPULATION: 64.2 million
TOTAL AREA: 386,660 sq miles (1,001,450 sq km)

DENSITY: 166 people per sq mile
LANGUAGES: Arabic*, French, English, Berber, Greek, Armenian
RELIGIONS: Muslim 94%, other 6%
ETHNIC MIX: Eastern Hamitic 90%, other (inc. Greek, Armenian) 10%
GOVERNMENT: Multiparty republic
CURRENCY: Pound = 100 piastres

SUDAN

THE LARGEST country in Africa, Sudan borders the Red Sea. In 1989, an army coup installed a military Islamic fundamentalist regime.

 GEOGRAPHY
Lies within the upper Nile basin. Mostly arid plains, with marshes in the south. Highlands border the Red Sea in the northeast.

CLIMATE
North is hot, arid desert with constant dry winds. Rainy season ranging from two months in the center, to eight in the south.

PEOPLE AND SOCIETY
Large number of ethnic and linguistic groups. Two million people are nomads, moving over ancient tribal areas in the south. Major social division is between Arabized Muslims in north, and mostly African, largely Christian or animist peoples in south. Attempts to impose Arab and Islamic values throughout Sudan have been the root cause of the civil war that has ravaged the south since 1983.

THE ECONOMY
Sudan is affected by drought and food shortages. Sesame seeds, cotton, gum arabic are cash crops.

◆ *INSIGHT: Sudan's Sudd plain contains the world's largest swamp*

FACT FILE

OFFICIAL NAME: Republic of Sudan
DATE OF FORMATION: 1956
CAPITAL: Khartoum
POPULATION: 27.4 million
TOTAL AREA: 967,493 sq miles (2,505,815 sq km)

DENSITY: 29 people per sq mile
LANGUAGES: Arabic*, other
RELIGIONS: Muslim 70%, traditional beliefs 20%, Christian 5%, other 5%
ETHNIC MIX: Arab 51%, Dinka 13%, Nuba 9%, Beja 7%, other 20%
GOVERNMENT: Military regime
CURRENCY: Pound = 100 piastres

ERITREA

LYING ON the shores of the Red Sea, Eritrea effectively seceded from Ethiopia in 1991, following a 30-year war for independence.

 GEOGRAPHY
Mostly rugged mountains, bush, and the Danakil Desert, which falls below sea level.

 CLIMATE
Warm in the mountains; desert areas are hot. Droughts from July onward are common.

PEOPLE AND SOCIETY
Nine main ethnic groups. Tigrinya-speakers are the largest in number. Strong sense of nationhood forged by the war. Women played important role in the war, fighting alongside men. Over 80% of people are subsistence farmers. Few live beyond the age of 45. Transitional government will hold multiparty elections in 1997.

◆ *INSIGHT: 75% of Eritreans are dependent upon aid for all, or part, of their annual food supply*

THE ECONOMY
Legacy of disruption and destruction from war. Susceptible to drought and famine. Most of the population live at subsistence level. Potential for mining of gold, copper, silver, and zinc. Possible foreign earnings from oil exports.

FACT FILE

OFFICIAL NAME: State of Eritrea
DATE OF FORMATION: 1993
CAPITAL: Asmara
POPULATION: 3.5 million
TOTAL AREA: 36,170 sq miles
(93,680 sq km)
DENSITY: 96 people per sq mile

LANGUAGES: Tigrinya*, Arabic*, Tigre, Afar, Bilen, Kunama, Nara
RELIGIONS: Coptic Christian 45%, Muslim 45%, other 10%
ETHNIC MIX: Nine main ethnic groups
GOVERNMENT: Provisional military government
CURRENCY: Ethiopian birr = 100 cents

DJIBOUTI

A CITY state with a desert hinterland, Djibouti lies in northeast Africa. Once known as French Somaliland, it became independent in 1977.

GEOGRAPHY
Mainly low-lying desert and semidesert, with a volcanic mountain range in the north.

CLIMATE
Hot all year round, with June–August temperatures reaching 109°F (45°C). Scant rainfall.

PEOPLE AND SOCIETY
Dominant ethnic groups are the Issas in the south and the mainly nomadic Afars in the north. Tensions between them developed into a guerrilla war in 1991. Smaller tribal groups make up the rest of the population, together with French and other European expatriates, and Arabs. Population was swelled by 20,000 Somali refugees in 1992. France still exerts considerable influence in Djibouti, supporting it financially and maintaining a naval base and a military garrison.

THE ECONOMY
Djibouti's major asset is its port in a key Red Sea location.

◆ *INSIGHT: Chewing the leaves of the mildly narcotic Qat shrub is an age-old social ritual in Djibouti*

FACT FILE
OFFICIAL NAME: Republic of Djibouti
DATE OF FORMATION: 1977
CAPITAL: Djibouti
POPULATION: 500,000
TOTAL AREA: 8,958 sq miles (23,200 sq km)
DENSITY: 55 people per sq mile

LANGUAGES: Arabic*, French*, Somali, Afar, other
RELIGIONS: Christian 87%, other 13%
ETHNIC MIX: Issa 35%, Afar 20%, Gadaboursis and Isaaks 28%, other (inc. Arab, European) 17%
GOVERNMENT: Single-party republic
CURRENCY: Franc = 100 centimes

ETHIOPIA

LOCATED IN northeast Africa, Ethiopia was a Marxist regime from 1974–1991. It has had a series of economic, civil, and natural crises.

GEOGRAPHY
Great Rift Valley divides mountainous northwest region from desert lowlands in northeast and southeast. Ethiopian Plateau is drained mainly by the Blue Nile.

CLIMATE
Generally moderate with summer rains. Highlands are warm, with night frost and snowfalls on the mountains.

PEOPLE AND SOCIETY
76 Ethiopian nationalities speak 286 languages. Oromo are largest group. In 1995, the first multiparty elections were held, ending four years of rule by transitional government, and beginning a new nine-state federation.

◆ INSIGHT: Solomon and the Queen of Sheba are said to have founded the Kingdom of Abyssinia (Ethiopia) c. 1000 B.C

THE ECONOMY
World's second poorest nation. Most people are subsistence farmers. Despite war-damaged infrastructure and periodic serious droughts, agricultural and industrial output are growing as it moves toward a market economy.

FACT FILE

OFFICIAL NAME: Undetermined
DATE OF FORMATION: 1903/1993
CAPITAL: Addis Ababa
POPULATION: 56.7 million
TOTAL AREA: 435,605 sq miles (1,128,221 sq km)
DENSITY: 130 people per sq mile

LANGUAGES: Amharic*, English, Arabic, Tigrinya, Orominga
RELIGIONS: Muslim 43%, Christian 37%, traditional beliefs, other 20%,
ETHNIC MIX: Oromo 40%, Amhara and Tigrean 32%, other 28%
GOVERNMENT: Multiparty republic
CURRENCY: Birr = 100 cents

SOMALIA

A SEMIARID state occupying the horn of Africa. Italian Somaliland and British Somaliland were united in 1960 to form an independent Somalia.

GEOGRAPHY
Highlands in the north, flatter scrub-covered land to the south. Coastal areas are more fertile.

CLIMATE
Very dry, except for the north coast, which is hot and humid. Interior has among world's highest average yearly temperatures.

PEOPLE AND SOCIETY
Clan system forms the basis of all commercial, political, and social activities. Most people are herders (Samaal) while the rest are farmers (Sab). Years of clan-based civil war have resulted in collapse of central government. US-led UN peacekeeping force was deployed, but it was withdrawn in 1994.

◆ INSIGHT: *Present-day Somalia was known to the Egyptians, Phoenicians, and Greeks as "the land of incense"*

THE ECONOMY
Somalia is heavily reliant on foreign aid, since all commodities except arms are in short supply. Formal economy has collapsed due to civil war and drought.

FACT FILE

OFFICIAL NAME: Somali Democratic Republic
DATE OF FORMATION: 1960
CAPITAL: Mogadishu
POPULATION: 9.5 million
TOTAL AREA: 246,200 sq miles (637,660 sq km)

DENSITY: 39 people per sq mile
LANGUAGES: Somali*, Arabic*, other
RELIGIONS: Sunni Muslim 99%, other (inc. Christian) 1%
ETHNIC MIX: Somali 98%, Bantu, Arab 1.5%, European, other 0.5%
GOVERNMENT: Transitional
CURRENCY: Shilling = 100 cents

UGANDA

UGANDA LIES landlocked in East Africa. It was ruled by one of Africa's more eccentric leaders, the dictator Idi Amin Dada, from 1971–1980.

GEOGRAPHY
Predominantly a large plateau with Ruwenzori mountain range and Great Rift Valley in the west. Lake Victoria in the southeast. Vegetation is of savanna type.

CLIMATE
Altitude and the influence of the lakes modify the equatorial climate. Rain falls throughout the year; spring is the wettest period.

PEOPLE AND SOCIETY
Predominantly rural population comprises 13 main ethnic groups. Since 1986, President Museveni has worked hard to break down traditional animosities. In 1993, he allowed the restoration of Uganda's four historical monarchies. New constitution will use a federal system with boundaries based on those of the old kingdoms.

THE ECONOMY
Coffee earns 93% of export income. Hydroelectric power is to be developed to replace 50% of oil imports. Reopening of mines should improve the economy.

◆ INSIGHT: Lake Victoria is the world's third largest lake

3000m/9843ft
2000m/6562ft
1000m/3281ft
500m/1640ft

FACT FILE
OFFICIAL NAME: Republic of Uganda
DATE OF FORMATION: 1962
CAPITAL: Kampala
POPULATION: 19.2 million
TOTAL AREA: 91,073 sq miles
(235,880 sq km)
DENSITY: 245 people per sq mile

LANGUAGES: English*, Luganda, Nkole, Chiga, Lango, Acholi, Teso
RELIGIONS: Catholic/Protestant 66%, traditional beliefs 18%, Muslim 16%
ETHNIC MIX: Buganda 18%, Banyoro 14%, Teso 9%, other 59%
GOVERNMENT: Multiparty republic
CURRENCY: Shilling = 100 cents

KENYA

KENYA STRADDLES the equator on Africa's east coast. It became a multiparty democracy in 1992 and has been led by President Moi since 1978.

GEOGRAPHY
Central plateau divided by Great Rift Valley. North of the equator is mainly semidesert. To the east lies a fertile coastal belt.

CLIMATE
Coast and Great Rift Valley are hot and humid. Plateau interior is temperate. Northeastern desert is hot and dry. Rain generally falls April–May and October–November.

PEOPLE AND SOCIETY
Kenya's 70 ethnic groups speak about 40 languages. Rural majority has strong clan and family links. One of the world's highest population growth rates, together with poverty, has exacerbated the recent surge in ethnic violence.

◆ *INSIGHT: Kenya has more than 40 game reserves and national parks, and two marine parks in the Indian Ocean*

THE ECONOMY
Tourism is the leading foreign exchange earner. Tea and coffee grown as cash crops. Large and diversified manufacturing sector.

5000m/16405ft
4000m/13124ft
3000m/9843ft
2000m/6562ft
1000m/3281ft
500m/1640ft
200m/656ft
Sea Level

0   100 km
0   100 miles

FACT FILE

OFFICIAL NAME: Republic of Kenya
DATE OF FORMATION: 1963
CAPITAL: Nairobi
POPULATION: 29.1 million
TOTAL AREA: 224,081 sq miles
(580,370 sq km)
DENSITY: 130 people per sq mile

LANGUAGES: Swahili*, English, Kikuyu, Luo, Kamba, other
RELIGIONS: Catholic/Protestant 66%, animist 26%, Muslim 6%, other 2%
ETHNIC MIX: Kikuyu 21%, Luhya 14%, Kamba 11%, other 54%
GOVERNMENT: Multiparty republic
CURRENCY: Shilling = 100 cents

RWANDA

R

RWANDA LIES just south of the equator in east central Africa. Since independence from France in 1962, ethnic tensions have dominated politics

GEOGRAPHY
Series of plateaus descends from ridge of volcanic peaks in the west to Akagera River on eastern border. Great Rift Valley also passes through this region.

CLIMATE
Tropical, tempered by the altitude. Two wet seasons are separated by a dry season, June–August. Heaviest rain in the west.

PEOPLE AND SOCIETY
Rwandans live a subsistence existence. Traditional family and clan structures are strong. For over 500 years the cattle-owning Tutsi were politically dominant over the land-owning Hutu. In 1959, violent revolt led to a reversal of the roles. The two groups have since been waging a spasmodic war. In the most recent outbreak of violence, in 1994, over 200,000 people died.

THE ECONOMY
All economic activity has been suspended due to ethnic conflict. Rwanda has few resources but during peace, it produces coffee. Possible oil and gas reserves

◆ INSIGHT: *Rwanda is Africa's most densely populated country*

FACT FILE
OFFICIAL NAME: Rwandese Republic
DATE OF FORMATION: 1962
CAPITAL: Kigali
POPULATION: 7.5 million
TOTAL AREA: 10,170 sq miles (26,340 sq km)
DENSITY: 737 people per sq mile

LANGUAGES: Kinyarwanda*, French*, Kiswahili
RELIGIONS: Catholic 65%, Protestant 9%, traditional beliefs 25%, other 1%
ETHNIC MIX: Hutu 90%, Tutsi 9%, Twa pygmy 1%
GOVERNMENT: Multiparty republic
CURRENCY: Franc = 100 centimes

BURUNDI

SMALL, DENSELY populated, and landlocked, Burundi lies just south of the equator, on the Nile–Congo watershed in Central Africa.

 GEOGRAPHY
Hilly with high plateaus in center and savanna in the east. Great Rift Valley on western side.

 CLIMATE
Temperate, with high humidity. Heavy and frequent rainfall, mostly October–May.

PEOPLE AND SOCIETY
Burundi's postindependence history has been dominated by ethnic conflict – with repeated large-scale massacres – between majority Hutu and the Tutsi, who control the army. Over 120,000 people, mostly Hutu, have been killed since 1992. Twa pygmies are not involved in the conflict. Most people are subsistence farmers.

◆ *INSIGHT: Burundi's birth rate is one of the highest in Africa. On average, families have seven children*

THE ECONOMY
Overwhelmingly agricultural economy. Small quantities of gold and tungsten. Potential of oil in Lake Tanganyika. Burundi has 5% of the world's nickel reserves.

2000m/6562ft	
1000m/3281ft	
500m/1640ft	

FACT FILE

OFFICIAL NAME: Republic of Burundi
DATE OF FORMATION: 1962
CAPITAL: Bujumbura
POPULATION: 5.8 million
TOTAL AREA: 10,750 sq miles (27,830 sq km)
DENSITY: 539 people per sq mile

LANGUAGES: Kirundi*, French*, Swahili, other
RELIGIONS: Catholic 62%, traditional beliefs 32%, Protestant 6%
ETHNIC MIX: Hutu 85%, Tutsi 13%, Twa pygmy 1%, other 1%
GOVERNMENT: Multiparty republic
CURRENCY: Franc = 100 centimes

CENTRAL AFRICAN REPUBLIC

A LANDLOCKED country lying between the basins of the Chad and Congo rivers. Its arid north sustains less than 2% of the population.

GEOGRAPHY
Comprises a low plateau, covered by scrub or savanna. Rain forests in the south. One of Africa's great rivers, the Ubangi, forms the border with Congo (Zaire).

CLIMATE
The south is equatorial; the north is hot and dry. Rain occurs all year round, with heaviest falls between July and October.

PEOPLE AND SOCIETY
Baya and Banda are largest ethnic groups, but Sango, spoken by minority river peoples in the south, is the *lingua franca.* Most political leaders since independence have come from the south. Women, as in other non-Muslim African countries, have considerable power. Large number of ethnic groups helps limit disputes.

THE ECONOMY
Dominated by subsistence farming. Exports include gold, diamonds, cotton, and timber. Country is self-sufficient in food production. Poor infrastructure.

◆ *INSIGHT: The country was severely depopulated in previous centuries by the Arab and European slave trades*

FACT FILE

OFFICIAL NAME: Central African Republic
DATE OF FORMATION: 1960
CAPITAL: Bangui
POPULATION: 3.3 million
TOTAL AREA: 240,530 sq miles (622,980 sq km)

DENSITY: 13 people per sq mile
LANGUAGES: French*, Sango, Banda
RELIGIONS: Christian 50%, traditional beliefs 27%, Muslim 15%, other 8%
ETHNIC MIX: Baya 34%, Banda 27%, Mandjia 21%, Sara 10%, other 8%
GOVERNMENT: Multiparty republic
CURRENCY: CFA franc = 100 centimes

CONGO (ZAIRE)

STRADDLING THE equator in east central Africa, this is one of Africa's largest countries. It achieved independence from Belgium in 1960.

 GEOGRAPHY
Rain forest basin of River Congo occupies 60% of the land. High mountain ranges stretch down the eastern border.

 CLIMATE
Tropical and humid. Distinct wet and dry seasons south of the equator. The north is mainly wet.

PEOPLE AND SOCIETY
12 main groups and around 190 smaller ones. Original inhabitants, Forest Pygmies, are now a marginalized group. Ethnic tensions inherited from colonial period were contained until 1990, since when outbreaks of ethnic violence have occurred.

◆ INSIGHT: *The rain forests comprise almost 6% of the world's, and 50% of Africa's, remaining woodlands*

THE ECONOMY
25 years of mismanagement have brought economy near to collapse. Hyperinflation. Minerals, including copper and diamonds, provide 85% of export earnings.

```
          2000m/6562ft
          1000m/3281ft
          500m/1640ft
          200m/656ft
          Sea Level

0          200 km
0          200 miles
```

FACT FILE

OFFICIAL NAME: Democratic Republic of the Congo
DATE OF FORMATION: 1960
CAPITAL: Kinshasa
POPULATION: 41.2 million
TOTAL AREA: 905,563 sq miles (2,345,410 sq km)
DENSITY: 45 people per sq mile

LANGUAGES: French*, Kiswahili, Tshiluba, Kikongo, Lingala
RELIGIONS: Christian 70%, traditional beliefs 20%, Muslim 10%
ETHNIC MIX: Bantu 23%, Hamitic 23%, other (inc. Pygmy) 54%
GOVERNMENT: Transitional
CURRENCY: Congolese Franc

NIGER

NIGER LIES landlocked in West Africa, but it is linked to the sea by its one permanent river, the Niger. It became independent of France in 1960.

 GEOGRAPHY
North and northeast regions are part of Sahara and Sahel. Aïr mountains in center rise high above the desert. Savanna in the south.

 CLIMATE
High temperatures for most of the year – around 95°F (35°C). The north is virtually rainless.

PEOPLE AND SOCIETY
A largely Islamic society. Women have limited rights and restricted access to education. Considerable tensions exist between Tuareg nomads in the north and groups in the south. Tuaregs have felt alienated from mainstream politics. They mounted a low-key revolt in 1990. Sense of community and egalitarianism among southern peoples helps to combat economic difficulties.

THE ECONOMY
Vast uranium deposits. Frequent droughts and southwest expansion of Sahara are problems.

◆ *INSIGHT: Niger's name is derived from the Tuareg word n'eghirren, meaning "flowing water"*

FACT FILE

OFFICIAL NAME: Republic of Niger
DATE OF FORMATION: 1960
CAPITAL: Niamey
POPULATION: 8.5 million
TOTAL AREA: 489,188 sq miles (1,267,000 sq km)
DENSITY: 18 people per sq mile

LANGUAGES: French*, Hausa, Djerma, Fulani, Tuareg, Teda
RELIGIONS: Muslim 85%, traditional beliefs 14%, Christian 1%
ETHNIC MIX: Hausa 56%, Djerma 22%, Fulani 9%, other 13%
GOVERNMENT: Multiparty republic
CURRENCY: CFA franc = 100 centimes

CHAD

LANDLOCKED IN north central Africa, Chad has been torn by intermittent periods of civil war since independence from France in 1960.

GEOGRAPHY
Mostly plateaus sloping west-ward to Lake Chad. Northern third is Sahara. Tibesti Mountains in north rise to 10,826 ft (3,300 m).

CLIMATE
Three distinct zones: desert in north, semiarid region in center, and tropics in south.

PEOPLE AND SOCIETY
Half the population live in southern fifth of the country. Northern third has only 100,000 people, mainly Muslim Toubeu nomads. Political strife between Muslims in north and Christians in south. Recent attempts to introduce multiparty system, after 30 years of military and one-party rule.

◆ *INSIGHT: Lake Chad is progressively drying up – it is now estimated to be just 20% of its size in 1970*

THE ECONOMY
One of Africa's poorest states. Vast majority of people involved in subsistence agriculture, notably cotton and cattle herding. Recent discovery of large oil deposits.

FACT FILE
OFFICIAL NAME: Republic of Chad
DATE OF FORMATION: 1960
CAPITAL: Ndjamena
POPULATION: 6 million
TOTAL AREA: 495,752 sq miles
(1,284,000 sq km)
DENSITY: 13 people per sq mile

LANGUAGES: French*, Sara, Maba
RELIGIONS: Muslim 44%, Christian 33%, traditional beliefs 23%
ETHNIC MIX: Bagirmi, Sara and Kreish 31%, Sudanic Arab 26%, Teda 7%, other 36%
GOVERNMENT: Transitional
CURRENCY: CFA franc = 100 centimes

MAURITANIA

SITUATED IN northwest Africa, two thirds of Mauritania's territory is desert. A former French colony, it achieved independence in 1960.

GEOGRAPHY
The Sahara, barren with scattered oases, covers the north. Savanna lands to the south.

CLIMATE
Generally hot and dry, aggravated by dusty *harmattan* wind. Summer rain in the south, virtually none in the north.

PEOPLE AND SOCIETY
The Maures control political life and dominate the minority black population. Ethnic tension centers on the oppression of blacks by Maures. Tens of thousands of blacks are estimated to be in slavery. Family solidarity among nomadic peoples is particularly strong.

◆ INSIGHT: *Slavery officially became illegal in Mauritania in 1980, but* de facto *slavery still persists*

THE ECONOMY
Agriculture and herding. Iron and copper mining. World's largest gypsum deposits. Rich fishing grounds. Large foreign debt.

FACT FILE
OFFICIAL NAME: Islamic Republic of Mauritania
DATE OF FORMATION: 1960
CAPITAL: Nouakchott
POPULATION: 2.2 million
TOTAL AREA: 395,953 sq miles (1,025,520 sq km)

DENSITY: 5 people per sq mile
LANGUAGES: French*, Hassaniyah Arabic, Wolof
RELIGIONS: Muslim 100%
ETHNIC MIX: Maure 80%, Wolof 7%, Tukulor 5%, other 8%
GOVERNMENT: Multiparty republic
CURRENCY: Ouguiya = 5 khoums

MALI

LANDLOCKED IN the heart of West Africa, Mali held its first free elections in 1992, more than 30 years after it gained independence from France.

GEOGRAPHY
Northern half lies in the Sahara. Inland delta of River Niger flows through grassy savanna region in the south.

CLIMATE
In the south, intensely hot, dry weather precedes the westerly rains. The north is almost rainless.

PEOPLE AND SOCIETY
Most people live in southern savanna region. Bambara are politically dominant. A few nomadic Fulani and Tuareg herders travel northern plains. Extended family provides social security. Tension between peoples of the south and Tuaregs in north.

THE ECONOMY
One of the poorest countries in the world. Less than 2% of land can be cultivated. Most people are farmers, herders, or river fishers. Gold deposits now being mined.

◆ INSIGHT: Tombouctou was the center of the huge Malinke empire during the 14th century

FACT FILE

OFFICIAL NAME: Republic of Mali
DATE OF FORMATION: 1960
CAPITAL: Bamako
POPULATION: 10.1 million
TOTAL AREA: 478,837 sq miles (1,240,190 sq km)
DENSITY: 21 people per sq mile

LANGUAGES: French*, Bambara, Fulani, Senufo, Soninké
RELIGIONS: Muslim 80%, traditional beliefs 18%, Christian 2%
ETHNIC MIX: Bambara 31%, Fulani 13%, Senufo 12%, other 44%
GOVERNMENT: Multiparty republic
CURRENCY: CFA franc = 100 centimes

SENEGAL

A FORMER French colony, Senegal achieved independence in 1960. Its capital, Dakar, stands on the westernmost cape of Africa.

GEOGRAPHY
Arid semidesert in the north. The south is mainly savanna bushland. Plains in the southeast.

CLIMATE
Tropical, with humid rainy conditions June–October, and drier season December–May. Coast is cooled by northern trade winds.

PEOPLE AND SOCIETY
Very little ethnic tension, due to considerable amount of interethnic marriage. Groups can be identified regionally. Dakar is a Wolof area, the Senegal River is dominated by the Toucouleur, and the Malinke mostly live in the east. The Diola in Casamance have felt politically excluded and this has led to unrest. A French-influenced class system is still prevalent and has become more apparent in recent years.

THE ECONOMY
70% of people are farmers – groundnuts are main export crop. Phosphate is mined. More industr than most West African countries.

◆ INSIGHT: Senegal's name derives from the Zenega Berbers who invade in the 1300s, bringing Islam with the

FACT FILE

OFFICIAL NAME: Republic of Senegal
DATE OF FORMATION: 1960
CAPITAL: Dakar
POPULATION: 7.9 million
TOTAL AREA: 75,950 sq miles (196,720 sq km)
DENSITY: 104 people per sq mile

LANGUAGES: French*, Wolof, Fulani, Serer, Diola, Malinke, Soninke
RELIGIONS: Muslim 92%, traditional beliefs 6%, Christian 2%
ETHNIC MIX: Wolof 46%, Fulani 25%, Serer 16%, Diola 7%, Malinke 6%
GOVERNMENT: Multiparty republic
CURRENCY: CFA franc = 100 centimes

GAMBIA

A NARROW state on the west coast of Africa, Gambia was renowned for its stability until its government was overthrown in a coup in 1994.

GEOGRAPHY
Narrow strip of land which borders River Gambia. Long, sandy beaches backed by mangrove swamps along river. Savanna and tropical forests higher up.

CLIMATE
Subtropical, with wet, humid months July–October and warm, dry season November–May.

PEOPLE AND SOCIETY
Little tension between various ethnic groups. Creole community, known as the Aku, is small but socially prominent. People are increasingly leaving rural areas for the towns, where average incomes are four times higher. Each year seasonal immigrants from neighboring states come to farm groundnuts. Women are active as traders.

THE ECONOMY
80% of the labor force is involved in agriculture. Groundnuts are the principal crop. The fisheries sector is being improved. Growth in tourism now halted by political instability. Most donor aid has been suspended until civilian rule is restored.

◆ INSIGHT: *Banjul's airport was upgraded by NASA in 1989, for Space Shuttle emergency landings*

SENEGAL 15°

Bakau
Serekunda ○BANJUL ○Farafenni   Georgetown
ATLANTIC   ○Brikama   Gambia   Basse
OCEAN   ○Gunjur   SENEGAL   Santa Su

200m/656ft
Sea Level

0   50 km
0   50 miles

FACT FILE

OFFICIAL NAME: Republic of The Gambia

DATE OF FORMATION: 1965

CAPITAL: Banjul

POPULATION: 900,000

TOTAL AREA: 4,363 sq miles (11,300 sq km)

DENSITY: 206 people per sq mile

LANGUAGES: English*, other

RELIGIONS: Muslim 85%, Christian 9%, traditional beliefs 6%

ETHNIC MIX: Mandinka 41%, Fulani 14%, Wolof 13%, other 32%

GOVERNMENT: Military regime

CURRENCY: Dalasi = 100 butut

CAPE VERDE

OFF THE west coast of Africa, in the Atlantic Ocean, lies the group of islands that make up Cape Verde, a Portuguese colony until 1975.

GEOGRAPHY
Ten main islands and eight smaller islets, all of volcanic origin. Mostly mountainous, with steep cliffs and rocky headlands.

CLIMATE
Warm and very dry. Subject to droughts that may last for years at a time.

PEOPLE AND SOCIETY
Most people are of mixed Portuguese-African origin; rest are largely African, descended from slaves or from more recent immigrants from the mainland. 50% of the population live on Santiago. Roman Catholicism and the extended family are strong. Some ethnic tension between islands.

◆ INSIGHT: *Poor soils and lack of surface water mean that Cape Verde must import 90% of its food*

THE ECONOMY
Most people are subsistence farmers. Fish is the main export. Only minerals produced are salt, and volcanic rock for cement.

FACT FILE

OFFICIAL NAME: Republic of Cape Verde
DATE OF FORMATION: 1975
CAPITAL: Praia
POPULATION: 400,000
TOTAL AREA: 1,556 sq miles (4,030 sq km)

DENSITY: 258 people per sq mile
LANGUAGES: Portuguese*, Creole
RELIGIONS: Roman Catholic 98%, Protestant 2%
ETHNIC MIX: Creole (*mestiço*) 71%, Black 28%, White 1%
GOVERNMENT: Multiparty republic
CURRENCY: Escudo = 100 centavos

GUINEA-BISSAU

KNOWN AS Portuguese Guinea during its days as a colony, Guinea-Bissau is situated on Africa's west coast, bordered by Senegal and Guinea.

GEOGRAPHY
Low-lying, apart from savanna highlands in northeast. Rain forests and swamps are found along coastal areas.

CLIMATE
Tropical, with wet season May–November and dry season December–April. Hot *harmattan* wind blows during dry season.

PEOPLE AND SOCIETY
Largest ethnic group is Balante, who live in the south. Though less than 2% of the population, the mixed Portuguese-African *mestiços* dominate top ranks of government and bureaucracy. Most people live on small family farms in self-contained villages. After 20 years of single-party rule, the first multiparty elections were held in 1994.

THE ECONOMY
Mostly subsistence farming – corn, sweet potatoes, cassava. Main cash crops are cashews, groundnuts, and palm kernels. Offshore oil as yet untapped.

◆ INSIGHT: *In 1974, Guinea-Bissau became the first Portuguese colony to gain independence*

FACT FILE
OFFICIAL NAME: Republic of Guinea-Bissau
DATE OF FORMATION: 1974
CAPITAL: Bissau
POPULATION: 1 million
TOTAL AREA: 13,940 sq miles (36,120 sq km)

DENSITY: 71 people per sq mile
LANGUAGES: Portuguese*, other
RELIGIONS: Traditional beliefs 54%, Muslim 38%, Christian 8%
ETHNIC MIX: Balante 27%, Fulani 22%, Malinke 12%, other 39%
GOVERNMENT: Multiparty republic
CURRENCY: Peso = 100 centavos

GUINEA

FACING THE Atlantic Ocean, on the west coast of Africa, Guinea became the first French colony in Africa to gain independence, in 1958.

 GEOGRAPHY
Coastal plains and mangrove swamps in west rise to forested or savanna highlands in the south. Semidesert in the north.

 CLIMATE
Tropical, with wet season April–October. Heavy annual rainfall. Hot *harmattan* wind blows from Sahara during dry season.

PEOPLE AND SOCIETY
Malinke and Fulani make up most of the population, but traditional rivalries between them have allowed coastal peoples such as the Susu to dominate politics. Daily life revolves around the extended family. Women gained influence under Marxist party rule from 1958–1984, but Muslim revival since then has reversed the trend. First multiparty elections held in 1995.

THE ECONOMY
Two thirds of people are farmers. Cash crops are palm oil, bananas, pineapples, and rice. Gold, diamond, and bauxite reserves.

◆ *INSIGHT: The colors of Guinea's flag represent the three words of the country's motto: work (red), justice (yellow), and solidarity (green)*

FACT FILE

OFFICIAL NAME: Republic of Guinea
DATE OF FORMATION: 1958
CAPITAL: Conakry
POPULATION: 6.3 million
TOTAL AREA: 94,926 sq miles (245,860 sq km)
DENSITY: 65 people per sq mile

LANGUAGES: French*, Fulani, Malinke, Susu, Kissi, other
RELIGIONS: Muslim 85%, Christian 8%, traditional beliefs 7%
ETHNIC MIX: Fulani 40%, Malinke 25%, Susu 12%, Kissi 7%, other 16%
GOVERNMENT: Multiparty republic
CURRENCY: Franc = 100 centimes

SIERRA LEONE

THE WEST African state of Sierra Leone achieved independence from the British in 1961. Today, it is one of the world's poorest nations.

GEOGRAPHY
Flat plain, running the length of the coast, stretches inland for 83 miles (133 km). Beyond, forests rise to highlands near neighboring Guinea in the northeast.

CLIMATE
Hot tropical weather, with very high rainfall and humidity. Dusty, northeastern *harmattan* wind blows November–April.

PEOPLE AND SOCIETY
Mende and Temne are major ethnic groups. Freetown's citizens are largely descended from slaves freed from Britain and the US, resulting in a strongly anglicized Creole culture. A military coup in 1992 halted plans to turn the government into a multiparty democracy. Rebel forces have been fighting the government since 1991; thousands have died in clashes.

THE ECONOMY
Vast majority of people are subsistance farmers. Cash crops include palm kernels, cocoa beans, and kola. Main export is diamonds.

◆ *INSIGHT: The British philanthropist Granville Sharp set up a settlement for freed slaves in Sierra Leone in 1787*

1000m/3281ft	
500m/1640ft	
200m/656ft	
Sea Level	

FACT FILE

OFFICIAL NAME: Republic of Sierra Leone

DATE OF FORMATION: 1961

CAPITAL: Freetown

POPULATION: 4.5 million

TOTAL AREA: 27,699 sq miles (71,740 sq km)

DENSITY: 162 people per sq mile

LANGUAGES: English*, Krio (Creole)

RELIGIONS: Traditional beliefs 52%, Muslim 40%, Christian 8%

ETHNIC MIX: Mende 34%, Temne 31%, Limba 9%, Kono 5%, other 21%

GOVERNMENT: Military regime

CURRENCY: Leone = 100 cents

LIBERIA

LIBERIA FACES the Atlantic Ocean in equatorial West Africa. Africa's oldest republic, it was established in 1847. Today it is torn by civil war.

GEOGRAPHY

Coastline of beaches and mangrove swamps rises to forested plateaus and highlands inland.

CLIMATE

High temperatures. Except in extreme southeast, there is only one wet season, May–October.

PEOPLE AND SOCIETY
Key social distinction has been between Americo-Liberians – descendants of freed slaves – and the indigenous tribal peoples. However, political assimilation and intermarriage have eased tensions. Inter-tribal tension is now a problem. A civil war has ravaged the country since 1990, with private armies competing for power.

◆ INSIGHT: *Liberia is named after the people liberated from US slavery who arrived in the 1800s*

THE ECONOMY
Civil war has led to collapse of economy – little commercial activity. Only 1% of land is arable. Estimated one billion tons of iron ore reserves at Mount Nimba.

FACT FILE
OFFICIAL NAME: Republic of Liberia
DATE OF FORMATION: 1847 / 1907
CAPITAL: Monrovia
POPULATION: 2.8 million
TOTAL AREA: 43,000 sq miles (111,370 sq km)
DENSITY: 75 people per sq mile

LANGUAGES: English*, Kpelle, Bassa Vai, Grebo, Kru, Kissi, Gola
RELIGIONS: Traditional beliefs 70%, Muslim 20%, Christian 10%
ETHNIC MIX: Kpelle 20%, Bassa 14%, Americo-Liberians 5%, other 61%
GOVERNMENT: Transitional
CURRENCY: Liberian $ = 100 cents

IVORY COAST

ONE OF the larger nations along the coast of West Africa, the Ivory Coast remains under the influence of its former colonial ruler, France.

 GEOGRAPHY
Sandy coastal strip backed by largely rain forest interior, and savanna plateaus in the north.

CLIMATE
High temperatures all year round. South has two wet seasons; north has one, with lower rainfall.

PEOPLE AND SOCIETY
More than 60 ethnic groups. President Houphouët-Boigny, who ruled from independence until 1993, promoted his own group, the Baoule. Succession of Konan Bedic, another Baoule, has annoyed other tribes. The extended family keeps laborers who migrate to the cities in contact with their villages.

THE ECONOMY
Cash crops include cocoa, coffee, palm oil, bananas, and rubber. Teak, mahogany, and ebony in rain forests. Oil reserves.

◆ INSIGHT: *The Basilica of Our Lady of the Peace in Yamoussoukro is the second largest church in the world. It holds up to 100,000 people*

FACT FILE

OFFICIAL NAME: Republic of the Ivory Coast
DATE OF FORMATION: 1960
CAPITAL: Yamoussoukro
POPULATION: 13.4 million
TOTAL AREA: 124,503 sq miles (322,463 sq km)

DENSITY: 107 people per sq mile
LANGUAGES: French*, Akran, other
RELIGIONS: Traditional beliefs 63%, Muslim 25%, Christian 12%
ETHNIC MIX: Baoule 23%, Bété 18%, Kru 17%, Malinke 15%, other 27%
GOVERNMENT: Multiparty republic
CURRENCY: CFA franc = 100 centimes

BURKINA

KNOWN AS Upper Volta until 1984, the West African state of Burkina has had military rulers for most of its postindependence history.

GEOGRAPHY
North of country is covered by the Sahara. South is largely savanna. Three main rivers are Black, White, and Red Voltas.

CLIMATE
Tropical. Dry, cool weather November–February. Erratic rain March–April, mostly in southeast.

PEOPLE AND SOCIETY
No ethnic group is dominant, but the Mossi have always played an important part in government. Extreme poverty has led to a strong sense of egalitarianism. The extended family is important, and reaches from villages into towns and cities. Women wield considerable power and influence within this system, but most are still denied access to education.

THE ECONOMY
Based on agriculture – cotton is most valuable cash crop – but not self-sufficient in food. Gold is the leading nonagricultural export.

◆ *INSIGHT: Poor soils and droughts mean that many men migrate seasonally to Ghana and the Ivory Coast for work*

FACT FILE

OFFICIAL NAME: Burkina
DATE OF FORMATION: 1960
CAPITAL: Ouagadougou
POPULATION: 9.8 million
TOTAL AREA: 105,870 sq miles (274,200 sq km)
DENSITY: 91 people per sq mile

LANGUAGES: French*, Mossi, Fulani, Tuareg, Dyula, Songhai
RELIGIONS: Traditional beliefs 65%, Muslim 25%, Christian 10%
ETHNIC MIX: Mossi 45%, Mande 10%, Fulani 10%, others 35%
GOVERNMENT: Multiparty republic
CURRENCY: CFA franc = 100 centimes

GHANA

ONCE KNOWN as the Gold Coast, Ghana in West Africa has experienced intermittent periods of military rule since independence in 1957.

 GEOGRAPHY
Mostly low-lying. West is covered by rain forest. Lake Volta – the world's third largest artificial lake – was created by damming the White Volta River.

 CLIMATE
Tropical. Two wet seasons in the south; one in the north.

PEOPLE AND SOCIETY
Around 75 ethnic groups. The largest is the Akan. Over 100 languages and dialects are spoken. Southern peoples are richer and more urban than those of the north. In recent years, tension between groups in the north has erupted into violence. Multiparty elections in 1992 confirmed former military leader Jerry Rawlings in power.

◆ INSIGHT: Ghana was the first British colony in Africa to gain independence

THE ECONOMY
Produces 15% of the world's cocoa. Hardwood trees such as maple and sapele are exploited. Gold, diamonds, bauxite, and manganese are major exports.

FACT FILE

OFFICIAL NAME: Republic of Ghana
DATE OF FORMATION: 1957
CAPITAL: Accra
POPULATION: 16.4 million
TOTAL AREA: 92,100 sq miles (238,540 sq km)
DENSITY: 178 people per sq mile

LANGUAGES: English*, Akan, Mossi, Ewe, Ga, Twi, Fanti, Gurma, other
RELIGIONS: Traditional beliefs 38%, Muslim 30%, Christian 24%, other 8%
ETHNIC MIX: Akan 52%, Mossi 15%, Ewe 12%, Ga 8%, other 13%
GOVERNMENT: Multiparty republic
CURRENCY: Cedi = 100 pesewas

TOGO

TOGO LIES sandwiched between Ghana and Benin in West Africa. The 1993–1994 elections were the first since its independence in 1960.

GEOGRAPHY
Central forested region bounded by savanna lands to the north and south. Mountain range stretches southwest to northeast.

CLIMATE
Coast hot and humid; drier inland. Rainy season March–July, with heaviest falls in the west.

PEOPLE AND SOCIETY
Harsh resentment between Ewe in the south and Kabye in the north. Kabye control military, but are far less developed than people of the south. Extended family is important. Tribalism and nepotism are key factors in everyday life. Some ethnic groups, such as the Mina, have matriarchal societies.

◆ INSIGHT: The "Nana Benz," the market-women of Lomé market, control Togo's retail trade

THE ECONOMY
Most people are farmers. Self-sufficient in basic foodstuffs. Main export crops are coffee, cocoa, and cotton. Half of all export revenues come from phosphate deposits with the world's highest mineral content.

500m/1640ft
200m/656ft
Sea Level

0   50 km
0   50 miles

FACT FILE

OFFICIAL NAME: Togolese Republic
DATE OF FORMATION: 1960
CAPITAL: Lomé
POPULATION: 3.9 million
TOTAL AREA: 21,927 sq miles (56,790 sq km)
DENSITY: 177 people per sq mile

LANGUAGES: French*, Ewe, Kabye, Gurma, other
RELIGIONS: Traditional beliefs 70%, Christian 20%, Muslim 10%
ETHNIC MIX: Ewe 43%, Kabye 26%, Gurma 16%, other 15%
GOVERNMENT: Multiparty republic
CURRENCY: CFA franc = 100 centimes

BENIN

STRETCHES NORTH from the West African coast. In 1990, it became one of the pioneers of African democratization, ending years of military rule.

GEOGRAPHY
Long, sandy coastal region. Numerous lagoons lie just behind the shoreline. Forested plateaus inland. Mountains in the northwest.

CLIMATE
Hot and humid in the south. Two rainy seasons. Hot, dusty *harmattan* winds blow during December–February dry season.

PEOPLE AND SOCIETY
Around 50 ethnic groups. Fon people in the south dominate politics. Other major groups are Adja and Yoruba. In the far north, Fulani follow a nomadic lifestyle. Tension between north and south, partly reflecting Muslim–Christian divide, and partly because south is more developed. Women hold positions of power in retail trade. Substantial differences in wealth reflect strongly hierarchical society.

THE ECONOMY
Mostly subsistence farming. Cash crops include cotton, cocoa beans, and coffee. Some oil and limestone are produced. France is the main aid donor.

◆ *INSIGHT:*
Benin trains
many
doctors,
but more
of them
work in
France than
in Benin

FACT FILE
OFFICIAL NAME: Republic of Benin
DATE OF FORMATION: 1960
CAPITAL: Porto-Novo
POPULATION: 5.1 million
TOTAL AREA: 43,480 sq miles
(112,620 sq km)
DENSITY: 117 people per sq mile

LANGUAGES: French*, Fon, Bariba, Yoruba, Adja, Houeda, Fulani
RELIGIONS: Traditional beliefs 70%, Muslim 15%, Christian 15%
ETHNIC MIX: Fon 39%, Yoruba 12%, Adja 10%, other 39%
GOVERNMENT: Multiparty republic
CURRENCY: CFA franc = 100 centimes

NIGERIA

 FOUR TIMES the size of the United Kingdom, from which it gained independence in 1960, Nigeria in West Africa is a federation of 30 states.

GEOGRAPHY
Coastal area of beaches, swamps, and lagoons gives way to rain forest, and then to savanna on high plateaus. Semidesert in north.

CLIMATE
South is hot, rainy, and humid for most of the year. Arid north has one very humid wet season. Jos plateau and highlands are cooler.

 PEOPLE AND SOCIETY
Some 250 ethnic groups: the largest are Hausa, Yoruba, Ibo, and Fulani. Tensions between groups constantly threaten national unity, although they have largely been contained in recent years. Members of one group tend to blame those of another for their problems, rather than the political system. Except in the Islamic north, women are allowed economic independence.

THE ECONOMY
Oil has been the economic mainstay since 1970s, accounting for 90% of export earnings.

◆ *INSIGHT: Nigeria is Africa's most populous state – one in every six Africans is Nigerian*

FACT FILE
OFFICIAL NAME: Federal Republic of Nigeria
DATE OF FORMATION: 1960
CAPITAL: Abuja
POPULATION: 115 million
TOTAL AREA: 356,668 sq miles (923,770 sq km)

DENSITY: 322 people per sq mile
LANGUAGES: English*, Hausa, Yoruba
RELIGIONS: Muslim 50%, Christian 40%, traditional beliefs 10%
ETHNIC MIX: Hausa 21%, Yoruba 20%, Ibo 17%, Fulani 9%, other 33%
GOVERNMENT: Military regime
CURRENCY: Naira = 100 kobo

CAMEROON

SITUATED ON the central West African coast, Cameroon was in effect a one-party state for 30 years. Multiparty elections were held in 1992.

 GEOGRAPHY
Over half the land is forested: equatorial rain forest in north, evergreen forest and wooded savanna in south. Mountains in the west.

 CLIMATE
South is equatorial, with plentiful rainfall, declining inland. Far north is beset by drought.

PEOPLE AND SOCIETY
Around 230 ethnic groups; no single group is dominant. Bamileke is the largest, but it has never held political power. Some tension between more affluent south and poorer north, albeit diminished by the ethnic diversity. Also rivalry between majority French-speakers and minority English-speakers.

◆ INSIGHT: *Cameroon's name derives from the Portuguese* camarões – *after the shrimp fished by the early explorers*

THE ECONOMY
Moderate oil reserves. Very diversified agricultural economy – timber, cocoa, coffee, rubber. Self-sufficient in food. Growing national debt owing to failure to adjust to falling oil revenues.

2000m/6562ft
1000m/3281ft
500m/1640ft
200m/656ft
Sea Level

0   100 km
0   100 miles

Lake
Chad

CHAD

NIGERIA   Maroua

Garoua

Ngaoundéré

Bamenda Kumbo   Meiganga

Bafoussam   CENTRAL
Kumba Nkongsamba   AFRICAN
Douala   REPUBLIC
YAOUNDÉ
Edéa   Mbalmayo

Ebolowa

ATLANTIC
OCEAN
EQ.
GUINEA GABON CONGO

FACT FILE

OFFICIAL NAME: Republic of Cameroon
DATE OF FORMATION: 1960
CAPITAL: Yaoundé
POPULATION: 13.6 million
TOTAL AREA: 183,570 miles
(475,440 sq km)
DENSITY: 75 people per sq mile

LANGUAGES: English*, French*, Fang, Bulu, Yaunde, Duala, Mbum
RELIGIONS: Traditional beliefs 51%, Christian 33%, Muslim 16%
ETHNIC MIX: Bamileke and Manum 20%, Fang 19%, other 61%
GOVERNMENT: Multiparty republic
CURRENCY: CFA franc = 100 centimes

EQUATORIAL GUINEA

COMPRISES THE mainland territory of Rio Muni and five islands on the west coast of central Africa. In 1993, the first free elections were held

 GEOGRAPHY
Islands are mountainous and volcanic. Mainland is lower, with mangrove swamps along coast.

 CLIMATE
Bioko is extremely wet and humid. The mainland is only marginally drier and cooler.

PEOPLE AND SOCIETY
The mainland is sparsely populated. Most people are Fang, who dominate politics. Ruling Mongomo clan have most of the wealth. Bioko populated mostly by Bubi and minority of Creoles known as *Fernandinos*. Extended family ties have remained strong despite disruptive social pressure during the years of dictatorship.

◆ INSIGHT: *Some 100,000 Equatorial Guineans now live outside the country, having fled its dictatorial regimes*

THE ECONOMY
Bioko generates the most income. Main exports are tropical timber and cocoa. Oil and gas reserves yet to be fully exploited.

2000m/6562ft	
1000m/3281ft	
500m/1640ft	
200m/656ft	
Sea Level	

FACT FILE

OFFICIAL NAME: Republic of Equatorial Guinea
DATE OF FORMATION: 1968
CAPITAL: Malabo
POPULATION: 400,000
TOTAL AREA: 10,830 sq miles (28,050 sq km)

DENSITY: 36 people per sq mile
LANGUAGES: Spanish*, Fang, other
RELIGIONS: Christian (mainly Roman Catholic) 89%, other 11%
ETHNIC MIX: Fang 72%, Bubi 14%, Duala 3%, Ibibio 2%, other 9%
GOVERNMENT: Multiparty republic
CURRENCY: CFA franc = 100 centimes

SAO TOME & PRINCIPE

A FORMER Portuguese colony off Africa's west coast, comprising two main islands and smaller islets. 1991 elections ended 15 years of Marxism.

 GEOGRAPHY
Islands are scattered across equator. São Tomé and Príncipe are heavily forested and mountainous.

 CLIMATE
Hot and humid, slightly cooled by Benguela Current. Plentiful rainfall, but dry July–August.

PEOPLE AND SOCIETY
Population is mostly black, although Portuguese culture predominates. Blacks run the political parties. Society is well integrated and free of racial prejudice. Wealth disparities are not great, although there is a growing business class. Extended family offers main form of social security. Príncipe assumed autonomous status in April 1995.

◆ INSIGHT: *The population is entirely of immigrant descent: the islands were uninhabited when colonized in 1470*

THE ECONOMY
Cocoa provides 90% of export earnings. Palm oil, pepper, and coffee are farmed. One of Africa's highest aid-to-population ratios.

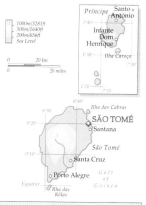

1000m/3281ft
500m/1640ft
200m/656ft
Sea Level

0   20 km
0   20 miles

Príncipe Santo António
Infante Dom Henrique
Ilha Caroço

Ilha das Cabras
SÃO TOMÉ
Santana
São Tomé
Santa Cruz
Porto Alegre
Gulf of Guinea
Equator
Ilha das Rôlas

FACT FILE

OFFICIAL NAME: Democratic Republic of Sao Tome and Principe
DATE OF FORMATION: 1975
CAPITAL: São Tomé
POPULATION: 121,000
TOTAL AREA: 372 sq miles (964 sq km)
DENSITY: 352 people per sq mile

LANGUAGES: Portuguese*, Portuguese Creole, other
RELIGIONS: Roman Catholic 90%, other Christian 10%
ETHNIC MIX: Black 90%, Portuguese and Creole 10%
GOVERNMENT: Multiparty republic
CURRENCY: Dobra = 100 centimos

GABON

A FORMER French colony straddling the equator on Africa's west coast. It returned to multiparty politics in 1990, after 22 years of one-party rule.

GEOGRAPHY

Low plateaus and mountains lie beyond the coastal strip. Two-thirds of the land is rain forest.

CLIMATE

Hot and tropical, with little distinction between seasons. Cold Benguela Current cools the coast.

PEOPLE AND SOCIETY
Some 40 different languages are spoken. The Fang, who live mainly in the north, are the largest ethnic group, but have yet to gain control of the government. Oil wealth has led to growth of an affluent middle class. Menial jobs are done by immigrant workers. Education follows the French system. With almost half its population living in towns, Gabon is one of Africa's most urbanized countries. The government is encouraging population growth.

THE ECONOMY
Oil is the main source of revenue. Tropical hardwoods are being exploited. Cocoa beans, coffee, and rice grown for export.

◆ INSIGHT: Libreville was founded as a settlement for freed French slaves in 184-

FACT FILE

OFFICIAL NAME: The Gabonese Republic
DATE OF FORMATION: 1960
CAPITAL: Libreville
POPULATION: 1.3 million
TOTAL AREA: 103,347 sq miles (267,670 sq km)

DENSITY: 13 people per sq mile
LANGUAGES: French*, Fang, other
RELIGIONS: Catholic, other Christian 96%, Muslim 2%, other 2%
ETHNIC MIX: Fang 36%, Mpongwe 15%, Mbete 14%, other 35%
GOVERNMENT: Multiparty republic
CURRENCY: CFA franc = 100 centimes

CONGO

ASTRIDE THE equator in west central Africa, this former French colony emerged from 20 years of Marxist-Leninist rule in 1990.

GEOGRAPHY
Mostly forest- or savanna-covered plateaus, drained by bangi and Congo River systems. arrow coastal plain is lined with nd dunes and lagoons.

CLIMATE
Hot, tropical. Temperatures rely fall below 86°F (30°C). Two et and two dry seasons. Rainfall heaviest south of the equator.

PEOPLE AND SOCIETY
One of the most tribally onscious nations in Africa. Four ain ethnic groups: Bakongo, angha, Teke, and Mboshi. Main nsions between Bakongo in the orth and Mboshi in the south. liddle class is sustained by oil ealth. Schools are run according the French system and are still ubject to inspection from Paris. ultiparty elections held in 1992.

THE ECONOMY
Oil is main source of revenue. Cash crops include sugar, coffee, cocoa, and palm oil. Substantial industrial base. Large foreign debt.

◆ *INSIGHT: In 1970, Congo became Africa's first declared communist state*

FACT FILE

OFFICIAL NAME: The Republic of the Congo

DATE OF FORMATION: 1960

CAPITAL: Brazzaville

POPULATION: 2.4 million

TOTAL AREA: 132,040 sq miles (342,000 sq km)

DENSITY: 18 people per sq mile

LANGUAGES: French*, Kongo, other

RELIGIONS: Catholic 50%, traditional beliefs 48%, other (inc. Muslim) 2%

ETHNIC MIX: Bakongo 48%, Teke 17%, Mboshi 17%, Sangha 5%, other 13%

GOVERNMENT: Multiparty republic

CURRENCY: CFA franc =100 centimes

ANGOLA

LOCATED IN southwest Africa, Angola was in an almost continuous state of civil war from 1975–1994, following independence from Portugal.

GEOGRAPHY
Most of the land is hilly and grass-covered. Desert in the south. Mountains in the center and north.

CLIMATE
Varies from temperate to tropical. Rainfall decreases north to south. Coast is cooler and dry.

PEOPLE AND SOCIETY
Civil war was fought by two groups. UNITA cast itself as sole representative of the Ovimbundu, in order to attack ruling Kimbundu-dominated MPLA. In 1991–92, MPLA abandoned Marxist rule and held free elections. UNITA lost, and resumed civil war. Up to 500,000 people died as a result. In 1995, UN troops were deployed to begin a phased demilitarization operation.

◆ INSIGHT: Angola has some of the world's richest alluvial diamond deposits

THE ECONOMY
Potentially one of Africa's richest countries, but civil war has hampered economic development. Oil and diamonds are exported.

FACT FILE
OFFICIAL NAME: Republic of Angola
DATE OF FORMATION: 1975
CAPITAL: Luanda
POPULATION: 10.3 million
TOTAL AREA: 481,551 sq miles
(1,246,700 sq km)
DENSITY: 21 people per sq mile

LANGUAGES: Portuguese*, other
RELIGIONS: Catholic/Protestant 64%, traditional beliefs 34%, other 2%
ETHNIC MIX: Ovimbundu 37%, Kimbundu 25%, Bakongo 13%, mixed 1%, other 24%
GOVERNMENT: Multiparty republic
CURRENCY: Kwanza = 100 lwei

ZAMBIA

ZAMBIA LIES landlocked at the heart of southern Africa. In 1991, it made a peaceful transition from single-party rule to multiparty democracy.

GEOGRAPHY
A high savanna plateau, broken by mountains in northeast. Vegetation mainly trees and scrub.

CLIMATE
Tropical, with three seasons: cool and dry, hot and dry, and wet. Southwest is prone to drought.

PEOPLE AND SOCIETY
One of the continent's most urbanized countries. More than 70 different ethnic groups, but it has been less affected by ethnic tensions than many African states. Largest group is Bemba in northeast. Other major groups are Tonga in the south, and Lozi in the west. Urban life has done little to change the traditionally subordinate role of women in the family and politics. Rural population live by subsistence farming.

THE ECONOMY
Copper mining is the main industry – exports bring in 80% of foreign income. However, domestic reserves are declining rapidly.

◆ INSIGHT: Zambia's Victoria Falls is known to Africans as Musi-o-Tunyi (The Smoke That Thunders)

FACT FILE
OFFICIAL NAME: Republic of Zambia
DATE OF FORMATION: 1964
CAPITAL: Lusaka
POPULATION: 8.9 million
TOTAL AREA: 290,563 sq miles (752,610 sq km)
DENSITY: 31 people per sq mile

LANGUAGES: English*, Bemba, Tonga, Nyanja, Lozi, Lunda
RELIGIONS: Christian 63%, traditional beliefs 35%, other 2%
ETHNIC MIX: Bemba 36%, Maravi 18%, Tonga 15%, other 31%
GOVERNMENT: Multiparty republic
CURRENCY: Kwacha = 100 ngwee

TANZANIA

THE EAST African state of Tanzania was formed in 1964 by the union of Tanganyika and Zanzibar. A third of its area is game reserve or national park.

 GEOGRAPHY
Mainland is mostly a high plateau lying to the east of the Great Rift Valley. Forested coastal plain. Highlands in the north and south.

CLIMATE
Tropical on the coast and Zanzibar. Semiarid on central plateau, semitemperate in the highlands. March–May rains.

PEOPLE AND SOCIETY
99% of people belong to one of 120 small ethnic Bantu groups. Arabs, Asians, and Europeans make up remaining population. Use of Swahili as *lingua franca* has eliminated ethnic rivalries. Politics is moving towards democracy.

◆ *INSIGHT: At 19,340 ft (5,895 m), Kilimanjaro in northeast Tanzania is Africa's highest mountain*

THE ECONOMY
Reliant on agriculture, including forestry and livestock. Cotton, coffee, tea, and cloves are cash crops. Diamonds are mined.

FACT FILE
OFFICIAL NAME: United Republic of Tanzania
DATE OF FORMATION: 1964
CAPITAL: Dodoma
POPULATION: 28.8 million
TOTAL AREA: 364,900 sq miles (945,090 sq km)

DENSITY: 79 people per sq mile
LANGUAGES: English*, Swahili*
RELIGIONS: Traditional beliefs 42%, Muslim 31%, Christian 27%
ETHNIC MIX: 120 ethnic Bantu groups 99%, other 1%
GOVERNMENT: Single-party republic
CURRENCY: Shilling = 100 cents

MALAWI

A FORMER British colony, Malawi lies landlocked in southeast Africa. Its name means "the land where the sun is reflected in the water like fire."

GEOGRAPHY
Lake Malawi takes up one fifth of the country. Highlands lie west of the lake. Much of the land is covered by forests and savanna.

CLIMATE
Mainly subtropical. South is hot and humid. Highlands are cooler. May–October dry season.

PEOPLE AND SOCIETY
Few ethnic tensions as most people share common Bantu origin. However, tensions between north and south have arisen in recent years. Northerners are increasingly disaffected by their lack of political representation. Many Asians are involved in the retail trade. Multi-party politics introduced in 1993.

◆ INSIGHT: *Lake Malawi is 353 miles (568 km) in length and contains at least 500 species of fish*

THE ECONOMY
Tobacco accounts for 76% of export earnings. Tea and sugar production. Coal, bauxite reserves.

2000m/6562ft
1000m/3281ft
500m/1640ft
200m/656ft
Sea Level

0   100 km
0   100 miles

FACT FILE
OFFICIAL NAME: Republic of Malawi
DATE OF FORMATION: 1964
CAPITAL: Lilongwe
POPULATION: 10.7 million
TOTAL AREA: 45,745 sq miles
(118,480 sq km)
DENSITY: 285 people per sq mile

LANGUAGES: English*, Chewa*, other
RELIGIONS: Protestant / Catholic 66%,
traditional beliefs 18%, other 16%
ETHNIC MIX: Maravi 55%, Lomwe
17%, Yao 13%, Ngoni 7%, other
(including Asian) 8%
GOVERNMENT: Multiparty republic
CURRENCY: Kwacha = 100 tambala

ZIMBABWE

THE FORMER British colony of Southern Rhodesia became fully independent as Zimbabwe in 1980, after 15 years of troubled white minority rule.

 GEOGRAPHY
High plateaus in center bordered by Zambezi River in the north and Limpopo in the south. Rivers crisscross central area.

 CLIMATE
Tropical, though moderated by the altitude. Wet season November–March. Drought is common in eastern highlands.

PEOPLE AND SOCIETY
Two main ethnic groups, Ndebele in the north, and Shona in the south. Shona outnumber Ndebele by four to one. Whites make up just 1% of the population. Because of past colonial rule, whites are generally far more affluent than blacks. This imbalance has been somewhat redressed by government policies to increase black education and employment. Families are large and 45% of people are under 15.

THE ECONOMY
Most broadly based African economy after South Africa. Virtually self-sufficient in food and energy. Tobacco is main cash crop.

◆ *INSIGHT: The city of Great Zimbabwe, after which the country is named, was built in the 8th century. Its ruins are found near Masvingo*

FACT FILE

OFFICIAL NAME: Republic of Zimbabwe
DATE OF FORMATION: 1980
CAPITAL: Harare
POPULATION: 10.9 million
TOTAL AREA: 150,800 sq miles (390,580 sq km)
DENSITY: 70 people per sq mile

LANGUAGES: English*, Shona, Ndebele
RELIGIONS: Syncretic (Christian and traditional beliefs) 50%, Christian 26%, traditional beliefs 24%
ETHNIC MIX: Shona 71%, Ndebele 16%, other 11%, White, Asian 2%
GOVERNMENT: Multiparty republic
CURRENCY: Zimbabwe $ = 100 cents

MOZAMBIQUE

MOZAMBIQUE LIES on the southeast African coast. It was torn by a civil war between the Marxist government and a rebel group from 1977 to 1992.

 GEOGRAPHY
Largely a savanna-covered plateau. Coast is fringed by coral reefs and lagoons. Zambezi River bisects country from east to west.

CLIMATE
Tropical. Hottest along the coast. Wet season usually March–October, but rains frequently fail.

PEOPLE AND SOCIETY
Racially diverse, but tensions in society are between northerners and southerners, rather than ethnic groups. Life is based around the extended family, which in some regions is matriarchal. Polygamy is fairly common. Government has faced huge task of resettling the one million war refugees. 90% of the population live in poverty.

◆ *INSIGHT: Maputo, the capital, has Africa's second largest harbor*

THE ECONOMY
Almost entirely dependent on foreign aid. 85% of the population is engaged in agriculture.

FACT FILE

OFFICIAL NAME: Republic of Mozambique
DATE OF FORMATION: 1975
CAPITAL: Maputo
POPULATION: 15.3 million
TOTAL AREA: 309,493 sq miles
(801,590 sq km)

DENSITY: 49 people per sq mile
LANGUAGES: Portuguese*, other
RELIGIONS: Traditional beliefs 60%, Christian 30%, Muslim 10%
ETHNIC MIX: Makua-Lomwe 47%, Tsonga 23%, Malawi 12%, other 18%
GOVERNMENT: Multiparty republic
CURRENCY: Metical = 100 centavos

NAMIBIA

LOCATED IN southwestern Africa, Namibia became free of South African control in 1990, after years of uncertainty and guerrilla activity.

GEOGRAPHY
Namib Desert stretches along coastal strip. Inland, a ridge of mountains rises to 8,200 ft (2,500 m). Kalahari Desert lies in the east.

CLIMATE
Almost rainless. Coast usually shrouded in thick fog, unless hot dry *berg* wind blows.

PEOPLE AND SOCIETY
Largest ethnic group, the Ovambo, live mainly in the north. Whites, including a large German community, are centred around Windhoek. Ethnic strife predicted at time of independence has not materialized. High illiteracy among blacks due to legacy of apartheid. Whites still control the economy.

◆ INSIGHT: *The Namib is the Earth's oldest, and one of its driest deserts*

THE ECONOMY
Third wealthiest country in sub-Saharan Africa. Varied mineral resources, including uranium and diamonds. Rich offshore fishing grounds. Lack of skilled labor.

Rundu
Tsumeb
Grootfontein
Otjiwarongo
Swakopmund ✦ WINDHOEK
Walvis Bay
Rehoboth
Lüderitz
Keetmanshoop

ANGOLA
ZAMBIA
Zambezi
BOTSWANA
Kalahari Desert
ATLANTIC OCEAN
Orange River
SOUTH AFRICA

```
2000m/6562
1000m/3281
500m/1640ft
200m/656ft
Sea Level
```

0   200 km
0   200 mi

FACT FILE
OFFICIAL NAME: Republic of Namibia
DATE OF FORMATION: 1990/1994
CAPITAL: Windhoek
POPULATION: 1.6 million
TOTAL AREA: 318,260 sq miles (824,290 sq km)
DENSITY: 5 people per sq mile

LANGUAGES: English*, Afrikaans, Ovambo, Kavango, German, other
RELIGIONS: Christian 90%, other 10%
ETHNIC MIX: Ovambo 50%, Kavango 9%, Herero 7%, Damara 7%, White 6%, other 21%
GOVERNMENT: Multiparty republic
CURRENCY: Rand = 100 cents

BOTSWANA

ONCE THE British protectorate of Bechuanaland, Botswana lies landlocked in southern Africa. Diamonds provide it with a prosperous economy.

GEOGRAPHY
Lies on vast plateau, high above sealevel. Hills in the east. Kalahari Desert in center and southwest. Swamps and saltpans elsewhere and in Okavango Basin.

CLIMATE
Dry and prone to drought. Summer wet season, April–October. Winters are warm, with cold nights.

PEOPLE AND SOCIETY
Tswana make up 75% of the population. San, or Kalahari Bushmen, the first inhabitants, have been marginalized. 72% of people live in rural areas. Traditional forms of authority such as the village *kgotla*, or parliament, remain important.

◆ INSIGHT: *Water, Botswana's most precious resource, is honored in the name of the currency – pula*

THE ECONOMY
Diamonds are the leading export. Also deposits of copper, nickel, coal, salt, soda ash. Beef is exported to Europe. Tourism aimed at wealthy wildlife enthusiasts.

FACT FILE

OFFICIAL NAME: Republic of Botswana
DATE OF FORMATION: 1966
CAPITAL: Gaborone
POPULATION: 1.4 million
TOTAL AREA: 224,600 sq miles (581,730 sq km)
DENSITY: 5 people per sq mile

LANGUAGES: English*, Tswana, Shona, San, Khoikhoi, Ndebele
RELIGIONS: Traditional beliefs 50%, Christian (mostly Anglican) 50%
ETHNIC MIX: Tswana 75%, Shona 12%, San 3%, White 1%, other 9%
GOVERNMENT: Multiparty republic
CURRENCY: Pula = 100 thebe

LESOTHO

THE KINGDOM of Lesotho is entirely surrounded by South Africa, which provides all its land transportation links with the outside world.

GEOGRAPHY
High mountainous plateau, cut by valleys and ravines. Maluti range in center. Drakensberg range in the east. Lowlands in the west.

CLIMATE
Temperate. Summers are hot and wet. Snow is frequent in the mountains in winter.

PEOPLE AND SOCIETY
Almost everyone is Basotho, although there are some South Asians, Europeans, and Taiwanese. Strong sense of national identity has tended to minimize ethnic tensions. Many men work as migrant laborers in South Africa, leaving 72% of households, and most of the farms, run by women.

◆ *INSIGHT: Lesotho has one of the highest literacy rates in Africa, and the highest female literacy rate – 84%*

THE ECONOMY
Few natural resources. Heavy reliance on incomes of its migrant workers. Subsistence farming is the main activity. Exports include livestock, wool, mohair.

3000m/9843ft
2000m/6562ft
1000m/328ft

0   50 km
0   50 mile

FACT FILE
OFFICIAL NAME: Kingdom of Lesotho
DATE OF FORMATION: 1966
CAPITAL: Maseru
POPULATION: 1.9 million
TOTAL AREA: 11,718 sq miles (30,350 sq km)

DENSITY: 162 people per sq mile
LANGUAGES: English*, Sesotho*, Zulu
RELIGIONS: Roman Catholic and other Christian 93%, other 7%
ETHNIC MIX: Basotho 99%, other 1%
GOVERNMENT: Constitutional monarchy
CURRENCY: Loti = 100 lisente

SWAZILAND

THE SOUTHERN African kingdom of Swaziland gained independence from Britain in 1968. It is economically dependent on South Africa.

GEOGRAPHY
Mainly high plateaus and mountains. Rolling grasslands and low scrub plains to the east. Pine forests on western border.

CLIMATE
Temperatures rise and rainfall declines as land descends eastward, from high to low *veld*.

PEOPLE AND SOCIETY
One of Africa's most homogenous states. Also among its most conservative, although it is now coming under pressure from urban-based modernizers. Political system promotes Swazi tradition and is dominated by a powerful monarchy. Society is patriarchal and focused around clans and chiefs.

◆ INSIGHT: *Polygamy is practised in Swaziland. When King Sobhuza died in 1982, he left 100 wives and 600 children*

THE ECONOMY
Sugarcane is the main cash crop. Others are pineapples, cotton, rice, and tobacco. Asbestos, coal, and wood pulp are also exported.

SOUTH AFRICA

Piggs Peak
Tshaneni
◇MBABANE
Siteki
✚ Manzini
Bhunya
Sidvokodvo
Hlathikulu
MOZAMBIQUE
Nhlangano
SOUTH AFRICA

1000m/3281ft
500m/1640ft
200m/656ft
Sea Level

0   25 km
0   25 miles

FACT FILE

OFFICIAL NAME: Kingdom of Swaziland
DATE OF FORMATION: 1968
CAPITAL: Mbabane
POPULATION: 800,000
TOTAL AREA: 6,703 sq miles (17,360 sq km)

DENSITY: 120 people per sq mile
LANGUAGES: Siswati*, English*, Zulu
RELIGIONS: Protestant and other Christian 60%, traditional beliefs 40%
ETHNIC MIX: Swazi 95%, other 5%
GOVERNMENT: Executive monarchy
CURRENCY: Lilangeni = 100 cents

SOUTH AFRICA

SOUTH AFRICA is the southernmost nation on the African continent. After 80 years of white minority rule, and racial segregation under apartheid from 1948, the country's first multiracial, multiparty elections were held in 1994.

GEOGRAPHY

Much of the country is grassland plateaus, drained in the west by the Orange River system and in the east by the Limpopo and its tributaries. Mountain ridges stretch across south. Drakensberg range overshadows eastern coastal lowlands.

CLIMATE

Warm, temperate, and dry. Interior of country gets most of its rain in summer. Coast around Cape Town has Mediterranean climate, with winter rains.

◆ *INSIGHT: South Africa dominates the world market in gold and diamonds. Over the past century, it has produced almost half of the world's gold*

PEOPLE AND SOCIETY

Since dismantling of apartheid in early 1990s, racial segregation has ended, but tensions remain. Some Zulus and whites have made demands for independent homelands. Government aims to redress social and economic imbalance between blacks and whites, focusing on education, housing, land reform.

THE ECONOMY

Africa's largest economy; highly diversified, with modern infrastructure. Growing manufacturing sector. Varied agriculture. Diamonds, gold, platinum, coal, silver, uranium, copper, and asbestos mined.

2000m/6562ft
1000m/3281ft
500m/1640ft
Sea Level

0   200 km
0   200 miles

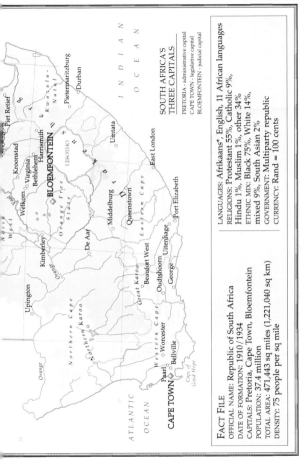

SOUTH AFRICA'S
THREE CAPITALS

PRETORIA - administrative capital
CAPE TOWN - legislative capital
BLOEMFONTEIN - judicial capital

LANGUAGES: Afrikaans*, English, 11 African languages
RELIGIONS: Protestant 55%, Catholic 9%,
Hindu 1%, Muslim 1%, other 34%
ETHNIC MIX: Black 75%, White 14%,
mixed 9%, South Asian 2%
GOVERNMENT: Multiparty republic
CURRENCY: Rand = 100 cents

FACT FILE
OFFICIAL NAME: Republic of South Africa
DATE OF FORMATION: 1910/1934
CAPITALS: Pretoria, Cape Town, Bloemfontein
POPULATION: 37.4 million
TOTAL AREA: 471,443 sq miles (1,221,040 sq km)
DENSITY: 75 people per sq mile

SEYCHELLES

A FORMER British colony, comprising 115 islands in the Indian Ocean. Under one-party rule for 16 years, it became a multiparty democracy in 1993.

GEOGRAPHY
Mostly low-lying coral atolls, but 40 islands, including the largest, Mahé, are mountainous and are the only granitic islands in the world.

CLIMATE
Tropical oceanic climate. Hot and humid all year round. Rainy season December–May.

PEOPLE AND SOCIETY
The islands were uninhabited when French settlers arrived in the 18th century. Today, the population is homogeneous – a result of inter-marriage between ethnic groups. Almost 90% of people live on Mahé. Living standards are among Africa's highest. Poverty is rare and the welfare system serves all.

◆INSIGHT: *Host to unique flora and fauna – it is the only country to have two natural World Heritage sites*

THE ECONOMY
Tourism is main source of income, based on appeal of beaches and exotic plants and animals. Tuna fished and canned for export. Virtually no mineral resources. All domestic requirements imported.

FACT FILE
OFFICIAL NAME: Republic of the Seychelles
DATE OF FORMATION: 1976
CAPITAL: Victoria
POPULATION: 69,000
TOTAL AREA: 108 sq miles (280 sq km)

DENSITY: 638 people per sq mile
LANGUAGES: Creole*, French, English
RELIGIONS: Catholic 90%, other 10%
ETHNIC MIX: Seychellois (mixed African, South Asian and European) 95%, Chinese and South Asian 5%
GOVERNMENT: Multiparty republic
CURRENCY: Rupee = 100 cents

COMOROS

COMOROS

Mozambique   Madagascar

IN THE Indian Ocean between Mozambique and Madagascar lie the Comoros, comprising three main islands and a number of smaller islets.

GEOGRAPHY
Main islands are of volcanic origin and are heavily forested. The remainder are coral atolls.

CLIMATE
Hot and humid all year round. November–May is hottest and wettest period.

PEOPLE AND SOCIETY
Country has absorbed diversity of people over the years: African, Arab, Polynesian, and Persian. Also Portuguese, Dutch, French, and Indian immigrants. Ethnic tension is rare. Wealth concentrated among political and business elite. Schools equipped to teach only basic literacy, hygiene, and agricultural skills. Politically unstable – frequent coup attempts have been made during 1990s.

THE ECONOMY
One of the world's poorest countries. 80% of people are farmers Vanilla and cloves are main cash crops. Lack of basic infrastructure.

◆INSIGHT: *The Comoros is the world's largest producer of ylang-ylang – an extract from trees used in manufacturing perfumes*

Grande Comore (Njazidja)

Koimbani

✈ MORONI

Foumbouni

Dembéni

INDIAN OCEAN

Mohéli (Mwali)

Fomboni

Mozambique Channel

Ouani

Mutsamudu

Moya

Anjouan (Nzwani)

1000m/3281ft
500m/1640ft
200m/656ft
Sea Level

0   20 km
0   20 miles

FACT FILE

OFFICIAL NAME: Federal Islamic Republic of the Comoros
DATE OF FORMATION: 1975
CAPITAL: Moroni
POPULATION: 600,000
TOTAL AREA: 8,865 sq miles (22,960 sq km)

DENSITY: 700 people per sq mile
LANGUAGES: Arabic*, French*, other
RELIGIONS: Muslim 86%, Roman Catholic 14%
ETHNIC MIX: Comorian 96%, Makua 2%, other (inc. French) 2%
GOVERNMENT: Islamic republic
CURRENCY: Franc = 100 centimes

MADAGASCAR

LYING IN the Indian Ocean, Madagascar is the world's fourth largest island. Free elections in 1993 ended 18 years of socialist government.

 GEOGRAPHY
More than two thirds of country is a savanna-covered plateau, which descends sharply to narrow coastal belt in the east.

CLIMATE
Tropical, and often hit by cyclones. Monsoons affect the east coast. Southwest is much drier.

PEOPLE AND SOCIETY
People are Malay-Indonesian in origin, intermixed with later migrants from African mainland. Main ethnic division is between Merina of the central plateau and the poorer *côtier* (coastal) peoples. Merina were the country's historic rulers. They remain the social elite, and largely run the government.

◆ *INSIGHT: 80% of Madagascar's plants, and many of its animal species, such as the lemur, are found nowhere else*

THE ECONOMY
Over 80% of people are farmers. Coffee is the most important cash crop. World's largest producer of vanilla. Shrimp are a valuable export commodity.

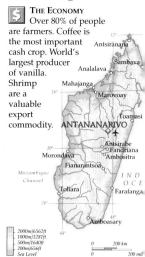

FACT FILE

OFFICIAL NAME: Democratic Republic of Madagascar
DATE OF FORMATION: 1960
CAPITAL: Antananarivo
POPULATION: 13.3 million
TOTAL AREA: 226,660 sq miles (587,040 sq km)

DENSITY: 57 people per sq mile
LANGUAGES: Malagasy*, French*
RELIGIONS: Traditional beliefs 52%, Catholic/Protestant 41%, Muslim 7%
ETHNIC MIX: Merina 26%, Betsimisaraka 15%, Betsileo 12%, other 47%
GOVERNMENT: Multiparty republic
CURRENCY: Franc = 100 centimes

MAURITIUS

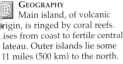

LOCATED TO the east of Madagascar in the Indian Ocean. Independent in 1968, as part of the Commonwealth, it became a republic in 1993.

 GEOGRAPHY
Main island, of volcanic origin, is ringed by coral reefs. Rises from coast to fertile central plateau. Outer islands lie some 311 miles (500 km) to the north.

CLIMATE
Warm and humid. March–December are hottest and wettest months, with tropical storms.

PEOPLE AND SOCIETY
Most people are descendants of laborers brought over from India in the 19th century. Small minority of French descent are the wealthiest group. Literacy rate for under-30s is 95%. Crime rates on the main island are fairly low; outer islands are virtually crime-free.

THE ECONOMY
Sugar, tourism, and clothing manufacture are main sources of income. Sugar accounts for 30% of exports. Potential as offshore financial center is being developed.

> INSIGHT: *The islands lie on what was once a land bridge between Asia and Africa – the Mascarene Archipelago*

FACT FILE

OFFICIAL NAME: Mauritius
DATE OF FORMATION: 1968
CAPITAL: Port Louis
POPULATION: 1.1 million
TOTAL AREA: 718 sq miles (1,860 sq km)
DENSITY: 1,532 people per sq mile

LANGUAGES: English*, French Creole, Hindi, Bhojpuri, Chinese
RELIGIONS: Hindu 52%, Catholic 26%, Muslim 17%, other 5%
ETHNIC MIX: Creole 55%, South Asian 40%, Chinese 3%, other 2%
GOVERNMENT: Multiparty republic
CURRENCY: Rupee = 100 cents

EUROPE

EUROPE IS the smallest continent after Australia, yet it has a wide range of climates, land forms, and types of vegetation. The tundra of the far north gives way to a cool, wet, heavily forested region. The North European Plain is well-drained, fertile, and rich in natural resources. The shores of the Mediterranean are generally warm, dry, and hilly. A great curve of mountain ranges, including the Pyrenees, Alps, and Carpathians, roughly divide the continent from north to south. To the east lie the rolling plains of European Russia and the Ukraine.

Greenland
(to Denmark)

Svalbard
(to Norway)

CANADA

A R C

Jan Mayen
(to Norway)

ICELAND

Norwegian
Sea

A T L A N T I C

O C E A N

Faeroe Is.
(to Denmark)

Shetland Is.

Orkney Is.

Outer
Hebrides

North
Sea

UNITED
KINGDOM

NOR

REP. OF
IRELAND

NETH.

GE

English Channel

BELGIUM

Seine

Thames

Rhine

Loire

FRANCE

SWITZ

Bay
of
Biscay

Mont Blanc
15,771 ft

C. Finisterre

ANDORRA

Maxsif
Central

MONACO

IT

PORTUGAL

Pyrenees

SPAIN

Corsica

Balearic Is.

Sardinia

Gibraltar
(to UK)

MOROCCO

ALGERIA

TUN

3000m/9843ft
2000m/6562ft
1000m/3281ft
200m/656ft
Sea Level
Below Sea Level

0   500 km
0   500 miles

Novaya Zemlya

Asiatic Russia

RUSSIAN FEDERATION

Ural Mountains

Irtysh

Kola Peninsula

Lake Onega

Lake Ladoga

FINLAND

European Russia

ONIA

KAZAKHSTAN

LATVIA

Volga

Aral Sea

UANIA

Don

UZBEKISTAN

BELARUS

Dnieper

Volga Delta
-92ft

Caspian Sea

TURKMENISTAN

UKRAINE

Balkan Mts.

MOLDAVA

Crimea

Caucasus

El'brus
18,510ft

GEOR

ARY

ROMANIA

Danube

Black Sea

AZ.

ARM.

YUGO

BULGARIA

TURKEY

IRAN

MAC

ANIA

GREECE

Aegean Sea

Crete

terranean Sea

B Y A

CONTINENTAL FACTS

HIGHEST POINT:
El'Brus, Caucasus Mts.,
European Russia
18,510 ft (5,642 m)

LOWEST POINT: Volga
Delta, Caspian Sea,
European Russia 92 ft
(28 m) below sea level

LARGEST LAKE:
Ladoga, European
Russia 7,100 sq miles
(18,390 sq km)

LONGEST RIVER:
Volga, European
Russia 2,290 miles
(3,699 km)

ICELAND

EUROPE'S WESTERNMOST country, Iceland lies in the north Atlantic, straddling the mid-Atlantic ridge. Its spectacular landscape is largely uninhabited.

 GEOGRAPHY
Grassy coastal lowlands, with fjords in the north. Central plateau of cold lava desert, glaciers, and geothermal springs. Around 200 volcanoes.

 CLIMATE
Location in middle of Gulf Stream moderates climate. Mild winters and brief, cool summers.

PEOPLE AND SOCIETY
Prosperous and homogeneous society includes only 4,000 foreign residents. High social mobility, free health care and heating (using geothermal power). Longevity rates are among the highest in the world. Equivocal attitude toward Europe accompanies increasing US influence. Strong emphasis on education and reading. Low crime rate, but concerns of alcohol abuse.

THE ECONOMY
Fish or fish products make up 80% of exports. Developing light industry produces knitwear, textiles, paint. Ecotourism potential.

◆ *INSIGHT: Iceland has the world's oldest parliament, founded in 930 A.D.*

FACT FILE

OFFICIAL NAME: Republic of Iceland
DATE OF FORMATION: 1944
CAPITAL: Reykjavik
POPULATION: 300,000
TOTAL AREA: 39,770 sq miles (103,000 sq km)

DENSITY: 8 people per sq mile
LANGUAGES: Icelandic*, other
RELIGIONS: Evangelical Lutheran 96%, other Christian 3%, other 1%
ETHNIC MIX: Icelandic (Norwegian-Celtic descent) 98%, other 2%
GOVERNMENT: Constitutional republic
CURRENCY: Krona = 100 aurar

NORWAY

THE KINGDOM of Norway traces the rugged western coast of Scandinavia. Settlements are largely restricted to southern and coastal areas.

GEOGRAPHY
Highly indented coast with fjords and tens of thousands of islands. Mountains and plateaus over most of the country.

CLIMATE
Mild coastal climate. Inland east is more extreme, with warm summers, and cold, snowy winters.

PEOPLE AND SOCIETY
Homogeneous, with some recent refugees from Bosnian conflict. Strong family tradition despite high divorce rate. Fair-minded consensus promotes female equality, boosted by generous childcare provision. Wealth more evenly distributed than in most developed countries.

THE ECONOMY
Europe's largest producer and exporter of oil and gas. Engineering, chemical, and metal industries.

▶ INSIGHT: At a point near Narvik, mainland Norway is only 4 miles (7 km wide)

FACT FILE

OFFICIAL NAME: Kingdom of Norway
DATE OF FORMATION: 1905/1930
CAPITAL: Oslo
POPULATION: 4.3 million
TOTAL AREA: 125,060 sq miles (323,900 sq km)
DENSITY: 34 people per sq mile

LANGUAGES: Norwegian* (Bokmal and Nynorsk), Lappish
RELIGIONS: Evangelical Lutheran 88%, other Christian 12%
ETHNIC MIX: Norwegian 95%, Lapp 1%, other 4%
GOVERNMENT: Constitutional monarchy
CURRENCY: Krone = 100 øre

ee also Overseas Territories pp 230–236

DENMARK

OCCUPIES THE Jutland peninsula and over 400 islands in Scandinavia. Greenland and the Faeroe islands are self-governing associated territories.

GEOGRAPHY
Fertile farmland covers two thirds of the terrain, which is among the flattest in the world. About 100 islands are inhabited.

CLIMATE
Damp, temperate climate with mild summers and cold, wet winters. Rainfall is moderate.

PEOPLE AND SOCIETY
Prosperous population maintains traditions of tolerance and welfare provision. High rates of divorce and cohabitation mean that almost 40% of children are brought up by unmarried couples or single parents. Over 75% of women work, due to generous state-funded childcare.

◆ INSIGHT: Denmark is Europe's oldest kingdom – the monarchy dates back to the 10th century

THE ECONOMY
Few natural resources but a diverse manufacturing base. Skilled work force a key to high-tech industrial success. Bacon, ham and dairy products are exported.

FACT FILE
OFFICIAL NAME: Kingdom of Denmark
DATE OF FORMATION: AD 960/1953.
CAPITAL: Copenhagen
POPULATION: 5.2 million
TOTAL AREA: 16,629 sq miles
(43,069 sq km)
DENSITY: 320 people per sq mile

LANGUAGES: Danish*, other
RELIGIONS: Evangelical Lutheran 91% other Protestant and Catholic 9%
ETHNIC MIX: Danish 96%, Faeroese and Inuit 1%, other 3%
GOVERNMENT: Constitutional monarchy
CURRENCY: Krone = 100 øre

see also Overseas Territories pp 230–236

SWEDEN

THE LARGEST Scandinavian country in both population and area, Sweden's strong industrial base helps to fund its extensive welfare system.

GEOGRAPHY
Heavily forested, with many lakes. Northern plateau extends beyond the Arctic Circle. Southern lowlands are widely cultivated.

CLIMATE
Southern coasts warmed by Gulf Stream. Northern areas have more extreme continental climate.

PEOPLE AND SOCIETY
Traditions of hard work and economic success are balanced by permissiveness and egalitarianism. High taxes pay for extensive childcare provision, medical protection, and state education. Most industries and the bulk of the population are based in and around the southern cities. A 15,000-strong minority of Sami (Lapps) live in the north.

INSIGHT: *Sweden has maintained a position of armed neutrality since 1815*

THE ECONOMY
Companies of global importance, including Volvo, Saab, SFK, Ericsson. Highly developed infrastructure. Up-to-date technology Skilled labor force.

FACT FILE

OFFICIAL NAME: Kingdom of Sweden
DATE OF FORMATION: 1809/1905
CAPITAL: Stockholm
POPULATION: 8.7 million
TOTAL AREA: 173,730 sq miles (449,960 sq km)
DENSITY: 55 people per sq mile

LANGUAGES: Swedish*, Finnish, Lappish, other
RELIGIONS: Evangelical Lutheran 94%, Catholic 2%, other 4%
ETHNIC MIX: Swedish 87%, Finnish and Lapp 1%, other European 12%
GOVERNMENT: Constitutional monarchy
CURRENCY: Krona = 100 öre

FINLAND

FINLAND'S DISTINCTIVE language and national identity have been influenced by both its Scandinavian and its Russian neighbors.

GEOGRAPHY
South and center are flat, with low hills and many lakes. Uplands and low mountains in the north. 60% of the land area is forested.

CLIMATE
Long, harsh winters with frequent snowfalls. Short, warmer summers. Rainfall is low, and decreases northward.

PEOPLE AND SOCIETY
More than half the population live in the five districts around Helsinki. The Swedish minority live mainly in the Åland Islands in the southwest. The Sami (Lapps) lead a seminomadic existence in the north. Over 50% of women go out to work, continuing a tradition of equality between the sexes.

◆ INSIGHT: *Finland has Europe's largest inland waterway system*

THE ECONOMY
Wood-based industries account for 40% of exports. Strong engineering and electronics sectors.

NORWAY

Inarijärvi

Lapland

SWEDEN

Arctic Circle

RUSS. FED.

Rovaniemi

500m/1640ft
200m/656ft
Sea Level

Oulu

0   100 km
0   100 miles

Gulf of Bothnia

Vaasa

Kuopio

Jyväskylä

Joensu

Haukivesi

Pori

Tampere

Saimaa

Lahti

Åland

Turku Vantaa

Kotka

Espoo HELSINKI

Baltic Sea

FACT FILE
OFFICIAL NAME: Republic of Finland
DATE OF FORMATION: 1917/1920
CAPITAL: Helsinki
POPULATION: 5 million
TOTAL AREA: 130,552 sq miles (338,130 sq km)
DENSITY: 42 people per sq mile

LANGUAGES: Finnish*, Swedish, Lappish
RELIGIONS: Evangelical Lutheran 89%, Greek Orthodox 1%, other 10%
ETHNIC MIX: Finnish 93%, Swedish 6%, other (inc. Sami) 1%
GOVERNMENT: Multiparty republic
CURRENCY: Markka = 100 pennia

ESTONIA

ESTONIA IS the smallest and most developed of the three Baltic states and has the highest standard of living of any former Soviet republic.

GEOGRAPHY
Flat, boggy, and partly forested, with over 1,500 islands. Lake Peipus forms much of the eastern border with Russia.

CLIMATE
Maritime, with some continental extremes. Harsh winters, cool summers, and damp springs.

PEOPLE AND SOCIETY
The Estonians are related linguistically and ethnically to the Finns. Friction between ethnic Estonians and the large Russian minority has led to assertion of Estonian culture and language, as well as job discrimination. Some post-independence political upheaval reflects disenchantment with free-market economics. Families are small; divorce rates are high.

THE ECONOMY
Agricultural machinery, electric motors, and ships are the leading manufactures. Strong timber industry. Increased trade links with Finland and Germany.

◆ INSIGHT: Estonia is still pressing for the return of territories ceded to Russia during the Soviet period

FACT FILE
OFFICIAL NAME: Republic of Estonia
DATE OF FORMATION: 1991
CAPITAL: Tallinn
POPULATION: 1.6 million
TOTAL AREA: 17,423 sq miles (45,125 sq km)

DENSITY: 94 people per sq mile
LANGUAGES: Estonian*, Russian
RELIGIONS: Evangelical Lutheran 98%, Eastern Orthodox, Baptist 2%
ETHNIC MIX: Estonian 62%, Russian 30%, Ukrainian 3%, other 5%
GOVERNMENT: Multiparty republic
CURRENCY: Kroon = 100 cents

LATVIA

SITUATED ON the east coast of the Baltic Sea. Like its Baltic neighbors, it became independent in 1991. It retains a large Russian population.

GEOGRAPHY
Flat coastal plain deeply indented by the Gulf of Riga. Poor drainage creates many bogs and swamps in the forested interior.

CLIMATE
Temperate: warm summers and cold winters. Steady rainfall throughout the year.

PEOPLE AND SOCIETY
Latvia is the most urbanized of the three Baltic states, with more than 70% of the population living in cities and towns. Delicate relations with Russia are dictated by a large Russian minority, and energy and infrastructure investment dating from the Soviet period. The status of women is on a par with that in Western Europe. The divorce rate is high.

THE ECONOMY
Transportation and defense equipment lead strong industrial sector. Developed papermaking industry. Good ports. Russia remains main trading partner.

◆ INSIGHT: Latvia's flag is said to represent a sheet stained with the blood of a 13th-century Latvian hero

FACT FILE
OFFICIAL NAME: Republic of Latvia
DATE OF FORMATION: 1991
CAPITAL: Riga
POPULATION: 2.7 million
TOTAL AREA: 24,938 sq miles
(64,589 sq km)
DENSITY: 109 people per sq mile

LANGUAGES: Latvian*, Russian
RELIGIONS: Evangelical Lutheran 85%, other Christian 15%
ETHNIC MIX: Latvian 52%, Russian 34%, Belorussian 5%, Ukrainian 4%, Polish 3%, other 2%
GOVERNMENT: Multiparty republic
CURRENCY: Lats = 100 santimi

LITHUANIA

 THE LARGEST and most powerful of the Baltic states, Lithuania was the first Soviet republic to declare independence from Moscow, in 1991.

GEOGRAPHY
Mostly flat with moors, bogs, and an intensively farmed central lowland. Numerous lakes and forested sandy ridges in the east.

CLIMATE
Coastal location moderates continental extremes. Cold winters, cool summers and steady rainfall.

PEOPLE AND SOCIETY
Homogeneous population, with Lithuanians forming a large majority. Strong Roman Catholic tradition and historical links with Poland. Better relations among ethnic groups than in other Baltic states and interethnic marriages are fairly common. However, some ethnic Russians and Poles see a threat of "Lithuanianization." Russian army presence until 1993, when all troops were withdrawn.

THE ECONOMY
Wide range of high-tech and heavy industries, includes textiles, engineering, shipbuilding, and food processing. Agricultural surpluses.

◆ INSIGHT: *The Baltic states produce two thirds of the world's amber – the fossilized sap of ancient trees. Most is found along Lithuania's "amber coast"*

FACT FILE

OFFICIAL NAME: Republic of Lithuania

DATE OF FORMATION: 1991

CAPITAL: Vilnius

POPULATION: 3.8 million

TOTAL AREA: 25,174 sq miles (65,200 sq km)

DENSITY: 151 people per sq mile

LANGUAGES: Lithuanian*, Russian

RELIGIONS: Roman Catholic 87%, Russian Orthodox 10%, other 3%

ETHNIC MIX: Lithuanian 80%, Russian 9%, Polish 8%, other 3%

GOVERNMENT: Multiparty republic

CURRENCY: Litas = 100 centas

POLAND

WITH ITS seven international borders and strategic location, Poland has always played an important role in European affairs.

GEOGRAPHY
Lowlands, part of the North European plain, cover most of the country. Carpathian Mountains run along the southern borders.

CLIMATE
Peak rainfall during hot summers. Cold winters with snow, especially in mountains.

PEOPLE AND SOCIETY
Ethnic homogeneity masks a number of tensions. Secular liberals criticize semiofficial status of Catholic Church; emerging wealth disparities resented by those unaffected by free-market reforms. German minority presses for action on Green issues. Many women hold policy-making posts.

◆ INSIGHT: Poland's eastern forests are home to Europe's largest remaining herds of European bison

THE ECONOMY
High growth, with foreign investment linked to government privatization program. Heavy industries still dominate, but service sector is quickly emerging

FACT FILE
OFFICIAL NAME: Republic of Poland
DATE OF FORMATION: 1918/1945
CAPITAL: Warsaw
POPULATION: 38.5 million
TOTAL AREA: 120,720 sq miles (312,680 sq km)

DENSITY: 320 people per sq mile
LANGUAGES: Polish*, German, other
RELIGIONS: Roman Catholic 95%, other (inc. Protestant and Eastern Orthodox) 5%
ETHNIC MIX: Polish 98%, other 2%
GOVERNMENT: Multiparty republic
CURRENCY: Zloty = 100 groszy

GERMANY

EUROPE'S STRONGEST economic power, Germany's democratic west and communist east were re-unified in 1990, after the fall of the east's regime.

 GEOGRAPHY
Coastal plains in the north, [ri]sing to rolling hills of central [re]gion. Alpine region in the south.

CLIMATE
Damp, temperate in northern [a]nd central regions. Continental [e]xtremes in mountainous south.

PEOPLE AND SOCIETY
Social and economic [di]fferences reflect former divisions. [S]ome prosperous Western Germans [re]sent added taxes since re-[u]nification. Far-right political [g]roups have emerged. Immigrant ["guest workers" – mainly Turks – [fa]ce citizenship problems and [o]ccasional racial attacks. Strong [f]eminist and Green movements.

◆ INSIGHT: *Germany's rivers and [ca]nals carry as much freight [a]s its roads*

$ THE ECONOMY
Massive exports of cars, heavy engineering, electronics, and chemicals. Postwar "miracle" powered by efficiency and good labor relations.

2000m/6562ft	
1000m/3281ft	
500m/1640ft	
200m/656ft	
Sea Level	

FACT FILE

OFFICIAL NAME: Federal Republic of Germany
DATE OF FORMATION: 1871 / 1990
CAPITAL: Berlin
POPULATION: 80.6 million
TOTAL AREA: 356,910 sq km (137,800 sq miles)

DENSITY: 598 people per sq mile
LANGUAGES: German*, Sorbian, other
RELIGIONS: Protestant 45%, Roman Catholic 37%, other 18%
ETHNIC MIX: German 92%, other 8%
GOVERNMENT: Multiparty republic
CURRENCY: Deutsche Mark = 100 pfennigs

NETHERLANDS

ASTRIDE THE delta of five major rivers in north-west Europe, the Netherlands has a long tradin tradition. Rotterdam is the world's largest port.

GEOGRAPHY
Mainly flat, with 27% of the land below sea level and protected by dunes, dikes, and canals. Low hills in the south and east.

CLIMATE
Mild, rainy winters and cool summers. Gales from the North Sea are common in autumn and winter.

PEOPLE AND SOCIETY
The Dutch see their country as the most tolerant in Europe. This reflects a long history of welcoming refugees and immigrants. Large urban concentration (89%) accounts for high population density. Laws concerning issues such as sexuality, euthanasia, and drug taking are among the world's most liberal.

◆ INSIGHT: *A century ago there were 10,000 windmills in the Netherlands, compared with only 1,000 today*

THE ECONOMY
Diverse industrial sector exports metals, machinery, chemicals, and electronics. Many high-profile multinationals.

FACT FILE
OFFICIAL NAME: Kingdom of the Netherlands
DATE OF FORMATION: 1815/1890
CAPITALS: Amsterdam, The Hague
POPULATION: 15.3 million
TOTAL AREA: 14,410 sq miles (37,330 sq km)

DENSITY: 1,165 people per sq mile
LANGUAGES: Dutch*, Frisian
RELIGIONS: Catholic 36%, Protestant 27%, other (inc. unaffiliated) 37%
ETHNIC MIX: Dutch 96%, other 4%
GOVERNMENT: Constitutional monarchy
CURRENCY: Guilder = 100 cents

see also Overseas Territories pp 230–23

BELGIUM

BELGIUM LIES in northwestern Europe. Its history has been marked by the division between its Flemish- and French-speaking communities.

GEOGRAPHY
Low-lying coastal plain covers two thirds of the country. Land becomes hilly and forested in the southeast (Ardennes) region.

CLIMATE
Maritime climate with Gulf stream influences. Temperatures are mild, with heavy cloud cover and rain. More rainfall and weather fluctuations on coast.

PEOPLE AND SOCIETY
Since 1970, Flemish-speaking regions have become more prosperous than those of the minority French-speakers (Walloons), overturning the traditional roles and increasing friction. In order to contain tensions, Belgium began to move toward federalism in 1980. Both groups now have their own governments and control most of their own affairs.

THE ECONOMY
Variety of industrial exports, including steel, glassware, cut diamonds, and textiles. Many foreign multinationals.

◆ INSIGHT: *The motorway network is extensive and so well lit that, along with the Great Wall of China, it is the most visible sight from space*

FACT FILE

OFFICIAL NAME: Kingdom of Belgium
DATE OF FORMATION: 1830
CAPITAL: Brussels
POPULATION: 10 million
TOTAL AREA: 12,780 sq miles (33,100 sq km)

DENSITY: 793 people per sq mile
LANGUAGES: French*, Dutch*, German*
RELIGIONS: Catholic 75%, other 25%
ETHNIC MIX: Flemish 58%, Walloon 32%, other European 6%, other 4%
GOVERNMENT: Constitutional monarchy
CURRENCY: Franc = 100 centimes

IRELAND

THE REPUBLIC of Ireland occupies 85% of the island of Ireland, with the remainder (Northern Ireland) being part of the United Kingdom.

 GEOGRAPHY
Low mountain ranges along an irregular coastline surround an inland plain punctuated by lakes, undulating hills and peat bogs.

 CLIMATE
The Gulf Stream accounts for the mild and wet climate. Snow is rare, except in the mountains.

PEOPLE AND SOCIETY
Although homogeneous in ethnicity and Catholic religion, the population show signs of change. Younger Irish question Vatican teachings on birth control, divorce, abortion. Many people still emigrate to find jobs. 1994 terrorist ceasefire in Northern Ireland tempered the traditional aim of reunification.

◆ INSIGHT: *About 20,000 people, in areas collectively known as the* Gaeltacht, *use Irish Gaelic as an everyday language*

THE ECONOMY
High unemployment tarnishe high-tech export successes and trade surplus. Highly educated work force. Efficient agriculture and food-processing industries.

1000m/3281ft
500m/1640ft
200m/656ft
Sea Level

Donegal
Donegal Bay
Sligo
NORTHERN IRELAND
Dundalk
54°
Irish Sea
Westport
Mullingar
Galway
Athlone
DUBLIN
Lough Derg
Dún Laoghaire
ATLANTIC OCEAN
Shannon Airport
Limerick
Wicklow Mts.
Kilkenny
Tralee
Tipperary
Wexford
Clonmel
Waterford
Killarney
52°
Cork
Celtic Sea
6°
10°
8°

0   50 km
0   50 mile

FACT FILE

OFFICIAL NAME: Republic of Ireland
DATE OF FORMATION: 1921 / 1922
CAPITAL: Dublin
POPULATION: 3.5 million
TOTAL AREA: 27,155 sq miles (70,280 sq km)

DENSITY: 133 people per sq mile
LANGUAGES: English*, Irish Gaelic*
RELIGIONS: Catholic 93%, Protestant (mainly Anglican) 5%, other 2%
ETHNIC MIX: Irish 95%, other (mainly British) 5%
GOVERNMENT: Multiparty republic
CURRENCY: Irish £ = 100 pence

UNITED KINGDOM

SEPARATED FROM continental Europe by the North Sea and the English Channel, the UK comprises England, Wales, Scotland, and Northern Ireland.

GEOGRAPHY
Mountainous in the north and west, undulating hills and lowlands in the south and east.

CLIMATE
Generally mild and temperate. Rainfall is heaviest in the west. Winter snow in mountainous areas.

PEOPLE AND SOCIETY
Although of mixed stock themselves, the British have an insular and ambivalent attitude toward Europe. The Welsh and Scottish are ethnically and culturally distinct. Asian and West Indian minorities in most cities. Class, the traditional source of division, is fading in the face of popular culture.

◆ INSIGHT: The UK has produced 90 nobel laureates – more than any other nation in the world, except from the US

THE ECONOMY
World leader in financial services, pharmaceuticals, and defense industries. Exports of steel, vehicles, aircraft, high-tech goods.

FACT FILE
OFFICIAL NAME: United Kingdom of Great Britain and Northern Ireland
DATE OF FORMATION: 1801/1922
CAPITAL: London
POPULATION: 57.8 million
TOTAL AREA: 94,550 sq miles (244,880 sq km)

DENSITY: 621 people per sq mile
LANGUAGES: English*, other
RELIGIONS: Protestant 52%, Catholic 9%, Muslim 3%, other 36%
ETHNIC MIX: English 81%, Scottish 10%, Welsh 2%, other 7%
GOVERNMENT: Constitutional monarchy
CURRENCY: £ sterling = 100 pence

see also Overseas Territories pp 230–236

FRANCE

STRADDLING WESTERN Europe from the English Channel to the Mediterranean Sea, France is one of the world's leading industrial powers.

 GEOGRAPHY
Broad plain covers northern half of the country. Tall mountain ranges in the east and southwest. Mountainous plateau in the center.

THE ECONOMY
Steel, chemicals, electronics, heavy engineering, wine, and aircraft typify a strong and diversified export sector.

CLIMATE
Three main climates: temperate and damp northwest; continental east; and Mediterranean south.

PEOPLE AND SOCIETY
Strong French national identity coexists with pronounced regional differences, including local languages. Long tradition of absorbing immigrants (European Jews, North African Muslims, economic migrants from Southern Europe). Catholic Church is no longer central to daily life.

◆ INSIGHT: *The French wine industry dates back to around 600 B.C.*

FACT FILE	
OFFICIAL NAME: The French Republic	LANGUAGES: French*, Provençal, German, Breton, Catalan, Basque
DATE OF FORMATION: 1685/1920	RELIGIONS: Catholic 90%, Protestant 2%, Jewish 1%, Muslim 1%, other 6%
CAPITAL: Paris	ETHNIC MIX: French 92%, North African 3%, German 2%, other 3%
POPULATION: 57.4 million	
TOTAL AREA: 551,500 sq km (212,930 sq miles)	GOVERNMENT: Multiparty republic
DENSITY: 270 people per sq mile	CURRENCY: Franc = 100 centimes

see also Overseas Territories pp 230–23

LUXEMBOURG

MAKING UP part of the plateau of the Ardennes in Western Europe, Luxembourg is Europe's last independent duchy and one of its richest states.

 GEOGRAPHY
Dense Ardennes forests in the north, low, open southern plateau. Undulating terrain throughout.

CLIMATE
Moist climate with warm summers and mild winters. Snow is common only in the Ardennes.

PEOPLE AND SOCIETY
Society is peaceable, despite large proportion of foreigners (half the work force and one third of the residents). Integration has been straightforward; most are fellow Western Europeans and Catholics, mainly from Italy and Portugal. High salaries and very low unemployment promote stability.

◆ INSIGHT: *Luxembourg's capital, Luxembourg, is home to over 980 investment funds and 192 banks – more than any other city in the world*

THE ECONOMY
Traditional industries such as steel-making have given way in recent years to a thriving banking and service sector. Tax-haven status attracts foreign companies.

□	500m/1640ft
□	200m/656ft
	Sea Level

0   10 km
0   10 miles

Clervaux

GERMANY

Ettelbrück

Mersch

Echternach

BELGIUM

✦ LUXEMBOURG

Pétange

Differdange

Esch-sur-Alzette

Dudelange

FRANCE

FACT FILE

OFFICIAL NAME: Grand Duchy of Luxembourg
DATE OF FORMATION: 1890
CAPITAL: Luxembourg
POPULATION: 400,000
TOTAL AREA: 998 sq miles (2,586 sq km)

DENSITY: 400 people per sq mile
LANGUAGES: Letzeburgish*, French*, German*, Italian, Portuguese, other
RELIGIONS: Catholic 97%, other 3%
ETHNIC MIX: Luxembourger 72%, Portuguese 9%, Italian 5%, other 14%
GOVERNMENT: Constitutional monarchy
CURRENCY: Franc = 100 centimes

MONACO

A JET-SET image and a thriving service sector define the modern identity of this tiny enclave on the Côte d'Azur in southeastern France.

GEOGRAPHY

A rocky promontory overlooking a narrow coastal strip that has been enlarged through land reclamation.

CLIMATE

Mediterranean. Summers are hot and dry; days with 12 hours of sunshine are not uncommon. Winters are mild and sunny.

PEOPLE AND SOCIETY

Less than 20% of residents are Monégasques. The rest are Europeans – mainly French – attracted by the tax-haven, upscale lifestyle. Nationals enjoy considerable privileges, including housing benefits to protect them from high housing prices, and the right of first refusal before foreigners can take a job. Women have equal status but only acquired the vote in 1962.

THE ECONOMY

Tourism and gambling are the mainstays. Banking secrecy laws and tax-haven conditions attract foreign investment. Almost totally dependent on imports due to lack of natural resources.

◆ INSIGHT: The Grimaldi princes (Rainier since 1949) have been Monaco's hereditary rulers for 700 years

FACT FILE

OFFICIAL NAME: Principality of Monaco
DATE OF FORMATION: 1861
CAPITAL: Monaco
POPULATION: 28,000
TOTAL AREA: 1.95 sq km (0.75 sq miles)

DENSITY: 37,333 people per sq mile
LANGUAGES: French*, Italian, other
RELIGIONS: Catholic 95%, other 5%
ETHNIC MIX: French 47%, Monégasque 17%, Italian 16%, other 20%
GOVERNMENT: Constitutional monarchy
CURRENCY: French franc = 100 centimes

ANDORRA

A TINY landlocked principality, Andorra lies high in the eastern Pyrenees between France and Spain. It held its first full elections in 1993.

GEOGRAPHY
High mountains, and six deep, glaciated valleys that drain into the River Valira as it flows into Spain.

CLIMATE
Cool, wet springs followed by dry, warm summers. Mountain snows linger until March.

PEOPLE AND SOCIETY
Immigration is strictly monitored and restricted by quota to French and Spanish nationals seeking employment. A referendum in 1993 ended 715 years of semifeudal status but society remains conservative. Divorce is illegal.

◆ INSIGHT: Andorra is a co-principality whose status dates back to the 13th century, the "princes" being the President of France and the Bishop of Urgel in Spain

THE ECONOMY
Tourism and duty-free sales dominate the economy. Banking secrecy laws and low consumer taxes promote investment and commerce. Dependence on imported food and raw materials.

FACT FILE

OFFICIAL NAME: Principality of Andorra

DATE OF FORMATION: 1278

CAPITAL: Andorra la Vella

POPULATION: 58,000

TOTAL AREA: 181 sq miles (468 sq km)

DENSITY: 320 people per sq mile

LANGUAGES: Catalan*, Spanish, other

RELIGIONS: Catholic 86%, other 14%

ETHNIC MIX: Catalan 61%, Spanish Castilian 30%, other 9%

GOVERNMENT: Parliamentary democracy

CURRENCY: French franc, Spanish peseta

PORTUGAL

FACING THE Atlantic on the western side of the Iberian peninsula, Portugal is the most westerly country on the European mainland.

GEOGRAPHY
The River Tagus bisects the country roughly east to west, dividing mountainous north from lower and more undulating south.

CLIMATE
North is cool and moist. South is warmer with dry, mild winters.

PEOPLE AND SOCIETY
Homogeneous and stable society, losing some of its conservative traditions. Small, well-assimilated immigrant population, mainly from former colonies. Urban areas and south are more socially progressive. North is more responsive to traditional Catholic values. Family ties remain all-important.

◆ INSIGHT: *Portugal is the world's leading producer of cork, which comes from the bark of the cork oak*

THE ECONOMY
Agricultural exports include grain, vegetables, fruits, and wine, but farming methods are outdated. Strong banking and tourism sectors

FACT FILE	
OFFICIAL NAME: Republic of Portugal	DENSITY: 277 people per sq mile
DATE OF FORMATION: 1140/1640	LANGUAGES: Portuguese*
CAPITAL: Lisbon	RELIGIONS: Catholic 97%, Protestant 1%, other 2%
POPULATION: 9.9 million	ETHNIC MIX: Portuguese 98%, African 1%, other 1%
TOTAL AREA: 35,670 sq miles (92,390 sq km)	GOVERNMENT: Multiparty republic
	CURRENCY: Escudo = 100 centavos

see also Overseas Territories pp 230–23

SPAIN

LODGED BETWEEN Europe, and Africa, the Atlantic, and the Mediterranean, Spain has occupied a pivotal position since it was united in 1492.

GEOGRAPHY
Mountain ranges in north, center, and south. Huge central plateau. Verdant valleys in north-west, Mediterranean lowlands.

CLIMATE
Maritime in north. Hotter and drier in south. Central plateau has an extreme climate.

PEOPLE AND SOCIETY
Ethnic regionalism, suppressed under General Franco's regime (1936–1975), is increasing. 17 regions are now autonomous. People remain church-going, although Catholic teachings on social issues are often flouted. Status of women rising quickly, with strong political representation.

THE ECONOMY
Outdated labor practices and low investment hinder growth. Heavy industry, textiles, and food-processing lead exports. Tourism and agriculture are important.

◆ INSIGHT: *Over 3,000 festivals and feasts take place each year in Spain*

ITALY

PROJECTING INTO the Mediterranean Sea in Southern Europe, Italy is an ancient land but also one of the continent's newest unified states.

 GEOGRAPHY
Appennino form the backbone of a rugged peninsula, extending from the Alps into the Mediterranean Sea. Alluvial plain in the north.

 CLIMATE
Mediterranean in the south. Seasonal extremes in mountains and on northern plain.

PEOPLE AND SOCIETY
Ethnically homogeneous, but gulf between prosperous, industrial north and poorer, agricultural south. Strong regional identities, especially on islands of Sicily and Sardinia. State institutions viewed as inefficient and corrupt. Allegiance to the family survives lessened influence of the Church.

◆ *INSIGHT: Italy was a collection of city states, dukedoms, and monarchies before it became a unified nation in 1871*

THE ECONOMY
World leader in industrial and product design and textiles. Strong tourism and agriculture sectors. Weak currency. Large public-sector debt.

FACT FILE

OFFICIAL NAME: Italian Republic
DATE OF FORMATION: 1871 / 1954
CAPITAL: Rome
POPULATION: 57.8 million
TOTAL AREA: 116,320 sq miles (301,270 sq km)
DENSITY: 512 people per sq mile

LANGUAGES: Italian*, German, French, Rhaeto-Romanic, Sardinian
RELIGIONS: Catholic 99%, other 1%
ETHNIC MIX: Italian 98%, other (inc. German, French, Greek, Slovenian, Albanian) 2%
GOVERNMENT: Multiparty republic
CURRENCY: Lira = 100 centesimi

MALTA

THE MALTESE archipelago lies off southern Sicily, midway between Europe and Africa. The only inhabited islands are Malta, Gozo, and Kemmuna.

 GEOGRAPHY
The main island of Malta has low hills and a ragged coastline with numerous harbors, bays, sandy beaches, and rocky coves. Gozo is more densely vegetated.

CLIMATE
Mediterranean climate. Many hours of sunshine throughout the year but very low rainfall.

PEOPLE AND SOCIETY
Over the centuries, the Maltese have been subject to Arab, Sicilian, Spanish, French, and English influences. Today, the population is socially conservative and devoutly Roman Catholic. Divorce is illegal. Many young Maltese go abroad to find work – notably to the United States and Australia – as opportunities for them on the islands are few.

THE ECONOMY
Tourism is the chief source of income. Offshore banking potential. Schemes to attract foreign high-tech industry. Almost all requirements have to be imported.

◆ INSIGHT: *The Maltese language has Phoenician origins but features Arabic etymology and intonation*

FACT FILE

OFFICIAL NAME: Republic of Malta
DATE OF FORMATION: 1964
CAPITAL: Valletta
POPULATION: 400,000
TOTAL AREA: 124 sq miles (320 sq km)
DENSITY: 3,250 people per sq mile

LANGUAGES: Maltese*, English
RELIGIONS: Catholic 98%, other (mostly Anglican) 2%
ETHNIC MIX: Maltese (mixed Arab, Sicilian, Norman, Spanish, Italian, English) 98%, other 2%
GOVERNMENT: Multiparty republic
CURRENCY: Lira = 100 cents

VATICAN CITY

THE VATICAN City, the seat of the Roman Catholic Church, is a walled enclave in the city of Rome. It is the world's smallest fully independent state.

GEOGRAPHY
Territory includes ten other buildings in Rome, plus the papal residence. The Vatican Gardens cover half the City's area.

CLIMATE
Mild winters with regular rainfall. Hot, dry summers with occasional thunderstorms.

PEOPLE AND SOCIETY
The Vatican has about 1,000 permanent inhabitants, including several hundred lay persons, and employs a further 3,400 lay staff. Citizenship can be acquired through stable residence and holding an office or job within the City. Reigning Pope has supreme legislative and judicial powers, and holds office for life. State maintains a neutral stance in world affairs and has observer status in many international organizations.

THE ECONOMY
Investments and voluntary contributions by Catholics world-wide (known as Peter's Pence), backed up by tourist revenue and issue of Vatican stamps and coins.

◆ *INSIGHT: The Vatican City is the only state to have Latin as an official language*

FACT FILE

OFFICIAL NAME: State of the Vatican City
DATE OF FORMATION: 1929
CAPITAL: Not applicable
POPULATION: 1,000
TOTAL AREA: 0.17 sq miles (0.44 sq km)

DENSITY: 5,910 people per sq mile
LANGUAGES: Italian*, Latin*, other
RELIGIONS: Catholic 100%
ETHNIC MIX: Italian 90%, Swiss 10% (including the Swiss Guard, which is responsible for papal security)
GOVERNMENT: Papal Commission
CURRENCY: Italian lira = 100 centesimi

SAN MARINO

PERCHED ON the slopes of Monte Titano in the Italian Appennino, San Marino has maintained its independence since the 4th century A.D.

GEOGRAPHY
Distinctive limestone outcrop of Monte Titano dominates wooded hills and pastures near Italy's Adriatic coast.

CLIMATE
Altitude and sea breezes moderate Mediterranean climate. Hot summers and cool, wet winters.

PEOPLE AND SOCIETY
Territory is divided into nine "castles," or districts. Tightly knit society, with 16 centuries of tradition. Strict immigration rules require 30-year residence before applying for citizenship. Catholic Church remains a more powerful influence in neighboring Italy. Living standards are similar to those of northern Italy.

◆ INSIGHT: Sales of postage stamps contribute 10% of the national income

THE ECONOMY
Tourism provides 60% of government income. Light industries – led by mechanical engineering and high-quality clothing – generate export revenue. Italian infrastructure is a boon.

FACT FILE

OFFICIAL NAME: Republic of San Marino
DATE OF FORMATION: AD 301/1862.
CAPITAL: San Marino
POPULATION: 23,000
TOTAL AREA: 24 sq miles (61 sq km)

DENSITY: 980 people per sq mile
LANGUAGES: Italian*, other
RELIGIONS: Catholic 96%, Protestant 2%, other 2%
ETHNIC MIX: Sammarinese 95%, Italian 4%, other 1%
GOVERNMENT: Multiparty republic
CURRENCY: Italian lira = 100 centesimi

SWITZERLAND

ONE OF the world's most prosperous countries, with a long tradition of neutrality in foreign affairs, it lies at the center of Western Europe.

GEOGRAPHY
Mostly mountainous, with river valleys. Alps cover 60% of its area; Jura in west cover 10%. Lowlands lie along east–west axis.

CLIMATE
Most rain falls in the warm summer months. Snowy winters, but milder and foggy away from the mountains.

PEOPLE AND SOCIETY
Composed of distinct Swiss-German, Swiss-French, and Swiss-Italian linguistic groups, but national identity is strong. Country divided into 26 autonomous cantons (states), each with control over housing and economic policy. Tensions over membership of EU, drug abuse, and role of guest workers in economy. Some young see society as regimented and conformist.

THE ECONOMY
Diversified economy relies on services – with strong tourism and banking sectors – and specialized industries (engineering, watches).

◆ *INSIGHT: Genève is the headquarters of many UN agencies, although Switzerland itself is not a UN member*

3000m/9843ft
2000m/6562ft
1000m/3281ft
500m/1640ft
200m/656ft

0   50 km
0   50 m

FACT FILE

OFFICIAL NAME: Swiss Confederation
DATE OF FORMATION: 1815
CAPITAL: Bern
POPULATION: 6.9 million
TOTAL AREA: 15,940 sq miles
(41,290 sq km)
DENSITY: 432 people per sq mile

LANGUAGES: German*, French*, Italian*, Romansch*, other
RELIGIONS: Catholic 48%, Protestant 44%, other 8%
ETHNIC MIX: German 65%, French 18%, Italian 10%, other 7%
GOVERNMENT: Federal republic
CURRENCY: Franc = 100 centimes

LIECHTENSTEIN

TUCKED IN the Alps between Switzerland and Austria, Liechtenstein became an independent principality of the Holy Roman Empire in 1719.

 GEOGRAPHY
Upper Rhine valley covers western third. Mountains and narrow valleys of the eastern Alps make up the remainder.

 CLIMATE
Warm, dry summers. Cold winters, with heavy snow in mountains December–March.

PEOPLE AND SOCIETY
Country's role as a financial center accounts for its many foreign residents (over 35% of the population), of whom half are Swiss and the rest mostly German. High standard of living results in few social tensions. Sovereignty cherished, despite close alliance with Switzerland, which handles its foreign relations and defense.

◆ INSIGHT: *Women in Liechtenstein only received the vote in 1984*

THE ECONOMY
Banking secrecy and low taxes attract foreign investment. Well-diversified exports include dental products, furniture, and chemicals.

| 0 | 4 km |
| 0 | 4 miles |

2000m/6562ft
1000m/3281ft
500m/1640ft
200m/656ft
Sea Level

Ruggell
Bendern
Mauren
Planken
Schaan
AUSTRIA
◇VADUZ
SWITZERLAND
Triesenberg
Triesen
Balzers

47°15'
47°10'
47°05'
9°30'
9°35'

FACT FILE

OFFICIAL NAME: Principality of Liechtenstein

DATE OF FORMATION: 1719

CAPITAL: Vaduz

POPULATION: 29,000

TOTAL AREA: 62 sq miles (160 sq km)

DENSITY: 468 people per sq mile

LANGUAGES: German*, Alemannish

RELIGIONS: Catholic 87%, Protestant 8%, other 5%

ETHNIC MIX: Liechtensteiner 63%, Swiss 15%, German 9%, other 13%

GOVERNMENT: Constitutional monarchy

CURRENCY: Swiss franc = 100 centimes

AUSTRIA

BORDERING EIGHT countries in the heart of Europe, Austria was created in 1920 after the collapse of the Austro-Hungarian Empire the previous year.

GEOGRAPHY
Mainly mountainous. Alps and foothills cover the west and south. Lowlands in the east are part of the Danube River basin.

CLIMATE
Temperate continental climate. Western Alpine regions have colder winters and more rainfall.

PEOPLE AND SOCIETY
Although all are German-speaking, Austrians consider themselves ethnically distinct from Germans. Minorities are few; there are a small number of Hungarians, Slovenes, and Croats, plus refugees from conflict in former Yugoslavia. Some Austrians are beginning to challenge patriarchal and class-conscious social values. Legislation reflects strong environmental concerns.

THE ECONOMY
Large manufacturing base, despite lack of energy resources. Skilled labor force the key to high-tech exports. Strong tourism sector.

◆ INSIGHT: Many of the world's great composers were Austrian, including Mozart, Haydn, Schubert, and Strauss

FACT FILE

OFFICIAL NAME: Republic of Austria
DATE OF FORMATION: 1918/1945
CAPITAL: Vienna
POPULATION: 7.8 million
TOTAL AREA: 32,375 sq miles (83,850 sq km)
DENSITY: 241 people per sq mile

LANGUAGES: German*, Croatian, Slovene, Hungarian (Magyar)
RELIGIONS: Catholic 85%, Protestant 6%, other 9%
ETHNIC MIX: German 99%, other (inc. Hungarian, Slovene, Croat) 1%
GOVERNMENT: Multiparty republic
CURRENCY: Schilling = 100 groschen

HUNGARY

HUNGARY IS bordered by seven states in Central Europe. It has changed its economic and political policies to develop closer ties with the EU.

GEOGRAPHY
Fertile plains in east and northwest; west and north are hilly. River Danube bisects the country from north to south.

CLIMATE
Continental. Wet springs; late, but very hot summers, and cold, cloudy winters.

PEOPLE AND SOCIETY
Ethnically homogenous and stable society, showing signs of stress since change to market economy. Most homes are overcrowded, due to a severe housing shortage. Since 1989, a middle class has emerged, but life for the unemployed and unskilled is harder than under communism. Concern over treatment of Hungarian nationals in neighboring states.

THE ECONOMY
Weak banking sector and unemployment hamper moves to open economy. Heavy industries and agriculture remain strong. Growing tourism and services.

◆ INSIGHT: *The Hungarian language is Asian in origin and has features not found in any other Western language*

FACT FILE

OFFICIAL NAME: Republic of Hungary
DATE OF FORMATION: 1918 / 1945
CAPITAL: Budapest
POPULATION: 10.5 million
TOTAL AREA: 35,919 sq miles (93,030 sq km)
DENSITY: 292 people per sq mile

LANGUAGES: Hungarian (Magyar)*, German, Slovak, other
RELIGIONS: Catholic 68%, Protestant 25%, other 7%
ETHNIC MIX: Hungarian (Magyar) 90%, German 2%, other 8%
GOVERNMENT: Multiparty republic
CURRENCY: Forint = 100 filler

CZECH REPUBLIC

ONCE PART of Czechoslovakia in Central Europe, it became independent in 1993, after peacefully dissolving its federal union with Slovakia.

GEOGRAPHY
Western territory of Bohemia is a plateau surrounded by mountains. Moravia, in the east, has hills and lowlands.

CLIMATE
Cool, sometimes cold winters, and warm summer months, which bring most of the annual rainfall.

PEOPLE AND SOCIETY
Secular and urban society, with high divorce rates. Czechs make up the vast majority of the population. The 300,000 Slovaks left after partition now form largest ethnic minority. Ethnic tensions are few, but there is some hostility towards the Gypsy community. A new commercial elite is emerging alongside ex-communist entrepreneurs.

THE ECONOMY
Traditional heavy industries (machinery, iron, car-making) have been successfully privatized. Large tourism revenues. Skilled labor force. Rising unemployment.

◆ *INSIGHT: The Czech Republic is the most polluted country in Europe. Acid rain has devastated many of its forests*

FACT FILE

OFFICIAL NAME: Czech Republic
DATE OF FORMATION: 1993
CAPITAL: Prague
POPULATION: 10.4 million
TOTAL AREA: 30,260 sq miles (78,370 sq km)
DENSITY: 343 people per sq mile

LANGUAGES: Czech*, Slovak, Romany, other
RELIGIONS: Catholic 44%, Protestant 6%, other Christian 12%, other 38%
ETHNIC MIX: Czech 85%, Moravian 13%, other (inc. Slovak, Gypsy) 2%
GOVERNMENT: Multiparty republic
CURRENCY: Koruna = 100 halura

SLOVAKIA

LANDLOCKED IN Central Europe, Slovakia has been independent since 1993. It is the less-developed half of the former Czechoslovakia.

GEOGRAPHY
Carpathian Mountains stretch along northern border with Poland. Southern lowlands include the fertile Danube plain.

CLIMATE
Continental. Moderately warm summers and steady rainfall. Cold winters with heavy snowfalls.

PEOPLE AND SOCIETY
Slovaks are largest and most dominant group. Tension between them and the Hungarian minority has increased, particularly over directive that Hungarians should adopt Slovak name endings. Before partition, many skilled Slovaks took jobs in Prague, but few have returned to help structure the new Slovakia. Catholic Church remains influential.

THE ECONOMY
Narrow emphasis on heavy industry, with poor record on innovation and capital investment. High inflation and unemployment. Growing tourism sector.

◆ INSIGHT: *Separation from the Czech Republic gave Slovakia full independence for the first time in over 1,000 years*

FACT FILE

OFFICIAL NAME: Slovak Republic

DATE OF FORMATION: 1993

CAPITAL: Bratislava

POPULATION: 5.3 million

TOTAL AREA: 19,100 sq miles (49,500 sq km)

DENSITY: 277 people per sq mile

LANGUAGES: Slovak*, Hungarian (Magyar), Romany, Czech, other

RELIGIONS: Catholic 80%, Protestant 12%, other 8%

ETHNIC MIX: Slovak 85%, Hungarian 9%, Czech 1%, other (inc. Gypsy) 5%

GOVERNMENT: Multiparty republic

CURRENCY: Koruna = 100 halura

SLOVENIA

NORTHERNMOST of the former Yugoslav republics, it has the closest links with Western Europe. In 1991, it gained independence with little violence.

GEOGRAPHY
Alpine terrain with hills and mountains. Forests cover almost half the country's area. Short Adriatic coastline.

CLIMATE
Mediterranean climate on small coastal strip. Alpine interior has continental extremes.

PEOPLE AND SOCIETY
Homogeneous population accounts for relatively peaceful transition to independence. Traditional links with Austria and Italy, each with Slovene populations, account for the "Alpine" rather than "Balkan" outlook. Wages are the highest in central Europe, but unemployment is rising. Institutional change is proceeding slowly.

THE ECONOMY
Competitive manufacturing industry. Prospects for growth in electronics industry. Well-developed tourist sector.

◆ *INSIGHT: Slovenia is a major producer of mercury, used in thermometers, barometers, and batteries*

1000m/3280ft	
500m/1640ft	
200m/656ft	
Sea Level	

FACT FILE

OFFICIAL NAME: Republic of Slovenia
DATE OF FORMATION: 1991
CAPITAL: Ljubljana
POPULATION: 2 million
TOTAL AREA: 7,820 sq miles (20,250 sq km)

DENSITY: 255 people per sq mile
LANGUAGES: Slovene*, Serbo-Croatian
RELIGIONS: Roman Catholic 96%, Muslim 1%, other 3%
ETHNIC MIX: Slovene 92%, Croat 3%, Serb 1%, other 4%
GOVERNMENT: Multiparty republic
CURRENCY: Tolar = 100 stotins

CROATIA

A FORMER Yugoslav republic. Postindependence fighting thwarted its plans to capitalize on its prime location along the east Adriatic coast.

GEOGRAPHY
Rocky, mountainous Adriatic [co]astline is dotted with islands. [In]terior is a mixture of wooded [m]ountains and broad valleys.

CLIMATE
The interior has a temperate [co]ntinental climate. Mediterranean [cl]imate along the Adriatic coast.

PEOPLE AND SOCIETY
Turbulence was triggered [b]y long-held ethnic hostilities. [O]pen warfare between Croats [an]d Serbs began in 1990. Some [ar]eas with local Serb majorities [a]chieved *de facto* autonomy after [fi]erce fighting in 1992. Destruction [w]as widespread; thousands of [pe]ople were made homeless.

▶ INSIGHT: *The Croatian language [u]ses the Roman alphabet, while Serbian [em]ploys Cyrillic (Russian) script*

THE ECONOMY
Economy was severely strained by fighting and influx of refugees. Potential for renewed success in manufacturing, tourism. Exports to the West have grown, despite conflict.

FACT FILE

OFFICIAL NAME: Republic of Croatia
DATE OF FORMATION: 1991
CAPITAL: Zagreb
POPULATION: 4.9 million
TOTAL AREA: 21,830 sq miles
(56,540 sq km)
DENSITY: 211 people per sq mile

LANGUAGES: Croatian*, Serbian
RELIGIONS: Roman Catholic 77%,
Orthodox Catholic 11%, Protestant
1%, Muslim 1%, other 10%
ETHNIC MIX: Croat 80%, Serb 12%,
Hungarian, Slovenian, other 8%
GOVERNMENT: Multiparty republic
CURRENCY: Kuna = 100 para

BOSNIA & HERZEGOVINA

DOMINATING THE western Balkans, Bosnia and Herzegovina was the focus of the bitter conflict surrounding the breakup of former Yugoslavia.

GEOGRAPHY
Hills and mountains, with narrow river valleys. Lowlands in the north. Mainly deciduous forest covers about half of the total area.

CLIMATE
Continental. Hot summers and cold, often snowy winters.

PEOPLE AND SOCIETY
Civil war between rival ethnic groups. Ethnic Bosnians (mainly Muslim) form the largest group, with large minorities of Serbs and Croats. Communities have been destroyed or uprooted ("ethnic cleansing") as Serbs and Croats established separate ethnic areas. The UN and Nato have been involved as peacekeepers.

◆ *INSIGHT: By 1995, over two million people had been made homeless and a further million had fled the country*

THE ECONOMY
Before 1991, Bosnia was home to five of former Yugoslavia's largest companies. It has the potential to become a thriving market economy with a strong manufacturing base.

FACT FILE
OFFICIAL NAME: The Republic of Bosnia and Herzegovina
DATE OF FORMATION: 1992
CAPITAL: Sarajevo
POPULATION: 3.5 million
TOTAL AREA: 19,741 sq miles (51,130 sq km)

DENSITY: 177 people per sq mile
LANGUAGES: Serbo-Croatian*, other
RELIGIONS: Muslim 40%, Orthodox Catholic 31%, other 29%
ETHNIC MIX: Bosnian 44%, Serb 31%, Croat 17%, other 8%
GOVERNMENT: Multiparty republic
CURRENCY: Dinar = 100 para

YUGOSLAVIA (SERBIA & MONTENEGRO)

THE FEDERAL Republic of Yugoslavia, comprising Serbia and Montenegro, is the successor state to the former Yugoslavia.

GEOGRAPHY

Fertile Danube plain in north, rolling uplands in center. Mountains in south, and behind narrow Adriatic coastal plain.

CLIMATE

Mediterranean along coast, continental inland. Hot summers and cold winters, with heavy snow.

PEOPLE AND SOCIETY

Social order has disintegrated since dissolution of the former Yugoslavia. Serbia was vilified in the international community for its role in the conflict in the region. Serbian concerns over Bosnia and Croatia have masked domestic tensions, particularly unrest among the Albanian population in the southern province of Kosovo.

> INSIGHT: *Belgrade means "White City." Its site has been settled for 7,000 years*

THE ECONOMY

Bosnian war and UN trade sanctions crippled the economy. Fuel and food shortages. Hyperinflation created a barter economy.

FACT FILE

OFFICIAL NAME: Federal Republic of Yugoslavia
DATE OF FORMATION: 1992
CAPITAL: Belgrade
POPULATION: 10.6 million
TOTAL AREA: 9,929 sq miles (25,715 sq km)

DENSITY: 270 people per sq mile
LANGUAGES: Serbo-Croatian*, other
RELIGIONS: Orthodox Catholic 65%, Muslim 19%, other 16%
ETHNIC MIX: Serb 63%, Albanian 14%, Montenegrin 6%, other 17%
GOVERNMENT: Multiparty republic
CURRENCY: Dinar = 100 para

ALBANIA

LYING AT the southeastern end of the Adriatic Sea, Albania held its first multiparty elections in 1991, after nearly five decades of communism.

 GEOGRAPHY
Narrow coastal plain. Interior is mostly hills and mountains. Forest and scrub cover over 40% of the land. Large lakes in the east.

CLIMATE
Mediterranean coastal climate, with warm summers and cool winters. Mountains receive heavy rains or snows in winter.

PEOPLE AND SOCIETY
Last eastern European country to move toward Western economic liberalism – pace of change remains a sensitive issue. Mosques and churches have reopened in what was once the world's only officially atheist state. Greek minority in the south suffers much discrimination.

◆ INSIGHT: The Albanians' name for their nation, Shqipërisë, means "Land of the Eagle"

THE ECONOMY
Oil and gas reserves plus high growth rate have potential to offset rudimentary infrastructure and lack of foreign investment.

FACT FILE
OFFICIAL NAME: Republic of Albania
DATE OF FORMATION: 1912/1913
CAPITAL: Tirana
POPULATION: 3.3 million
TOTAL AREA: 11,100 sq miles (28,750 sq km)

DENSITY: 312 people per sq mile
LANGUAGES: Albanian*, Greek
RELIGIONS: Muslim 70%, Greek Orthodox 20%, Roman Catholic 10%
ETHNIC MIX: Albanian 96%, Greek 2%, other (inc. Macedonian) 2%
GOVERNMENT: Multiparty republic
CURRENCY: Lek = 100 qindars

MACEDONIA

LANDLOCKED in the southern Balkans, Macedonia is affected by sanctions imposed on its northern trading partners and by Greek antagonism.

 GEOGRAPHY
Mainly mountainous or hilly, with deep river basins in center. Plains in northeast and southwest.

CLIMATE
Continental climate with wet springs and dry autumns. Heavy snowfalls in northern mountains.

PEOPLE AND SOCIETY
Slav Macedonians comprise two thirds of the population. Officially 20% are Albanian, although Albanians claim they account for 40%. Tensions between the two groups have so far been restrained. Greek government is hostile toward the state because it suspects it may try to absorb northern Greece – also called Macedonia – in a "Greater Macedonia." Social structures remain essentially socialist.

THE ECONOMY
Serbian sanctions paralyze exports, but foreign aid and grants boost foreign exchange reserves. Growing private sector. Thriving black market in the capital.

◆ INSIGHT: Lake Ohrid is the deepest lake in Europe at 964 ft (294 m)

FACT FILE

OFFICIAL NAME: Former Yugoslav Republic of Macedonia
DATE OF FORMATION: 1991
CAPITAL: Skopje
POPULATION: 1.9 million
TOTAL AREA: 9,929 sq miles (25,715 sq km)

DENSITY: 192 people per sq mile
LANGUAGES: Macedonian, Serbo-Croatian (no official language)
RELIGIONS: Christian 80%, Muslim 20%
ETHNIC MIX: Macedonian 67%, Albanian 20%, Turkish 4%, other 9%
GOVERNMENT: Multiparty republic
CURRENCY: Denar = 100 deni

BULGARIA

LOCATED IN southeastern Europe, Bulgaria has made slow progress toward democracy since the fall of its communist regime in 1990.

 GEOGRAPHY
Mountains run east–west across center and along southern border. Danube plain in north, Thracian plain in southeast.

CLIMATE
Warm summers and snowy winters, especially in mountains. East winds bring seasonal extremes.

PEOPLE AND SOCIETY
Government has sought to assimilate separate ethnic groups, thereby suppressing cultural identities. Large exodus of Bulgarian Turks in 1989. Recent privatization program has left many Turks landless and prompted further emigration. Gypsies suffer much discrimination. Female equality exists only in theory. Ruling party, mainly ex-communists, have resisted change.

THE ECONOMY
Political and technical delays hinder privatization program. Good agricultural production – including grapes for the well-developed wine industry – and tobacco.

◆ INSIGHT: Shaking one's head implies "yes" in Bulgaria while a nod means "no"

FACT FILE

OFFICIAL NAME: Republic of Bulgaria
DATE OF FORMATION: 1908/1923
CAPITAL: Sofia
POPULATION: 8.9 million
TOTAL AREA: 42,822 sq miles (110,910 sq km)
DENSITY: 211 people per sq mile

LANGUAGES: Bulgarian*, Turkish, Macedonian, Romany, Armenian
RELIGIONS: Christian 85%, Muslim 13%, Jewish 1%, other 1%
ETHNIC MIX: Bulgarian 85%, Turkish 9%, Macedonian 3%, Gypsy 3%
GOVERNMENT: Multiparty republic
CURRENCY: Lev = 100 stotinki

GREECE

GREECE IS the southernmost Balkan nation. Surrounded by the Mediterranean, Aegean, and Ionian seas, it has a strong seafaring tradition.

 GEOGRAPHY
Mountainous peninsula with over 2,000 islands. Large central plain along the Aegean coast.

 CLIMATE
Mainly Mediterranean with dry, hot summers. Alpine climate in northern mountain areas.

PEOPLE AND SOCIETY
Postwar industrial development altered the dominance of agriculture and seafaring. Rural exodus to industrial cities has been stemmed but over half the population now live in the two largest cities. Age-old culture and Greek Orthodox Church balance social mobility.

THE ECONOMY
High inflation and poor investment work against strong economic sectors: tourism, shipping, agriculture. Thriving black market.

◆ INSIGHT: *The Parthenon in Athens has suffered more erosion in the last 20 years than in the previous 2,000*

FACT FILE

OFFICIAL NAME: Hellenic Republic
DATE OF FORMATION: 1830/1947
CAPITAL: Athens
POPULATION: 10.2 million
TOTAL AREA: 50,961 sq miles (131,990 sq km)
DENSITY: 203 people per sq mile

LANGUAGES: Greek*, Turkish, Albanian, Macedonian
RELIGIONS: Greek Orthodox 98%, Muslim 1%, other (mainly Roman Catholic and Jewish) 1%
ETHNIC MIX: Greek 98%, other 2%
GOVERNMENT: Multiparty republic
CURRENCY: Drachma = 100 lepta

ROMANIA

ROMANIA LIES on the Black Sea coast. Since the overthrow of its communist regime in 1989, it has been slowly converting to a free-market economy.

 GEOGRAPHY
Carpathian Mountains encircle Transylvanian plateau. Wide plains to the south and east. River Danube on southern border.

CLIMATE
Continental. Hot, humid summers and cold, snowy winters. Very heavy spring rains.

PEOPLE AND SOCIETY
Since 1989, there has been a rise in Romanian nationalism, aggravated by the hardships brought by economic reform. Incidence of ethnic violence has also risen, particularly toward Hungarians and Gypsies. Decrease in population in recent years due to emigration and falling birth rate.

◆ *INSIGHT: Romania is the only nation with a Romance language that does not have a Roman Catholic background*

THE ECONOMY
Outdated, polluting heavy industries and unmechanized agricultural sector. Wages have fallen since demise of communism. High number of small-scale foreign joint ventures. Tourism potential.

	2000m/6562ft
	1000m/3281ft
	500m/1640ft
	200m/656ft
	Sea Level

0   50 km
0   50 miles

FACT FILE

OFFICIAL NAME: Romania
DATE OF FORMATION: 1947
CAPITAL: Bucharest
POPULATION: 23.4 million
TOTAL AREA: 91,700 sq miles (237,500 sq km)
DENSITY: 255 people per sq mile

LANGUAGES: Romanian*, Hungarian
RELIGIONS: Romanian Orthodox 70%, Roman Catholic 6%, Protestant 6%, Greek Catholic 3%, other 15%
ETHNIC MIX: Romanian 89%, Hungarian 8%, other (inc. Gypsy) 3%
GOVERNMENT: Multiparty republic
CURRENCY: Leu = 100 bani

MOLDOVA

SMALLEST AND most densely populated of the ex-Soviet republics, Moldova has strong linguistic and cultural links with Romania to the west.

GEOGRAPHY
Steppes and hilly plains, drained by Dniester and Prut rivers.

CLIMATE
Warm summers and relatively mild winters. Moderate rainfall, evenly spread throughout the year.

PEOPLE AND SOCIETY
Shared heritage with Romania defines national identity, although in 1994 Moldovans voted against possible unification with Romania. Most of the population is engaged in intensive agriculture. The 1994 constitution granted special autonomous status to the Gagauz people in the south (Orthodox Christian Turks), and to the Slav peoples on the east bank of the River Dniester.

$ THE ECONOMY
Well-developed agricultural sector: wine, tobacco, cotton, food processing. Light manufacturing. Progress in establishing markets for exports. High unemployment.

◆ INSIGHT: Moldova's vast underground wine vaults contain entire "streets" of bottles built into rock quarries

---

FACT FILE

OFFICIAL NAME: Republic of Moldova
DATE OF FORMATION: 1991
CAPITAL: Chișinău
POPULATION: 4.4 million
TOTAL AREA: 13,000 sq miles (33,700 sq km)
DENSITY: 338 people per sq mile

LANGUAGES: Moldovan*, Russian
RELIGIONS: Romanian Orthodox 98%, Jewish 1%, other 1%
ETHNIC MIX: Moldovan (Romanian) 65%, Ukrainian 14%, Russian 13%, Gagauz 4%, other 4%
GOVERNMENT: Multiparty republic
CURRENCY: Leu = 100 bani

BELARUS

FORMERLY KNOWN as White Russia, Belarus lies landlocked in Eastern Europe. It reluctantly became independent of the USSR in 1991.

GEOGRAPHY
Mainly plains and low hills. Dnieper and Dvina rivers drain eastern lowlands. Vast Pripet Marshes in the southwest.

CLIMATE
Extreme continental climate. Long, subfreezing, but mainly dry winters, and hot summers.

PEOPLE AND SOCIETY
Only 2% of people are non-Slav; ethnic tension is minimal. Entire population have right to citizenship, although only 11% are fluent in Belarussian. Slowest of the ex-Soviet states to implement political reform, a post-Soviet constitution not adopted until 1994. Wealth is held by a small ex-communist elite. Fallout from 1986 Chornobil' nuclear disaster in Ukraine seriously affected Bela-russians' health and environment.

THE ECONOMY
Food processing and heavy industries stagnate while politician argue over market reforms. Low unemployment but high inflation.

◆ *INSIGHT: The number of cancer an leukemia cases is 10,000 above the pre Chornobil' annual average*

FACT FILE	
OFFICIAL NAME: Republic of Belarus	LANGUAGES: Belarussian*, Russian
DATE OF FORMATION: 1991	RELIGIONS: Russian Orthodox 60%, Catholic 8%, other (inc. Uniate, Protestant, Muslim, Jewish) 32%
CAPITAL: Minsk	ETHNIC MIX: Belarussian 78%, Russian 13%, Polish 4%, other 5%
POPULATION: 10.3 million	
TOTAL AREA: 80,154 sq miles (207,600 sq km)	GOVERNMENT: Multiparty republic
DENSITY: 127 people per sq mile	CURRENCY: Rouble = 100 kopeks

UKRAINE

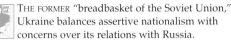

THE FORMER "breadbasket of the Soviet Union," Ukraine balances assertive nationalism with concerns over its relations with Russia.

GEOGRAPHY
Mainly fertile steppes and forests. Carpathian Mountains in southwest, Crimean chain in south. Pripet Marshes in northwest.

CLIMATE
Mainly continental climate, with distinct seasons. Southern Crimea has Mediterranean climate.

PEOPLE AND SOCIETY
Over 90% of the population in western Ukraine is Ukrainian. However, in several cities in the east and south, Russians form a majority. In the Crimea, the Tartars comprise around 10% of the population. At independence in 1991, most Russians accepted Ukrainian sovereignty. However, tensions are now rising as both groups adopt more extremist nationalist policies.

THE ECONOMY
Hyperinflation, corruption, and hostility from economic elite stifle any reforms. Heavy industries and agriculture largely unchanged since independence.

◆ INSIGHT: *The name Ukraine means "frontier," a reference to the country's position along the Russian border*

FACT FILE

OFFICIAL NAME: Ukraine
DATE OF FORMATION: 1991
CAPITAL: Kiev
POPULATION: 52.2 million
TOTAL AREA: 223,090 sq miles
(603,700 sq km)
DENSITY: 233 people per sq mile

LANGUAGES: Ukrainian*, Russian, Tartar
RELIGIONS: Mostly Ukrainian Orthodox, with Roman Catholic, Protestant and Jewish minorities
ETHNIC MIX: Ukrainian 73%, Russian 22%, other (inc. Tartar) 5%
GOVERNMENT: Multiparty republic
CURRENCY: Karbovanets (coupons)

RUSSIAN FEDERATION

 STILL THE world's largest state, despite the break-up of the USSR in 1991, the Russian Federation is struggling to capitalize on its diversity.

GEOGRAPHY
Ural Mountains divide European steppes and forests from tundra and forests of Siberia. South-central deserts and mountains.

CLIMATE
Continental in European Russia. Elsewhere from subarctic to Mediterranean and hot desert.

PEOPLE AND SOCIETY
Ethnic Russians now make up 80% of the population, but there are many minority groups. 57 nationalities have territorial status, a further 95 lack their own territory. 1994 war with Chechnya indicated potential for ethnic crisis. Wealth disparities, rising crime, and black market activities have accompanied reforms. Extremist politicians have exploited standard-of-living and ethnic concerns. Strong resurgence of religious practice since late 1980s.

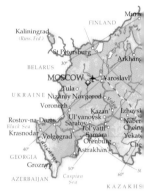

◆ *INSIGHT: The Trans-Siberian railroad, which runs 5,800 miles (9,335 km) from Moscow to Vladivostok, is the world's longest. It crosses seven time zones*

FACT FILE

OFFICIAL NAME: Russian Federation
DATE OF FORMATION: 1991
CAPITAL: Moscow
POPULATION: 149.2 million
TOTAL AREA: 6,592,800 sq miles (17,075,400 sq km)

DENSITY: 5 people per sq mile
LANGUAGES: Russian*, other
RELIGIONS: Russian Orthodox 80%, other (inc. Jewish, Muslim) 20%
ETHNIC MIX: Russian 80%, Tatar 4%, Ukrainian 3%, other 13%
GOVERNMENT: Multiparty republic
CURRENCY: Rouble = 100 kopeks

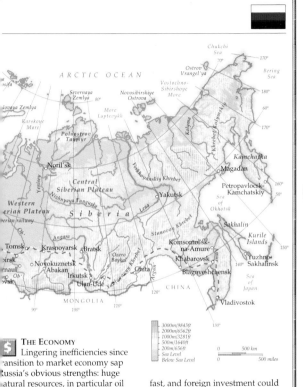

THE ECONOMY

Lingering inefficiencies since transition to market economy sap Russia's obvious strengths: huge natural resources, in particular oil and gas, precious metals, timber, and hydrocarbons. Enormous engineering and scientific base. Privatization, which is proceeding fast, and foreign investment could transform industry and agriculture. Many of the skills developed under communism are not relevant in a competitive economy.

159

ASIA

THE LARGEST, highest, and most populous
continent in the world, Asia is separated from
Africa by the Red Sea and bounded in the north
by the Arctic Ocean. In the extreme north, both
land and sea are frozen for most of the year.
Asia's great central mass of mountains and
plateaus, including the highest in the world –
the Himalayas – forms a barrier between North
and South Asia. Vast alluvial plains border its
major rivers: the Ganges, Ob, Mekong, Chang
Jiang (Yangtze), and Yellow Rivers. Asia has
important mineral resources, particularly the
oil and natural gas deposits of the Arab states.

CONTINENTAL FACTS

HIGHEST POINT:
Mt. Everest, Nepal
29,029 ft (8,848 m)

LOWEST POINT:
Dead Sea
About half of Bangladesh
lies between sea level
and 25 ft (8 m)

LARGEST LAKE:
Caspian Sea
143,205 sq miles
(371,000 sq km)

LONGEST RIVER:
Chang Jiang (Yangtze),
China 3,965 miles
(6,380 km)

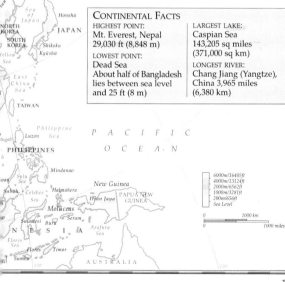

6000m/16405ft	
4000m/13124ft	
2000m/6562ft	
1000m/3281ft	
200m/656ft	
Sea Level	

0   1000 km

0   1000 miles

AZERBAIJAN

SITUATED ON the western coast of the Caspian Sea, Azerbaijan was the first Soviet republic to declare independence from Moscow in 1991.

 GEOGRAPHY
Caucasus Mountains in west, including Naxçivan enclave in south of Armenia. Flat, low-lying terrain on the coast of the Caspian Sea.

 CLIMATE
Continental with pronounced seasonal extremes. Low rainfall, with peak months during summer.

PEOPLE AND SOCIETY
Azerbaijanis now form a large majority. Thousands of Armenians, Russians, and Jews have left as a result of rising nationalism among Azerbaijanis. Racial hostility against those who remain is increasing. Influx of half a million Azerbaijani refugees fleeing war with Armenia over the disputed enclave of Nagorno Karabakh. Once-effective social security system has collapsed.

THE ECONOMY
Oil and gas have considerable potential. War is a major drain on state resources. Market reforms attract foreign interest.

◆ *INSIGHT: The fire-worshipping Zoroastrian faith originated in Azerbaijan in the 6th century B.C.*

FACT FILE

OFFICIAL NAME: Republic of Azerbaijan
DATE OF FORMATION: 1991
CAPITAL: Baku
POPULATION: 7.3 million
TOTAL AREA: 33,436 sq miles (86,600 sq km)
DENSITY: 218 people per sq mile

LANGUAGES: Azerbaijani*, Russian, Armenian, other
RELIGIONS: Muslim 83%, Armenian Apostolic , Russian Orthodox 17%
ETHNIC MIX: Azerbaijani 83%, Russian 6%, Armenian 6%, other 5%
GOVERNMENT: Multiparty republic
CURRENCY: Manat = 100 gopik

ARMENIA

SMALLEST OF the former USSR's republics, Armenia lies in the Lesser Caucasus Mountains. Since 1988, it has been at war with Azerbaijan.

GEOGRAPHY
Rugged and mountainous, with expanses of semidesert and a large lake in the east, Sevana Lich.

CLIMATE
Continental climate, little rainfall in the lowlands. Winters are often bitterly cold.

PEOPLE AND SOCIETY
Strong commitment to Christianity, and to Armenian culture. Minority groups are well integrated. War with Azerbaijan over the enclave of Nagorno Karabakh has meant 100,000 Armenians living in Azerbaijan forced to return home to live in poverty. In 1988, 25,000 people died in an earthquake in the west.

$ THE ECONOMY
Few natural resources, though lead, copper, and zinc are mined. Main agricultural products are wine, tobacco, olives, and rice. Well-developed machine-building and manufacturing – includes textiles and bottling of mineral water.

◆ INSIGHT: In the 4th century, Armenia became the first country to adopt Christianity as its state religion

FACT FILE	LANGUAGES: Armenian*, Azerbaijani, Russian, Kurdish
OFFICIAL NAME: Republic of Armenia	RELIGIONS: Armenian Apostolic 90%, other Christian and Muslim 10%
DATE OF FORMATION: 1991	ETHNIC MIX: Armenian 93%,
CAPITAL: Yerevan	Azerbaijani 3%, Russian, Kurdish 4%
POPULATION: 3.6 million	GOVERNMENT: Multiparty republic
TOTAL AREA: 11,505 sq miles (29,000 sq km)	CURRENCY: Dram = 100 Iouma
DENSITY: 312 people per sq mile	

TURKEY

LYING PARTLY in Europe, but mostly in Asia, Turkey's position gives it significant influence i the Mediterranean, Black Sea and Middle East.

GEOGRAPHY
Asian Turkey (Anatolia) is dominated by two mountain ranges, separated by a high, semidesert plateau. Coastal regions are fertile.

CLIMATE
Coast has a Mediterranean climate. Interior has cold, snowy winters and hot, dry summers.

PEOPLE AND SOCIETY
The Turks are racially diverse. Many are refugees or descendants of refugees, often from the Balkans or other territories once under Russian rule. However, the sense of national identity is strong. Since 1984, southeastern region has been the scene of a civil war waged by the Kurdish minority, demanding their rights within the country.

THE ECONOMY
Since the early 1980s, textiles manufacturing, and construction sectors all booming. Tourism is als a major foreign currency earner.

◆ INSIGHT: Turkey had two of the seven wonders of the ancient world: the tomb of King Mausolus at Halicarnassus (now Bodrum), and the temple of Artemis at Ephesus

FACT FILE

OFFICIAL NAME: Republic of Turkey
DATE OF FORMATION: 1923/1939
CAPITAL: Ankara
POPULATION: 63.1 million
TOTAL AREA: 300,950 sq miles (779,450 sq km)

DENSITY: 210 people per sq mile
LANGUAGES: Turkish*, Kurdish, Arabic, Circassian, Armenian
RELIGIONS: Muslim 99%, other 1%
ETHNIC MIX: Turkish 80%, Kurdish 17%, other 3%
GOVERNMENT: Multiparty republic
CURRENCY: Turkish lira = 100 krural

GEORGIA

LOCATED ON the eastern shore of the Black Sea, Georgia has been torn by civil war since achieving independence from the USSR in 1991.

GEOGRAPHY
Kura valley lies between Caucasus Mountains in the north and Lesser Caucasus range in south. Lowlands along the Black Sea coast.

CLIMATE
Subtropical along the coast, changing to continental extremes at high altitudes. Rainfall is moderate.

PEOPLE AND SOCIETY
Paternalistic society, with strong family, cultural, and literary traditions. Georgians are the majority group. An uneasy truce has followed 1990–1993 civil war, and the political scene remains volatile. In 1994, another civil war was fought, as ethnic Abkhazians attempted to secede from Georgia. Around one in five Georgians live in poverty, but a small, wealthy elite is found in the capital.

THE ECONOMY
Food processing and wine production are the main industries. Economy has broken down due to war and severance of links with other former Soviet republics.

◆ INSIGHT: *Western Georgia was the land of the legendary Golden Fleece of Greek mythology*

3000m/9843ft
2000m/6562ft
1000m/3281ft
500m/1640ft
200m/656ft
Sea Level

0   100 km
0   100 miles

FACT FILE
OFFICIAL NAME: Republic of Georgia
DATE OF FORMATION: 1991
CAPITAL: Tbilisi
POPULATION: 5.5 million
TOTAL AREA: 26,911 sq miles
(69,700 sq km)
DENSITY: 205 people per sq mile

LANGUAGES: Georgian*, Russian, other
RELIGIONS: Georgian Orthodox 70%,
Russian Orthodox 10%, other 20%
ETHNIC MIX: Georgian 69%,
Armenian 9%, Russian 6%,
Azerbaijani 5%, other 11%
GOVERNMENT: Republic
CURRENCY: Coupons

LEBANON

LEBANON IS dwarfed by its two powerful neighbors, Syria and Israel. The country is rebuilding after 14 years of civil war.

1989

GEOGRAPHY
Behind a narrow coastal plain, two parallel mountain ranges run the length of the country, separated by the fertile El Beqaa valley.

CLIMATE
Hot summers, with high humidity on the coast. Mild winters.

PEOPLE AND SOCIETY
Population is split between Christians and Muslims. Although in the minority, Christians have been the traditional rulers. In 1975, civil war broke out between the two groups. A settlement, which gave the Muslims more power, was reached in 1989. Elections in 1992 brought greater hope of stability. A huge gulf exists between the poor and a small, immensely rich elite.

◆ *INSIGHT: The Cedar of Lebanon has been the nation's symbol for 2,000 years*

THE ECONOMY
Infrastructure wrecked by civil war. Postwar opportunity to regain position as Arab center for banking and services. Potentially a major producer of wine and fruit.

3000m/9843ft	
2000m/6562ft	
1000m/3281ft	
500m/1640ft	
200m/656ft	
Sea Level	

FACT FILE
OFFICIAL NAME: Republic of Lebanon
DATE OF FORMATION: 1944
CAPITAL: Beirut
POPULATION: 2.9 million
TOTAL AREA: 4,015 sq miles (10,400 sq km)
DENSITY: 712 people per sq mile

LANGUAGES: Arabic*, French, Armenian, English
RELIGIONS: Muslim (mainly Shi'a) 57%, Christian (mainly Maronite) 43%
ETHNIC MIX: Arab 93% (Lebanese 83%, Palestinian 10%), other 7%
GOVERNMENT: Multiparty republic
CURRENCY: Pound = 100 piastres

SYRIA

STRETCHING FROM the eastern Mediterranean to the River Tigris, Syria's borders were created on its independence from France in 1946.

 GEOGRAPHY
Northern coastal plain is backed by a low range of hills. The River Euphrates cuts through a vast interior desert plateau.

CLIMATE
Mediterranean coastal climate. Inland areas are arid. In winter, snow is common on the mountains.

 PEOPLE AND SOCIETY
Most Syrians live near the coast, where the biggest cities are sited. 90% are Muslim, including the politically dominant Alawis. In the north and west are groups of Kurds, Armenians, and Turkish-speaking peoples. Some 300,000 Palestinian refugees have also settled in Syria. They, together with the urban unemployed, make up the poorest groups in a growing gulf between rich and poor.

THE ECONOMY
High defense spending is major drain on economy. Exporter of crude oil. Agriculture is thriving: crops include cotton, wheat, olives.

◆ *INSIGHT: Aramaic, the language of the Bible, is still spoken in two villages in Syria*

FACT FILE

OFFICIAL NAME: Syrian Arab Republic
DATE OF FORMATION: 1946
CAPITAL: Damascus
POPULATION: 13.8 million
TOTAL AREA: 71,500 sq miles (185,180 sq km)

DENSITY: 187 people per sq mile
LANGUAGES: Arabic*, French, Kurdish, Armenian, Circassian, Aramaic
RELIGIONS: Sunni Muslim 74%, other Muslim 16%, Christian 10%
ETHNIC MIX: Arab 90%, other 10%
GOVERNMENT: Single-party republic
CURRENCY: Pound = 100 piastres

CYPRUS

CYPRUS LIES in the eastern Mediterranean. Since 1974, it has been partitioned between the Turkish-occupied north and the Greek south.

 GEOGRAPHY
Mountains in the center-west give way to a fertile plain in the east, flanked by hills to the northeast.

 CLIMATE
Mediterranean. Summers are hot and dry. Winters are mild, with snow in the mountains.

PEOPLE AND SOCIETY
Majority of the population is Greek Christian. Since the 16th century, a minority community of Turkish Muslims has lived in the north of the island. In 1974 Turkish troops occupied the north, which was proclaimed the Turkish Republic of Northern Cyprus, but is recognized only by Turkey. The north remains poor, while the south, where the tourist industry is booming, is richer.

THE ECONOMY
In the south, tourism is the key industry. Shipping and light manufacturing also important. In the north, the main exports are citrus fruits and live animals.

◆ INSIGHT: *The buffer zone that divides Cyprus is manned by UN forces, at an estimated cost of $100m a year*

FACT FILE

OFFICIAL NAME: Republic of Cyprus
DATE OF FORMATION: 1960/1983
CAPITAL: Nicosia
POPULATION: 700,000
TOTAL AREA: 3,572 sq miles
(9,251 sq km)

DENSITY: 198 people per sq mile
LANGUAGES: Greek*, Turkish, other
RELIGIONS: Greek Orthodox 77%, Muslim 18%, other 5%
ETHNIC MIX: Greek 77%, Turkish 18%, other (mostly British) 5%
GOVERNMENT: Multiparty republic
CURRENCY: Cypriot £/Turkish lira

ISRAEL

CREATED AS a new state in 1948, on the east coast of the Mediterranean. Following wars with its Arab neighbors, it has extended its boundaries.

 GEOGRAPHY
Coastal plain. Desert in the south. In the east lie the Great Rift Valley and the Dead Sea – the lowest point on the Earth's surface.

CLIMATE
Summers are hot and dry. Wet season, March–November, is mild.

 PEOPLE AND SOCIETY
Large numbers of Jews settled in Palestine before Israel was founded. After World War II there was a huge increase in immigration. Sephardi Jews from the Middle East and Mediterranean are now in the majority, but Ashkenazi Jews from Central Europe still dominate politics and business. Palestinians in Gaza and Jericho gained limited autonomy in 1994.

◆ INSIGHT: *All Jews worldwide have the right of Israeli citizenship*

THE ECONOMY
Huge potential of industrial, agricultural, and manufacturing products. Major exporter of mineral salts. Important banking sector.

The West Bank, Gaza Strip and Golan Heights have been occupied by Israel since the Six Day War in 1967

Palestinians gained limited home rule of the Gaza Strip and Jericho in 1994

1000m/3281ft
500m/1640ft
200m/656ft
Sea Level
Below Sea Level

0   50 km
0   50 miles

FACT FILE
OFFICIAL NAME: State of Israel
DATE OF FORMATION: 1948/1982
CAPITAL: Jerusalem
POPULATION: 5.4 million
TOTAL AREA: 7,992 sq miles
(20,700 sq km)
DENSITY: 653 people per sq mile

LANGUAGES: Hebrew*, Arabic, Yiddish, German, Russian, Polish, Romanian, Persian, English
RELIGIONS: Jewish 83%, Muslim 13%, Christian 2%, other 2%
ETHNIC MIX: Jewish 83%, Arab 17%
GOVERNMENT: Multiparty republic
CURRENCY: New shekel = 100 agorat

JORDAN

THE KINGDOM of Jordan lies east of Israel. In 1993 King Hussein responded to calls for greater democracy by agreeing to multiparty elections.

GEOGRAPHY
Mostly desert plateaus, with occasional saltpans. Lowest parts lie along eastern shore of Dead Sea and East Bank of the River Jordan.

CLIMATE
Hot, dry summers. Cool, wet winters. Areas below sea level very hot in summer, and warm in winter.

PEOPLE AND SOCIETY
A predominantly Muslim country with a strong national identity, Jordan's population has Bedouin roots. There is a Christian minority and a large Palestinian population who have moved to Jordan from Israeli-occupied territory. Jordan gave up its claim to the West Bank to the PLO in 1988. The monarchy's power base lies among the rural tribes, which also provide the backbone of the military.

THE ECONOMY
Phosphates, chemicals, and fertilizers are principal exports. Skilled, educated work force.

◆ INSIGHT: *King Hussein, who succeeded to the throne in 1952, is the longest-reigning Arab ruler*

FACT FILE
OFFICIAL NAME: Hashemite Kingdom of Jordan
DATE OF FORMATION: 1946/1976
CAPITAL: Amman
POPULATION: 4.4 million
TOTAL AREA: 34,440 sq miles (89,210 sq km)

DENSITY: 125 people per sq mile
LANGUAGES: Arabic*, other
RELIGIONS: Muslim 95%, Christian 5%
ETHNIC MIX: Arab 98% (Palestinian 49%), Armenian 1%, Circassian 1%
GOVERNMENT: Constitutional monarchy
CURRENCY: Dinar = 1,000 fils

SAUDI ARABIA

OCCUPYING MOST of the Arabian peninsula, the oil- and gas-rich kingdom of Saudi Arabia covers an area the size of Western Europe.

GEOGRAPHY
Mostly desert or semidesert plateau. Mountain ranges in the west run parallel to the Red Sea and drop steeply to a coastal plain.

CLIMATE
In summer, temperatures often soar above 118°F (48°C), but in winter they may fall below freezing. Rainfall is rare.

PEOPLE AND SOCIETY
Most Saudis are Sunni Muslims who follow the strictly orthodox *wahabi* interpretation of Islam and embrace *sharia* (Islamic law) in their daily lives. Women are obliged to wear the veil, cannot hold driver's licenses, and have no role in public life. The Al-Saud family have been absolutist rulers since 1932. With the support of the religious establishment, they control all political life.

THE ECONOMY
Vast oil and gas reserves. Other minerals include coal, iron, and gold. Most food is imported.

◆ *INSIGHT: Over two million Muslims a year make the* haj – *the pilgrimage to the holy city of Mecca*

| 2000m/6562ft |
| 1000m/3281ft |
| 500m/1640ft |
| 200m/656ft |
| Sea Level |

FACT FILE

OFFICIAL NAME: Kingdom of Saudi Arabia

DATE OF FORMATION: 1932 / 1981

CAPITAL: Riyadh

POPULATION: 16.5 million

TOTAL AREA: 829,995 sq miles (2,149,690 sq km)

DENSITY: 18 people per sq mile

LANGUAGES: Arabic*, other

RELIGIONS: Sunni Muslim 85%, Shi'a Muslim 14%, Christian 1%

ETHNIC MIX: Arab 90%, Yemeni 8%, other Arab 1%, other 1%

GOVERNMENT: Absolute monarchy

CURRENCY: Riyal = 100 malalah

YEMEN

LOCATED IN southern Arabia, Yemen was formerly two countries: a socialist regime in the south, and a republic in the north, which united in 1990.

 GEOGRAPHY
Mountainous north with fertile strip along the Red Sea. Arid desert and mountains in south and east.

CLIMATE
Desert climate, modified by altitude, which affects temperatures by as much as 54°F (12°C).

 PEOPLE AND SOCIETY
Yemenis are almost entirely of Arab and Bedouin descent. The majority are Sunni Muslims, of the Shafi sect. In rural areas and in the north, Islamic orthodoxy is strong and most women wear the veil. Tension continues to exist between the south, led by the cosmopolitan city of 'Adan, and the more conservative north. Clashes between their former armies escalated into a brief civil war in 1994.

THE ECONOMY
Poor economic development due to political instability. Large oil and gas reserves discovered in 1984. Agriculture is the largest employer.

◆ *INSIGHT: Al Mukha (Mokha) on the Red Sea gave its name to the first coffee beans to be exported to Europe in the 17th and 18th centuries*

| 3000m/9843ft |
| 2000m/6562ft |
| 1000m/3281ft |
| 500m/1640ft |
| 200m/656ft |
| Sea Level |

0   100 km
0   100 miles

FACT FILE

OFFICIAL NAME: Republic of Yemen
DATE OF FORMATION: 1990
CAPITAL: Sana
POPULATION: 13 million
TOTAL AREA: 203,849 sq miles (527,970 sq km)
DENSITY: 62 people per sq mile

LANGUAGES: Arabic*, other
RELIGIONS: Sunni Muslim 55%, Shi'a Muslim 42%, other 3%
ETHNIC MIX: Arab 95%, Afro-Arab 3%, South Asian, African, European 2%
GOVERNMENT: Multiparty republic
CURRENCY: Rial (North), Dinar (South) – both are legal currency

OMAN

SITUATED ON the eastern coast of the Arabian peninsula, Oman is the least developed of the Gulf states, despite modest oil exports.

 GEOGRAPHY
Mostly gravel desert, with mountains in the north and south. Some narrow fertile coastal strips.

 CLIMATE
Blistering heat in the north. Summer temperatures often climb above 110°F (44°C). Southern uplands receive rains June–September.

PEOPLE AND SOCIETY
Most Omanis still live on the land, especially in the south. The majority are Ibadi Muslims who follow an appointed leader, the Imam. Ibadism is not opposed to freedom for women, and a few women hold positions of authority. Baluchis from Pakistan are the largest group of foreign workers.

◆ INSIGHT: Until the late 1980s, Oman was closed to all but business or official visitors

THE ECONOMY
Oil accounts for most export revenue. Gas is set to eventually supplant oil. Other exports include fish, dates, limes, and coconuts.

FACT FILE

OFFICIAL NAME: Sultanate of Oman
DATE OF FORMATION: 1650 / 1951
CAPITAL: Muscat
POPULATION: 1.7 million
TOTAL AREA: 82,030 sq miles (212,460 sq km)
DENSITY: 21 people per sq mile

LANGUAGES: Arabic*, Baluchi, other
RELIGIONS: Ibadi Muslim 75%, other Muslim 11%, Hindu 14%
ETHNIC MIX: Arab 75%, Baluchi 15%, other (mainly South Asian) 10%
GOVERNMENT: Monarchy with Consultative Council
CURRENCY: Rial = 1,000 baizas

UNITED ARAB EMIRATES

BORDERING THE Persian Gulf on the northern coast of the Arabian peninsula is the United Arab Emirates, a federation of seven states.

GEOGRAPHY
Mostly flat, semiarid desert with sand dunes, saltpans, and occasional oases. Cities are watered by extensive irrigation systems.

CLIMATE
Summers are humid, despite minimal rainfall. Sand-laden *shamal* winds blow in winter and spring.

PEOPLE AND SOCIETY
People are mostly Sunni Muslims of Bedouin descent, and largely city-dwellers. In theory, women enjoy equal rights with men. Poverty is rare. Emirians make up only one fifth of the population. They are outnumbered by immigrants who arrived during 1970s oil boom. Western expatriates are permitted a virtually unrestricted lifestyle. Islamic fundamentalism, however, is a growing force among the young.

THE ECONOMY
Major exporter of oil and natural gas. Fish and shellfish are caught in the Persian Gulf, as well as oysters for their pearls. Most food and raw materials are imported

◆ INSIGHT: *At present levels of production, the country's crude oil reserves should last for over 100 years*

FACT FILE
OFFICIAL NAME: United Arab Emirates
DATE OF FORMATION: 1971
CAPITAL: Abu Dhabi
POPULATION: 1.7 million
TOTAL AREA: 32,278 sq miles
(83,600 sq km)
DENSITY: 52 people per sq mile

LANGUAGES: Arabic*, Farsi
(Persian), Urdu, Hindi, English
RELIGIONS: Sunni Muslim 77%,
Shi'a Muslim 19% other 4%
ETHNIC MIX: South Asian 50%, Emirian
19%, other Arab 23%, other 8%
GOVERNMENT: Federation of monarchs
CURRENCY: Dirham = 100 fils

QATAR

PROJECTING NORTH from the Arabian peninsula into the Persian Gulf, Qatar's reserves of oil and gas make it one of the region's wealthiest states.

GEOGRAPHY
Flat, semiarid desert with [sa]nd dunes and saltpans. Vegetation [li]mited to small patches of scrub.

CLIMATE
Hot and humid. Summer [te]mperatures soar to over 104°F [(4]0°C). Rainfall is rare.

PEOPLE AND SOCIETY
Only one in five Qataris is [n]ative-born. Most of the population [a]re guest workers from the Indian [su]bcontinent, Iran, and North [A]frica. Qataris were once nomadic [b]edouins, but since advent of oil [w]ealth, have become city-dwellers. [A]s a result, the north is dotted [w]ith abandoned villages. Political [an]d religious life is dominated by [th]e ruling Al-Thani family.

◆ INSIGHT: *There are over 700 [m]osques in the capital, Doha*

THE ECONOMY
Steady supply of crude oil and huge gas reserves, plus related industries. Economy is heavily dependent on foreign work force. All raw materials and most foods, except vegetables, are imported.

FACT FILE

OFFICIAL NAME: State of Qatar
DATE OF FORMATION: 1971
CAPITAL: Doha
POPULATION: 500,000
TOTAL AREA: 4,247 sq miles (11,000 sq km)
DENSITY: 117 people per sq mile

LANGUAGES: Arabic*, Farsi (Persian), Urdu, Hindi, English
RELIGIONS: Sunni Muslim 86%, Hindu 10%, Christian 4%
ETHNIC MIX: Arab 40%, South Asian 35%, Persian 12%, other 13%
GOVERNMENT: Absolute monarchy
CURRENCY: Riyal = 100 dirhams

BAHRAIN

BAHRAIN IS an archipelago of 33 islands between the Qatar peninsula and the Saudi Arabian mainland. Only three islands are inhabited.

GEOGRAPHY
All islands are low-lying. The largest, Bahrain Island, is mainly sandy plains and salt marshes.

CLIMATE
Summers are hot and humid. Winters are mild. Low rainfall.

PEOPLE AND SOCIETY
Largely Muslim population is divided between Shi'a majority and Sunni minority. Tensions between the two groups. Ruling Sunni class hold the best jobs in bureaucracy and business. Shi'ites tend to do menial work. Al-Khalifa family has ruled since 1783. Regime is autocratic and political dissent is not tolerated. Bahrain is the most liberal of the Gulf States. Women have access to education and jobs.

THE ECONOMY
Main exports are refined petroleum and aluminum products. As oil reserves run out, gas is of increasing importance. Bahrain is also the Arab world's major offshore banking center.

◆ INSIGHT: *Bahrain was the first Gulf emirate to export oil, in the 1930s*

FACT FILE
OFFICIAL NAME: State of Bahrain
DATE OF FORMATION: 1971
CAPITAL: Manama
POPULATION: 500,000
TOTAL AREA: 263 sq miles (680 sq km)
DENSITY: 1,911 people per sq mile

LANGUAGES: Arabic*, English, Urdu
RELIGIONS: Muslim (Shi'a majority) 85%, Christian 7%, other 8%
ETHNIC MIX: Arab 73%, South Asian 14%, Persian 8%, other 5%
GOVERNMENT: Absolute monarchy (emirate)
CURRENCY: Dinar = 1,000 fils

KUWAIT

KUWAIT LIES on the north of the Persian Gulf. The state was a British protectorate from 1914 until 1961, when full independence was granted.

 GEOGRAPHY
Low-lying desert. Lowest land in the north. Cultivation is only possible along the coast.

CLIMATE
Summers are very hot and dry. Winters are cooler, with some rain and occasional frost.

 PEOPLE AND SOCIETY
Oil-rich monarchy, ruled by the Al-Sabah family. Oil wealth has attracted workers from India, Pakistan, and other Arab states. In 1990, Iraq invaded Kuwait, claiming it as a province. A US-led alliance, backed by the UN, ousted Iraqi forces following a short war in 1991. Many foreign workers expelled after the war, in attempt to ensure Kuwaiti majority.

THE ECONOMY
Oil and gas production has been restored to pre-invasion levels. Skilled labor, raw materials, and food have to be imported. Vulnerability to Iraqi attack deters Western industrial investment.

INSIGHT: During the Gulf War, 800 of Kuwait's 950 oil wells were damaged

FACT FILE

OFFICIAL NAME: State of Kuwait
DATE OF FORMATION: 1961/1981
CAPITAL: Kuwait City
POPULATION: 1.8 million
TOTAL AREA: 6,880 sq miles (17,820 sq km)
DENSITY: 291 people per sq mile

LANGUAGES: Arabic*, English, other
RELIGIONS: Muslim 92%, Christian 6%, other 2%
ETHNIC MIX: Arab 85%, South Asian 9%, Persian 4%, other 2%
GOVERNMENT: Constitutional monarchy
CURRENCY: Dinar = 1,000 fils

IRAQ

IRAQ IS situated in the central Middle East. Since the removal of the monarchy in 1958, it has experienced considerable political turmoil.

GEOGRAPHY
Mainly desert. Rivers Tigris and Euphrates water fertile regions and create southern marshland. Mountains along northeast border.

CLIMATE
South has hot, dry summers and mild winters. North has dry summers, but winters can be harsh in the mountains. Rainfall is low.

PEOPLE AND SOCIETY
Population mainly Arab and Kurdish. Small minorities of Turks and Persians. After coming to power in 1979, President Saddam Hussein led the country into an inconclusive war with Iran (1980–1988). In 1990, invasion of Kuwait precipitated the Gulf War against UN forces. In recent years, drainage schemes in the southern marshlands have threatened the ancient and unique lifestyle of the Marsh Arabs.

THE ECONOMY
Gulf War and resulting UN sanctions had a devastating effect Iraq is unable to sell its oil on the international market.

◆ INSIGHT: As Mesopotamia, Iraq wa the site where the Sumerians establish the world's first civilization c. 4,000 B.c.

3000m/9843ft	
2000m/6562ft	
1000m/3281ft	
500m/1640ft	
200m/656ft	
Sea Level	

FACT FILE
OFFICIAL NAME: Republic of Iraq
DATE OF FORMATION: 1932/1981
CAPITAL: Baghdad
POPULATION: 21 million
TOTAL AREA: 169,235 sq miles (438,320 sq km)
DENSITY: 125 people per sq mile

LANGUAGES: Arabic*, Kurdish, Turkish, Farsi (Persian)
RELIGIONS: Shi'a Muslim 63%, Sunni Muslim 34%, other 3%
ETHNIC MIX: Arab 79%, Kurdish 16%, Persian 3%, Turkish 2%
GOVERNMENT: Single-party republic
CURRENCY: Dinar = 1,000 fils

RAN

SINCE THE 1979 revolution led by Ayatollah Khomeini, the Middle Eastern country of Iran has become the world's largest theocracy.

GEOGRAPHY
High desert plateau with large saltpans in the east. West and north are mountainous. Fertile coastal land borders Caspian Sea.

CLIMATE
Mostly desert climate. Hot summers, and bitterly cold winters. Area around the Caspian Sea is more temperate.

PEOPLE AND SOCIETY
Many ethnic groups, including Persians, Azerbaijanis, and Kurds. Large number of refugees, mainly from Afghanistan. Since 1979 Islamic revolution, political life has been dominated by militant Islamic idealism. Mullahs' belief that adherence to religious values is more important than economic welfare has resulted in declining living standards. The role of women in public life is restricted.

THE ECONOMY
One of the world's biggest oil producers. Government restricts contact with the West, blocking acquisition of vital technology. High unemployment and inflation.

◆ INSIGHT: *In Iran, a total of 109 offenses carry the death penalty*

3000m/9843ft	
2000m/6562ft	
1000m/3281ft	
500m/1640ft	
200m/656ft	
Sea Level	

0   200 km

0   200 miles

FACT FILE
OFFICIAL NAME: Islamic Republic of Iran
DATE OF FORMATION: 1906
CAPITAL: Tehran
POPULATION: 68.7 million
TOTAL AREA: 636,293 sq miles (1,648,000 sq km)

DENSITY: 108 people per sq mile
LANGUAGES: Farsi (Persian)*, other
RELIGIONS: Shi'a Muslim 95%, Sunni Muslim 4%, other 1%
ETHNIC MIX: Persian 52%, Azerbaijani 24%, Kurdish 9%, other 15%
GOVERNMENT: Islamic republic
CURRENCY: Rial = 100 dinars

TURKMENISTAN

STRETCHING FROM the Caspian Sea into the desert of Central Asia, the ex-Soviet state of Turkmenista has adjusted better than most to independence.

GEOGRAPHY

Low Karakumy desert covers 80% of the country. Mountains on southern border with Iran. Fertile Amu Darya valley in north.

CLIMATE
Arid desert climate with extreme summer heat, but sub-freezing winter temperatures.

PEOPLE AND SOCIETY
Before Czarist Russia annexed the country in 1884, the Turkmen were a largely nomadic tribal people. Today, the tribal unit remains strong, with most of the population clustered around desert oases. Generally peaceful relations between Turkmen and Uzbek and Russian minorities. Resurgence of Islam fosters ties with its Muslim neighbors to the south.

THE ECONOMY
Abundant reserves of natural gas. Least industrialized of the ex-Soviet states. Large cotton crop, bu most food has to be imported.

◆ INSIGHT: Ashgabat is a breeding cent for the Akhal-Teke, a prized race horse able to maintain its speed in the desert

FACT FILE

OFFICIAL NAME: Republic of Turkmenistan
DATE OF FORMATION: 1991
CAPITAL: Ashgabat
POPULATION: 4 million
TOTAL AREA: 188,455 sq miles (488,100 sq km)

DENSITY: 21 people per sq mile
LANGUAGES: Turkmen*, Uzbek, other
RELIGIONS: Muslim 85%, Eastern Orthodox 10%, other 5%
ETHNIC MIX: Turkmen 72%, Russian 9%, Uzbek 9%, other 10%
GOVERNMENT: Single-party republic
CURRENCY: Manat = 100 tenge

UZBEKISTAN

SHARING THE Aral Sea coastline with its northern neighbor, Kazakhstan, Uzbekistan lies on the ancient Silk Road between Asia and Europe.

GEOGRAPHY
Arid and semi-arid plains much of the west. Fertile, irrigated eastern farmland below peaks of the western Pamirs.

CLIMATE
Harsh continental climate. Summers can be extremely hot and dry, winters are cold.

PEOPLE AND SOCIETY
Complex ethnic make-up, with potential for racial and regional conflict. Ex-communists are in firm control, but traditional social patterns based on family, religion, clan, and region have reemerged. Population is concentrated in the fertile east. High birth rates, continued low status of women. Constitutional measures aim to control influence of Islam.

THE ECONOMY
Strong agricultural sector, led by cotton production. Large unexploited deposits of oil and natural gas, gold, and uranium. Very limited economic reform.

◆ INSIGHT: *The Aral Sea has shrunk to half of the area it covered in 1960, due to diversion of rivers for irrigation*

FACT FILE
OFFICIAL NAME: Republic of Uzbekistan

DATE OF FORMATION: 1991

CAPITAL: Tashkent

POPULATION: 21.9 million

TOTAL AREA: 439,733 sq miles (1,138,910 sq km)

DENSITY: 122 people per sq mile

LANGUAGES: Uzbek*, Russian, other

RELIGIONS: Muslim 88%, other (mostly Eastern Orthodox) 12%

ETHNIC MIX: Uzbek 71%, Russian 8%, Tajik 5%, Kazakh 4%, other 12%

GOVERNMENT: Single-party republic

CURRENCY: Sum = 100 teen

KAZAKHSTAN

LARGEST OF the former Soviet republics, mineral-rich Kazakhstan has the potential to become the major Central Asian economic power.

GEOGRAPHY
Mainly steppe. Volga delta and Caspian Sea in the west. Central plateau. Mountains in the east. Semidesert in the south.

CLIMATE
Dry continental. Hottest summers in desert south, coldest winters in northern steppes.

PEOPLE AND SOCIETY
Kazakhs only just outnumber Russians in a multiethnic society. Stable relations with Russia, plus increased international profile, preserve relative harmony. Few Kazakhs maintain a nomadic lifestyle, but Islam and loyalty to the three Hordes (clan federations) remain strong. Wealth is concentrated among former communists in the capital.

THE ECONOMY
Vast mineral resources, notably gas, oil, coal, uranium, and gold. Increasing foreign investment, but living standards have fallen with market reforms to date.

◆ *INSIGHT: Russia's space program was based at Baykonur, in the south*

FACT FILE

OFFICIAL NAME: Republic of Kazakhstan
DATE OF FORMATION: 1991
CAPITAL: Alma-Ata
POPULATION: 17.2 million
TOTAL AREA: 1,049,150 sq miles (2,717,300 sq km)

DENSITY: 16 people per sq mile
LANGUAGES: Kazakh*, Russian, other
RELIGIONS: Muslim 47%, other 53% (mostly Russian Orthodox, Lutheran)
ETHNIC MIX: Kazakh 40%, Russian 38%, Ukrainian 6%, other 16%
GOVERNMENT: Multiparty republic
CURRENCY: Tenge = 100 tein

MONGOLIA

LYING BETWEEN Russia and China, Mongolia is a vast and isolated country with a tiny population. Over two-thirds of the country is desert.

GEOGRAPHY
High steppe plateau, with mountains in the north. Lakes in the north and west. Desert region of the Gobi dominates the south.

CLIMATE
Continental. Mild summers, and long, dry, very cold winters, with heavy snowfall. Temperatures can drop to −30°C (−22°F).

PEOPLE AND SOCIETY
Mongolia was unified by Genghis Khan in 1206 and was later absorbed into Manchu China. It became a communist People's Republic in 1924, and after 66 years of Soviet-style communist rule, introduced democracy in 1990. Most Mongolians still follow a traditional nomadic way of life, living in circular felt tents called *gers*. Others live on state-run farms.

THE ECONOMY
Rich in oil, coal, copper, and other minerals, which were barely exploited under communism. In 1990s, some shift in agriculture away from traditional herding and toward a market economy.

◆ INSIGHT: *Horse-racing, wrestling, and archery are the national sports. During the* Nadam *festival each July, competitions are held all over Mongolia*

RUSSIAN FEDERATION

Ölgiy · Moron · Sühbaatar · Darhan
Hovd · Erdenet · ULAN BATOR · Kerulen · Choybalsan
Altay · Saynshand
Gobi · Dalandzadgad
CHINA

0 — 400 km
0 — 400 miles

3000m/9843ft
2000m/6562ft
1000m/3281ft
500m/1640ft

FACT FILE

OFFICIAL NAME: Mongolia
DATE OF FORMATION: 1924
CAPITAL: Ulan Bator
POPULATION: 2.4 million
TOTAL AREA: 604,247 sq miles
(1,565,000 sq km)
DENSITY: 3.6 people per sq mile

LANGUAGES: Khalkha Mongol*, Turkic, Russian, Chinese
RELIGIONS: Predominantly Tibetan Buddhist, with a Muslim minority
ETHNIC MIX: Khalkha Mongol 90%, Kazakh 4%, Chinese 2%, other 4%
GOVERNMENT: Multiparty republic
CURRENCY: Tughrik = 100 möngös

KYRGYZSTAN

A MOUNTAINOUS, landlocked state in Central Asia. The most rural of the ex-Soviet republics, it only gradually developed its own cultural nationalism.

GEOGRAPHY
Mountainous spurs of Tien Shan range have glaciers, alpine meadows, forests, and narrow valleys. Semi-desert in the west.

CLIMATE
Varies from permanent snow and cold deserts at altitude to hot deserts in low regions.

PEOPLE AND SOCIETY
Ethnic Kyrgyz majority status dates only from the late 1980s, and is due to their higher birth rate. Considerable tension between Kyrgyz and other groups, particularly Uzbeks. Large Russian community no longer wields power, but is seen as necessary for transfer of skills. Concerns over rising crime rate and opium poppy cultivation accompany political reforms.

THE ECONOMY
Still dominated by the state and tradition of collective farming. Small quantities of commercially exploitable coal, oil, and gas. Great hydroelectric power potential.

◆ INSIGHT: *Kyrgyz folklore is based around the 1,000-year-old epic poem, Manas, which takes a week to recite*

FACT FILE
OFFICIAL NAME: Kyrgyz Republic
DATE OF FORMATION: 1991
CAPITAL: Bishkek
POPULATION: 4.6 million
TOTAL AREA: 76,640 sq miles (198,500 sq km)
DENSITY: 60 people per sq mile

LANGUAGES: Kyrgyz*, Russian, Uzbek
RELIGIONS: Muslim 65%, other (mostly Russian Orthodox) 35%
ETHNIC MIX: Kyrgyz 52%, Russian 21%, Uzbek 13%, other (mostly Kazakh and Tajik) 14%
GOVERNMENT: Mutiparty republic
CURRENCY: Som = 100 teen

TAJIKISTAN

LIES LANDLOCKED on the western slopes of the
Pamirs in Central Asia. The Tajiks' language
and traditions are similiar to those of Iran.

GEOGRAPHY
Mainly mountainous: bare
slopes of Pamir ranges cover most
of the country. Small but fertile
Fergana Valley in northwest.

CLIMATE
Continental extremes in
valleys. Bitterly cold winters in
mountains. Low rainfall.

PEOPLE AND SOCIETY
Conflict between Tajiks,
Persian people, and
minority Uzbeks (of Turkic
origin), coupled with civil
war between supporters of
the government and Tajik
Islamic rebels. Despite a
ceasefire in late 1994, clashes
continued in 1995. Already
low living standards have
been worsened by the
conflict. Many Russians have
left to escape discrimination.

THE ECONOMY
Formal economy crippled
by conflict. All sectors in decline;
barter economy is widespread.
Uranium potential and hydroelectric schemes depend on peace.

◆ *INSIGHT: Carpet-making, an ancient
tradition learned from Persia, was a
major source of revenue before the war*

FACT FILE

OFFICIAL NAME: Republic
of Tajikistan
DATE OF FORMATION: 1991
CAPITAL: Dushanbe
POPULATION: 5.7 million
TOTAL AREA: 55,251 sq miles
(143,100 sq km)

DENSITY: 101 people per sq mile
LANGUAGES: Tajik*, Uzbek, Russian
RELIGIONS: Sunni Muslim 85%,
Shi'a Muslim 5%, other 10%
ETHNIC MIX: Tajik 62%, Uzbek 24%,
Russian 4%, Tartar 2%, other 8%
GOVERNMENT: Single-party republic
CURRENCY: Tajik rouble = 100 kopeks

AFGHANISTAN

LANDLOCKED IN southwestern Asia, about three quarters of Afghanistan is inaccessible. Civil war means the country effectively has no government

GEOGRAPHY
Predominantly mountainous. Highest range is the Hindu Kush. Mountains are bordered by fertile plains. Desert plateau in the south.

CLIMATE
Harsh continental. Hot, dry summers. Cold winters with heavy snow, especially in Hindu Kush.

PEOPLE AND SOCIETY
In 1979, Soviet forces invaded to support communist government against Islamic guerrillas. Last Soviet troops pulled out in 1989. Civil war continues between Pashtuns, the country's traditional rulers, and minority groups of Tajiks, Hazaras, and Uzbeks. Health and education systems have collapsed. Many Afghans are nomadic sheep farmers and most live in extreme poverty.

THE ECONOMY
Economy has collapsed. The largest sector, agriculture, has been damaged. Illicit opium trade is the main currency earner.

◆ INSIGHT: The UN estimates that it will take 100 years to remove the ten million landmines laid in the country

FACT FILE
OFFICIAL NAME: Islamic State of Afghanistan
DATE OF FORMATION: 1919
CAPITAL: Kābul
POPULATION: 20.5 million
TOTAL AREA: 251,770 sq miles (652,090 sq km)

DENSITY: 75 people per sq mile
LANGUAGES: Persian*, Pashtu*, other
RELIGIONS: Sunni Muslim 84%, Shi'a Muslim 15%, other 1%
ETHNIC MIX: Pashtun 38%, Tajik 25%, Hazara 19%, Uzbek 6%, other 12%
GOVERNMENT: Mujahideen coalition
CURRENCY: Afghani = 100 puls

PAKISTAN

ONCE A part of British India, Pakistan was created in 1947 as an independent Muslim state. Today, it is divided into four provinces.

GEOGRAPHY
East and south is great flood plain drained by River Indus. Hindu Kush range in north. West is semi-desert plateau and mountains.

CLIMATE
Temperatures can soar to 122°F (50°C) in south and west, and fall to −4°F (−20°C) in the Hindu Kush.

PEOPLE AND SOCIETY
Majority Punjabis control bureaucracy and the army. Many tensions with minority groups. Vast gap between rich and poor. Bonded laborers, often recent converts to Islam, or Christians, form the underclass. Strong family ties, reflected in dynastic and nepotistic political system.

► INSIGHT: In 1988, Pakistan elected the first female prime minister in the Muslim world

THE ECONOMY
Leading producer of cotton and rice, but unpredictable weather conditions often affect the crop. Oil, gas reserves. Inefficient, haphazard government economic policies.

5000m/16405ft
4000m/13124ft
3000m/9843ft
2000m/6562ft
1000m/3281ft
500m/1640ft
200m/656ft
Sea Level

CHINA

Hindu Kush

Karakoram Range

Khyber Pass

ISLĀMĀBĀD

Peshāwar
Rawalpindi
Sargodha
Faisalābād
Siālkot
Gujrānwāla
Lahore

AFGHANISTAN

Quetta

Punjab

Multān
Bahāwalpur

IRAN   Baluchistan

Sukkur

Thar Desert

INDIA

Sindh

Hyderābād

Karāchi

Arabian Sea

0   200 km

0   200 miles

FACT FILE

OFFICIAL NAME: Islamic Republic of Pakistan
DATE OF FORMATION: 1947 / 1972
CAPITAL: Islāmābād
POPULATION: 144.5 million
TOTAL AREA: 307,374 sq miles (796,100 sq km)

DENSITY: 470 people per sq mile
LANGUAGES: Urdu*, Punjabi, other
RELIGIONS: Sunni Muslim 77%, Shi'a Muslim 20%, Hindu 2%, Christian 1%
ETHNIC MIX: Punjabi 56%, Sindhi 13%, Pashtun 8%, other 23%
GOVERNMENT: Multiparty republic
CURRENCY: Rupee = 100 paisa

NEPAL

NEPAL LIES between India and China, on the shoulder of the southern Himalayan mountains. It is one of the world's poorest countries.

GEOGRAPHY
Mainly mountainous. Includes some of the highest mountains in the world, such as Mt. Everest. Flat, fertile river plains in the south.

CLIMATE
July–October warm monsoon. Rest of year dry, sunny, mild. Valley temperatures in Himalayas may average 14°F (–10°C).

PEOPLE AND SOCIETY
Few ethnic tensions, despite the variety of ethnic groups, including the Sherpas in the north, Terai peoples in the south, and the Newars, found mostly in the Kathmandu valley. Women's subordinate position enshrined in law. Hindu women are the most restricted. In 1991, first democratic elections for over 30 years ended period of absolute rule by the king.

THE ECONOMY
90% of the people work on the land. Crops include rice, corn and millet. Dependent on foreign aid. Tourism is growing. Great potential for hydroelectric power.

◆ *INSIGHT: Southern Nepal was the birthplace of Buddha (Prince Siddhartha Gautama) in 563 B.C*

FACT FILE
OFFICIAL NAME: Kingdom of Nepal
DATE OF FORMATION: 1769
CAPITAL: Kathmandu
POPULATION: 21.1 million
TOTAL AREA: 54,363 sq miles (140,800 sq km)
DENSITY: 388 people per sq mile

LANGUAGES: Nepali*, Maithilli, other
RELIGIONS: Hindu 90%, Buddhist 5%, Muslim 3%, other 2%
ETHNIC MIX: Nepalese 58%, Bihari 19%, Tamang 6%, other 17%
GOVERNMENT: Constitutional monarchy
CURRENCY: Rupee = 100 paisa

BHUTAN

PERCHED IN the eastern Himalayas between India and China, the landlocked kingdom of Bhutan is largely closed to the outside world.

GEOGRAPHY
Low, tropical southern strip rising through fertile central valleys to high Himalayas in the north. Two thirds of the land is forested.

CLIMATE
South is tropical, north is alpine, cold, and harsh. Central valleys warmer in east than west.

PEOPLE AND SOCIETY
The king is absolute monarch, head of both state and government. Most people originate from Tibet, and are devout Buddhists. 25% are Hindu Nepalese, who settled in the south. Bhutan has 20 languages. In 1988, Dzongkha (a Tibetan dialect) was made the official language and Nepali was banned. Many southerners deported as illegal immigrants, creating fierce ethnic tensions.

THE ECONOMY
Reliant upon aid from, and trade with, India. 80% of people farm their own plots of land and herd cattle and yaks. Development of cash crops for Asian markets.

◆ INSIGHT: TV is banned on the grounds that it might dilute Bhutanese values

5000m/16405ft
4000m/13124ft
3000m/9843ft
2000m/6562ft
1000m/3281ft
500m/1640ft
200m/656ft
Sea Level

FACT FILE

OFFICIAL NAME: Kingdom of Bhutan
DATE OF FORMATION: 1865
CAPITAL: Thimphu
POPULATION: 1.7 million
TOTAL AREA: 18,147 sq miles (47,000 sq km)
DENSITY: 93 people per sq mile

LANGUAGES: Dzongkha*, Nepali, other
RELIGIONS: Mahayana Buddhist 70%, Hindu 24%, Muslim 5%, other 1%
ETHNIC MIX: Bhutia 61%, Gurung 15%, Assamese 13%, other 11%
GOVERNMENT: Constitutional monarchy
CURRENCY: Ngultrum = 100 chetrum

INDIA

SEPARATED FROM the rest of Asia by the Himalaya mountain range, India forms a subcontinent. It is the world's second most populous country.

GEOGRAPHY
Three main regions: Himalayan mountains; northern plain between Himalayas and Vindhya Mountains; southern Deccan plateau. The Ghats are smaller mountain ranges on the east and west coasts.

CLIMATE
Varies greatly according to latitude, altitude, and season. Most of India has three seasons: hot, wet, and cool. In summer, the north is usually hotter than the south, with temperatures often over 104°F (40°C).

PEOPLE AND SOCIETY
Cultural and religious pressures encourage large families. Today, nationwide awareness campaigns aim to promote the idea of smaller families. Most Indians are Hindu. Each Hindu is born into one of thousands of castes and subcastes, which determine their future status and occupation. Middle class enjoys a very comfortable lifestyle, but at least 30% of Indians live in extreme poverty. In Bombay alone, over 100,000 people live on the streets.

◆ INSIGHT India's national animal, the tiger, was chosen by the Mohenjo-Daro civilization as its emblem, 4,000 years ago

PAKISTAN

25°

Rann
of
Gulf   Kachchh
of   Ahr
Kachchh   Jammagar

20°

5000m/16405ft
4000m/13124ft
3000m/9843ft
2000m/6562ft
1000m/3281ft
500m/1640ft
200m/656ft
Sea Level

A r a b i a n
S e a

0   200 km
0   200 miles

FACT FILE
OFFICIAL NAME: Republic of India
DATE OF FORMATION: 1947/1961
CAPITAL: New Delhi
POPULATION: 953 million
TOTAL AREA: 1,269,338 sq miles
(3,287,590 sq km)
DENSITY: 751 people per sq mile

LANGUAGES: Hindi*, English*, other
RELIGIONS: Hindu 83%, Muslim 11%,
Christian 2%, Sikh 2%, other 2%
ETHNIC MIX: Indo-Aryan 72%,
Dravidian 25%, Mongoloid
and other 3%
GOVERNMENT: Multiparty republic
CURRENCY: Rupee = 100 paisa

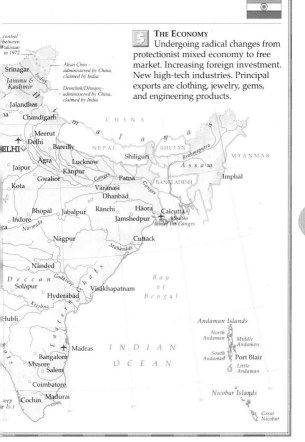

THE ECONOMY
Undergoing radical changes from protectionist mixed economy to free market. Increasing foreign investment. New high-tech industries. Principal exports are clothing, jewelry, gems, and engineering products.

'control' between Pakistan in 1972

Aksai Chin - administered by China, claimed by India

Demchok/Dêmqog - administered by China, claimed by India

Srinagar

Jammu & Kashmir

Jalandhar

Chandīgarh

CHINA

Meerut

Delhi

DELHI

Bareilly

NEPAL

BHUTAN

MYANMAR

Himalaya

Agra

Lucknow

Shiliguri

Assam

Brahmaputra

Jaipur

Kānpur

Ganges

Patna

BANGLADESH

Imphāl

Kota

Gwalior

Vārānasi

Dhanbād

Bhopāl

Jabalpur

Rānchi

Hāora

Calcutta

Indore

Narmada

Jamshedpur

Mouths of the Ganges

Nāgpur

Cuttack

Mahanādi

Nānded

Deccan

Godāvari

Bay of Bengal

Solāpur

Visākhapatnam

Hyderābād

Krishna

Hubli

Eastern Ghats

Madras

INDIAN

Bangalore

OCEAN

Mysore

Salem

Coimbatore

Cochin

Madurai

Andaman Islands

North Andaman

Middle Andaman

South Andaman

Port Blair

Little Andaman

Nicobar Islands

Great Nicobar

MALDIVES

MÁLDIVES · *India* · *Sri Lanka*

THE MALDIVES is an archipelago of 1,190 small coral islands set in the Indian Ocean, southwest of Sri Lanka. Only 202 islands are inhabited.

GEOGRAPHY
Low-lying islands and coral atolls. The larger ones are covered in lush, tropical vegetation.

CLIMATE
Tropical. Rain in all months, but heaviest June–November, during monsoon. Violent storms occasionally hit northern islands.

PEOPLE AND SOCIETY
Maldivians are descended from Sinhalese, Dravidian, Arab, and black ancestors. About 25% of the population, who are all Sunni Muslim, live on Male'. Tourism has grown in recent years, but resort islands are separate from settler islands. Politics is restricted to a small group of influential families, and is based around family and clan loyalties rather than formal parties. New young elite is pressing for a more liberal political system.

THE ECONOMY
Too dependent on fluctuating tourist industry, which is the economic mainstay. Fish, especially bonito and tuna, are the leading exports.

◆ INSIGHT: *Rising sea levels, brought about by global warming and climatic changes, are threatening to submerge the islands*

Ihavandip Atoll

Faadh Ae

Horsburgh Atoll

Ari Atoll

Mu A

Ma

F

Mu Ato

Kolhu Atoll

Hadhdhunmathi Atoll

One and Half Degree Cha

North Huva Atoll

Sou Huva Ato

INDIAN OCEAN

200m/656ft Sea Level

Equator

0   100 km
0   100 miles

73

Addu A
Gan

FACT FILE
OFFICIAL NAME: Republic of Maldives
DATE OF FORMATION: 1965
CAPITAL: Male'
POPULATION: 200,000
TOTAL AREA: 116 sq miles (300 sq km)

DENSITY: 1,734 people per sq mile
LANGUAGES: Dhivehi (Maldivian)*, Sinhala, Tamil
RELIGIONS: Sunni Muslim 100%
ETHNIC MIX: Maldivian 99%, Sinhalese and other South Asian 1%
GOVERNMENT: Republic
CURRENCY: Rufiyaa = 100 laari

SRI LANKA

SEPARATED FROM India by the narrow Palk Strait, Sri Lanka comprises one large island and several coral islets to the northwest.

 GEOGRAPHY
Main island is dominated by rugged central highlands. Fertile northern plains dissected by rivers. Much of the land is tropical jungle.

 CLIMATE
Tropical, with breezes on the coast and cooler air in highlands. Northeast is driest and hottest.

PEOPLE AND SOCIETY
Majority Sinhalese are mostly Buddhist; minority Tamils are mostly Muslim or Hindu. Since independence from Britain in 1948, Tamils have felt sidelined, and support for secession has grown. Long-standing tensions between the groups erupted into civil war in 1983. Tamils demand an independent state in the north and east.

◆ INSIGHT: *Sri Lanka elected the world's first woman prime minister in 1960*

THE ECONOMY
World's largest tea exporter. Manufacturing now accounts for 60% of export earnings. Civil war is a drain on government funds and deters investors and tourists.

FACT FILE
OFFICIAL NAME: Democratic Socialist Republic of Sri Lanka
DATE OF FORMATION: 1948
CAPITAL: Colombo
POPULATION: 17.9 million
TOTAL AREA: 25,332 sq miles (65,610 sq km)

DENSITY: 710 people per sq mile
LANGUAGES: Sinhala*, Tamil, English
RELIGIONS: Buddhist 70%, Hindu 15%, Christian 8%, Muslim 7%
ETHNIC MIX: Sinhalese 74%, Tamil 18%, Sri Lankan Moor 7%, other 1%
GOVERNMENT: Multiparty republic
CURRENCY: Rupee = 100 cents

BANGLADESH

BANGLADESH LIES at the north of the Bay of Bengal. It seceded from Pakistan in 1971 and, after much political instability, returned to democracy in 1991.

GEOGRAPHY
Mostly flat alluvial plains and deltas of the Brahmaputra and Ganges rivers. Southeast coasts are fringed with mangrove forests.

CLIMATE
Hot and humid. During the monsoon, water level can rise 20 feet (six meters) above sea level, flooding two thirds of the country.

PEOPLE AND SOCIETY
Bangladesh has suffered from a cycle of floods, cyclones, famine, political corruption, and military coups. Although 55% of people still live below the poverty line, living standards have improved in past decade. By providing independent income, textile trade is a factor in growing emancipation of women.

◆ *INSIGHT: Since 1960, there have been six cyclones with winds of over 100 mph*

THE ECONOMY
Heavily dependent on foreign aid. Agriculture is vulnerable to unpredictable climate. Bangladesh accounts for 80% of world jute fiber exports. Expanding textile industry.

FACT FILE

OFFICIAL NAME: People's Republic of Bangladesh
DATE OF FORMATION: 1971
CAPITAL: Dhaka
POPULATION: 122.2 million
TOTAL AREA: 55,598 sq miles (143,998 sq km)

DENSITY: 2,317 people per sq mile
LANGUAGES: Bangla*, Urdu, Chakma, Marma (Margh), other
RELIGIONS: Muslim 83%, Hindu 16%, other (Buddhist, Christian) 1%
ETHNIC MIX: Bengali 98%, other 2%
GOVERNMENT: Multiparty republic
CURRENCY: Taka = 100 paisa

BURMA (MYANMAR)

BURMA FORMS the eastern shores of the Bay of Bengal and the Andaman Sea in Southeast Asia. It gained independence from Britain in 1948.

GEOGRAPHY
Fertile Irrawaddy basin in the center. Mountains to the west, Shan plateau to the east. Tropical rain forest covers much of the land.

CLIMATE
Tropical. Hot summers, with high humidity, and warm winters.

PEOPLE AND SOCIETY
Under socialist military rule since 1962, Burma has suffered widespread political repression and ethnic conflict. Minority groups maintain low-level guerrilla activity against the state. 1990 election was won by opposition democratic party. Its leader, Aung San Suu Kyi, was placed under house arrest. She was released in 1995.

◆ INSIGHT: Burma is the world's biggest teak exporter, although reserves are diminishing rapidly

THE ECONOMY
Under socialism, Burma has plunged from prosperity to poverty. Nationwide black market, on which prices are soaring. Main products are teak, rice, and gems.

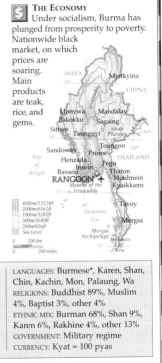

FACT FILE

OFFICIAL NAME: Union of Myanmar

DATE OF FORMATION: 1948

CAPITAL: Rangoon (Yangon)

POPULATION: 47.5 million

TOTAL AREA: 261,200 sq miles (676,550 sq km)

DENSITY: 182 people per sq mile

LANGUAGES: Burmese*, Karen, Shan, Chin, Kachin, Mon, Palaung, Wa

RELIGIONS: Buddhist 89%, Muslim 4%, Baptist 3%, other 4%

ETHNIC MIX: Burman 68%, Shan 9%, Karen 6%, Rakhine 4%, other 13%

GOVERNMENT: Military regime

CURRENCY: Kyat = 100 pyas

THAILAND

THAILAND LIES at the heart of mainland Southeas[t] Asia. Continuing rapid industrialization has resulted in massive congestion in the capital.

GEOGRAPHY
One third is occupied by a low plateau, drained by tributaries of the Mekong River. Fertile central plain. Mountains in the north.

CLIMATE
Tropical. Hot, humid March–May, monsoon rains May–October, cooler season November–March.

PEOPLE AND SOCIETY
The king is head of state. Criticism of him is not tolerated. Buddhism is national binding force. North and northeast are home to about 600,000 hill tribespeople, with their own languages and culture. Sex tourism is a problem. Women from the poor northeast enter prostitution in Bangkok and Pattaya.

◆ INSIGHT: Thailand, meaning "land of the free," is the only Southeast Asian nation never to have been colonized

THE ECONOMY
Rapid economic growth. Rise[?] in manufacturing. Chief world exporter of rice and rubber. Gas reserves. Successful tourist industr[y]

MYANMAR — LAOS
Mekong
Chiang Mai
Udon Thani
LAO[S]
Salween
Khon Kaen
Phitsanulok
Ubon
Ratchatha[ni]
Nakhon Sawan
Nakhon Ratchasir[i]
BANGKOK
Thon Buri — Samut Prakan
Ratchaburi — Pattaya
CAMBO[DIA]
Gulf
of
Thailand
Chumphon
Isthmus
of
Kra
Nakhon Si
Thammarat

| 2000m/6562ft |
| 1000m/3281ft |
| 500m/1640ft |
| 200m/656ft |
| Sea Level |

Phuket
Songkhla
Hat Yai
Malay Peninsula
Andaman Sea
MALAYSIA

0   200 km
0   200 mile

FACT FILE
OFFICIAL NAME: Kingdom of Thailand
DATE OF FORMATION: 1822 / 1887
CAPITAL: Bangkok
POPULATION: 56.9 million
TOTAL AREA: 198,116 sq miles
(513,120 sq km)
DENSITY: 286 people per sq mile

LANGUAGES: Thai*, Chinese, Malay,
Khmer, Mon, Karen, Miao, English
RELIGIONS: Buddhist 95%, Muslim
4%, other (inc. Hindu, Christian) 1%
ETHNIC MIX: Thai 75%, Chinese 14%,
Malay 4%, Khmer 3%, other 4%
GOVERNMENT: Constitutional monarchy
CURRENCY: Baht = 100 stangs

LAOS

A FORMER French colony, independent in 1953, Laos lies landlocked in Southeast Asia. It has been under communist rule since 1975.

 GEOGRAPHY
Largely forested mountains, broadening in the north to a plateau. Lowlands along Mekong valley.

CLIMATE
Monsoon rains September–May. Rest of the year is hot and dry.

PEOPLE AND SOCIETY
Over 60 ethnic groups. Lowland Laotians (*Lao Loum*), live along Mekong River and are wet-rice farmers. Upland Laotians (*Lao Theung*) and mountain top Laotians (*Lao Soung*) practice slash-and-burn farming. Government efforts to halt this traditional farming method, which can destroy forests and watersheds, have been resisted.

THE ECONOMY
One of the world's 20 least-developed nations. Government began to introduce market-oriented reforms in 1986. Potential for timber, mining, garment manufacturing.

▶ INSIGHT: *In the early 1990s, Laos and Thailand built a "Friendship Bridge" across the Mekong at Vientiane*

FACT FILE

OFFICIAL NAME: Lao People's Democratic Republic
DATE OF FORMATION: 1953
CAPITAL: Vientiane
POPULATION: 4.6 million
TOTAL AREA: 91,428 sq miles (236,800 sq km)

DENSITY: 52 people per sq mile
LANGUAGES: Lao*, Miao, Yao, other
RELIGIONS: Buddhist 85%, Christian 2%, Muslim 1%, other 12%
ETHNIC MIX: Lao Loum 56%, Lao Theung 34%, Lao Soung 10%
GOVERNMENT: Single-party republic
CURRENCY: Kip = 100 cents

CAMBODIA

LOCATED ON the Indochinese Peninsula in South east Asia, Cambodia has emerged from two decades of civil war and invasion from Vietnam

GEOGRAPHY
Mostly low-lying basin. Tônlé Sap (Great Lake) drains into the Mekong River. Forested mountains and plateau east of the Mekong.

CLIMATE
Tropical. High temperatures throughout the year. Heavy rainfall during May–October monsoon.

PEOPLE AND SOCIETY
Under Pol Pot's Marxist Khmer Rouge regime between 1975 and 1979, over one million Cambodians died. Half a million more went into exile in Thailand. Effects of revolution and civil war are still felt and are reflected in the world's highest rate of orphans and widows. Free elections held under UN supervision in 1993 brought fragile stability, although the Khmer Rouge, still led by Pol Pot, continues its armed struggle.

THE ECONOMY
Economy is still recovering from civil war. Loss of skilled workers as result of Khmer Rouge anti-bourgeois atrocities in 1970s. Modest trade in rubber and timber

◆ INSIGHT: *Cambodia has many impressive temples, dating from when it was the center of the Khmer empire*

FACT FILE
OFFICIAL NAME: State of Cambodia
DATE OF FORMATION: 1953
CAPITAL: Phnom Penh
POPULATION: 9 million
TOTAL AREA: 69,000 sq miles (181,040 sq km)
DENSITY: 130 people per sq mile

LANGUAGES: Khmer*, French, other
RELIGIONS: Buddhist 88%, Muslim 2%, Christian 1%, other 9%
ETHNIC MIX: Khmer 94%, Chinese 4%, Vietnamese 1%, other 1%
GOVERNMENT: Constitutional monarchy
CURRENCY: Riel = 100 sen

VIETNAM

SITUATED ON the eastern coast of the Indochinese Peninsula, the country is still rebuilding after the devastating 1962–1975 Vietnam War.

 GEOGRAPHY
Heavily forested mountain range separates northern Red river delta lowlands from southern Mekong delta in the south.

CLIMATE
Cool winters in north; south tropical, with even temperatures.

 PEOPLE AND SOCIETY
Partitioned in 1954, the communist north reunited the nation after the Vietnam War, in which two million people died. Women outnumber men, largely because of war deaths. Resettling of lowlanders in mountain regions has put pressure on farming and forest resources. Family life is based on kinship groups within village clans.

▶ INSIGHT: *A new mammal species, the Vu Quang Ox, was recently discovered in the forests of north Vietnam*

THE ECONOMY
After years of stagnation, the economy is recovering. Government seeking transfer to market economy. Growing steel, oil, gas, car industries.

FACT FILE

OFFICIAL NAME: Socialist Republic of Viet-Nam
DATE OF FORMATION: 1976
CAPITAL: Hanoi
POPULATION: 76.2 million
TOTAL AREA: 127,243 sq miles (329,560 sq km)

DENSITY: 599 people per sq mile
LANGUAGES: Vietnamese*, other
RELIGIONS: Buddhist 55%, Catholic 7%, Muslim 1%, other 37%
ETHNIC MIX: Vietnamese 88%, Chinese 4%, Thai 2%, other 6%
GOVERNMENT: Single-party republic
CURRENCY: Dong = 10 hao = 100 xu

MALAYSIA

MALAYSIA'S THREE separate territories stretch ove 1,240 miles (2,000 km) from the Malay Peninsula to the northeastern area of the island of Borneo.

GEOGRAPHY
Peninsular Malaysia (Malaya) has mountain ranges along its axis. Almost three quarters of the land is tropical rain forest or swamp forest. Territories of Sabah and Sarawak in Borneo are rugged and forested.

CLIMATE
Equatorial. Warm, with year-round rainfall. Heaviest rain March–May and September–November.

◆ INSIGHT: Malaysia accounts for almost half of world timber exports

PEOPLE AND SOCIETY
Indigenous Malays are the largest ethnic group, but Chinese have traditionally controlled most economic activity. Malays favored i education and jobs since 1970s in order to address imbalance. Labor shortages attract many immigrants from other Southeast Asian states.

THE ECONOMY
Rapid growth since 1980s. Successful electronics, car industrie: Leading producer of rubber, palm oil, pepper, tin, tropical hardwoods.

FACT FILE
OFFICIAL NAME: Malaysia
DATE OF FORMATION: 1957/1965
CAPITAL: Kuala Lumpur
POPULATION: 20.6 million
TOTAL AREA: 127,317 sq miles
(329,750 sq km)
DENSITY: 161 people per sq mile

LANGUAGES: Malay*, Chinese*, Tamil
RELIGIONS: Muslim 53%, Buddhist and Confucian 30%, other 17%
ETHNIC MIX: Malay and aborigine 60%, Chinese 30%, Indian 8%, other 2%
GOVERNMENT: Federal constitutional monarchy
CURRENCY: Ringgit = 100 cents

INDONESIA

THE WORLD'S largest archipelago, Indonesia's 13,677 islands are scattered over 3,000 miles (5,000 km), from the Indian Ocean to the Pacific Ocean.

GEOGRAPHY
Mountains, tropical swamps, rain forests, and over 200 volcanoes, many still active. Most larger islands have coastal lowlands.

CLIMATE
Predominantly tropical monsoon. Hilly areas are cooler. June–September dry season.

◆ INSIGHT: *Indonesia is the fifth most populous country in the world; 40% of its people are aged under 15*

PEOPLE AND SOCIETY
A mosaic of different cultures and languages. Islam, urbanization, and national language, Bahasa Indonesia, are unifying factors. Papuans of Irian Jaya, East Timorese, and Aceh of north Sumatra, denied autonomy, are all in conflict with government.

THE ECONOMY
Varied resources, especially energy. Timber, minerals, fishing, are all important. Rice is the main cash crop for the rural population.

FACT FILE

OFFICIAL NAME: Republic of Indonesia

DATE OF FORMATION: 1949 / 1963

CAPITAL: Jakarta

POPULATION: 200.6 million

TOTAL AREA: 735,555 sq miles (1,904,570 sq km)

DENSITY: 273 people per sq mile

LANGUAGES: Bahasa Indonesia*, 250 (est.) languages or dialects

RELIGIONS: Muslim 87%, Christian 10%, Hindu 2%, Buddhist 1%

ETHNIC MIX: Javanese 45%, Sundanese 14%, Madurese 8%, other 33%

GOVERNMENT: Multiparty republic

CURRENCY: Rupiah = 100 sen

SINGAPORE

A CITY state linked to the southernmost tip of the Malay Peninsula by a causeway, Singapore is one of Asia's most important commercial centers

 GEOGRAPHY
Little remains of the original vegetation on Singapore island. The other 54 much smaller islands are swampy jungle.

 CLIMATE
Equatorial. Hot and humid, with heavy rainfall all year round.

PEOPLE AND SOCIETY
Dominated by the Chinese, who make up three quarters of the community. English-speaking Straits Chinese and newer Mandarin-speakers are now well integrated. There is a significant foreign work force. Society is highly regulated and government campaigns to improve public behavior are frequent. Crime is limited and punishment can be severe.

THE ECONOMY
Highly successful financial, banking and manufacturing sector. Produces 50% of the world's computer disk drives. All food and energy has to be imported.

◆ *INSIGHT: Singapore has full employment, and the world's highest rate of home ownership and national savings*

FACT FILE
OFFICIAL NAME: Republic of Singapore
DATE OF FORMATION: 1965
CAPITAL: Singapore City
POPULATION: 2.8 million
TOTAL AREA: 239 sq miles (620 sq km)

DENSITY: 11,715 people per sq mile
LANGUAGES: Malay*, Chinese*, other
RELIGIONS: Buddhist 30%, Christian 20%, Muslim 17%, other 33%
ETHNIC MIX: Chinese 76%, Malay 15%, South Asian 7%, other 2%
GOVERNMENT: Multiparty republic
CURRENCY: Singapore $ = 100 cents

BRUNEI

LYING ON the northwestern coast of the island of Borneo, Brunei is surrounded and divided in two by the Malaysian state of Sarawak.

GEOGRAPHY
Mostly dense lowland rain forest and mangrove swamps. Mountains in the southeast.

CLIMATE
Tropical. Six-month rainy season with very high humidity.

PEOPLE AND SOCIETY
Malays benefit from positive discrimination. Many in Chinese community are stateless. Independent from the UK since 1984, Brunei is ruled by decree of the Sultan. In 1990, "Malay Muslim Monarchy" was introduced, promoting Islamic values as state ideology. Women less restricted than in some Muslim states.

THE ECONOMY
Oil and natural gas reserves yield one of the world's highest standards of living. Massive overseas investments. Major consumer of high-tech audio equipment, VCRs, and Western designer clothes.

◆ INSIGHT: *The Sultan spent US $450 million building the world's largest palace at Bandar Seri Begawan*

FACT FILE

OFFICIAL NAME: The Sultanate of Brunei
DATE OF FORMATION: 1984
CAPITAL: Bandar Seri Begawan
POPULATION: 300,000
TOTAL AREA: 2,228 sq miles (5,770 sq km)

DENSITY: 134 people per sq mile
LANGUAGES: Malay*, English, Chinese
RELIGIONS: Muslim 63%, Buddhist 14%, Christian 10%, other 13%
ETHNIC MIX: Malay 69%, Chinese 18%, other 13%
GOVERNMENT: Absolute monarchy
CURRENCY: Brunei $ = 100 cents

PHILIPPINES

AN ARCHIPELAGO of 7,107 islands between the South China Sea and the Pacific. After 21 years of dictatorship, democracy was restored in 1986

GEOGRAPHY
Larger islands are forested and mountainous. Over 20 active volcanoes. Frequent earthquakes.

CLIMATE
Tropical. Warm and humid all year round. Typhoons occur in rainy season, June–October.

PEOPLE AND SOCIETY
Over 100 ethnic groups. Most Filipinos are of Malay origin, and Christian. Catholic Church is the dominant cultural force. It opposes state-sponsored family planning programs designed to curb accelerating population growth. Women have traditionally played a prominent part in society. Many enter the professions. Half the population live on the poverty line.

◆ INSIGHT: *The Philippines is the only Christian state in Asia*

THE ECONOMY
Now open to outside investment. Agricultural productivity is rising. Power failures limit scope for expansion. Weak infrastructure.

FACT FILE
OFFICIAL NAME: Republic of the Philippines
DATE OF FORMATION: 1946
CAPITAL: Manila
POPULATION: 66.5 million
TOTAL AREA: 115,831 sq miles (300,000 sq km)

DENSITY: 569 people per sq mile
LANGUAGES: Pilipino*, English*, other
RELIGIONS: Catholic 83%, Protestant 9%, Muslim 5%, other 3%
ETHNIC MIX: Filipino 96%, Chinese 2%, other 2%
GOVERNMENT: Multiparty republic
CURRENCY: Peso = 100 centavos

TAIWAN

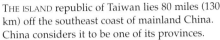

THE ISLAND republic of Taiwan lies 80 miles (130 km) off the southeast coast of mainland China. China considers it to be one of its provinces.

GEOGRAPHY
Mountain region covers two thirds of the island. Highly fertile lowlands and coastal plains.

CLIMATE
Tropical monsoon. Hot and humid. Typhoons July–September. Snow falls in mountains in winter.

PEOPLE AND SOCIETY
Most Taiwanese are Han Chinese, descendants of 17th-century settlers from the mainland. Taiwan came into existence in 1949, when the government was expelled from Beijing (then Peking) by the communists under Mao. 100,000 Nationalists arrived and established themselves as ruling class. Taiwan is diplomatically isolated and cannot gain representation at the UN.

THE ECONOMY
One of the world's most successful economies, based on small, adaptable manufacturing companies. Goods include televisions, calculators, footwear.

◆ INSIGHT: *Taiwan has the world's second largest foreign currency reserves*

FACT FILE
OFFICIAL NAME: Republic of China (Taiwan)
DATE OF FORMATION: 1949
CAPITAL: Taipei
POPULATION: 20.8 million
TOTAL AREA: 13,969 sq miles (36,179 sq km)
DENSITY: 1,489 people per sq mile
LANGUAGES: Mandarin*, other
RELIGIONS: Buddhist, Confucian, and Taoist 93%, Christian 5%, other 2%
ETHNIC MIX: Taiwanese 84%, mainland Chinese 14%, other 2%
GOVERNMENT: Multiparty republic
CURRENCY: New Taiwan $ = 100 cents

CHINA

CHINA COVERS a vast area of East Asia. From the founding of Communist China in 1949 until his death in 1976, Mao Zedong dominated the nation

GEOGRAPHY
Huge physical diversity. Great mountain chains and world's highest plateau in west. Arid basin in north and northeast. Deserts in northwest. South is mountainous. Rolling hills and plains in east.

CLIMATE
North and west are semiarid or arid, with extreme temperature variations. South and east are warmer and more humid, with rain throughout the year. Winter temperatures vary with latitude. Summer temperatures are more uniform, rising above 21°C (70°F).

THE ECONOMY
Moving rapidly toward a market-oriented economy. Vast mineral reserves. Increasingly diversified industrial sector. Low wage costs. Self-sufficient in food.

♦ INSIGHT: *China has the world's oldest continuous civilization. Its recorded history began 4,000 years ago, with the Shang dynasty*

FACT FILE

OFFICIAL NAME: People's Republic of China
DATE OF FORMATION: 1949/1950
CAPITAL: Beijing
POPULATION: 1,234.3 million
TOTAL AREA: 3,628,166 sq miles (9,396,960 sq km)

DENSITY: 340 people per sq mile
LANGUAGES: Mandarin*, other
RELIGIONS: Confucian 20%, Buddhist 6%, Taoist 2%, other 72%
ETHNIC MIX: Han 93%, Zhaung 1%, Hui 1%, other 5%
GOVERNMENT: Single-party republic
CURRENCY: Yuan = 10 jiao = 100 fen

PEOPLE AND SOCIETY
Most people are Han Chinese.
Rest of population belong to one of
55 minority nationalities, or recognized ethnic groups. Policy of resettling Han Chinese in remote regions is deeply resented and has led to uprisings. Government has relaxed one-child family policy for minorities after some small groups brought close to extinction. Han Chinese still face controls.

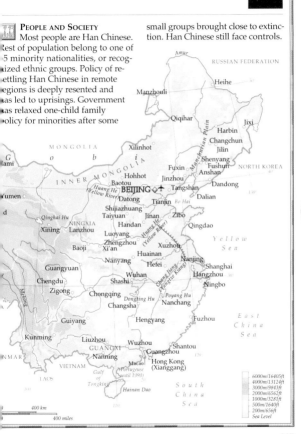

NORTH KOREA

NORTH KOREA comprises the northern half of the Korean peninsula. A communist state since 1948, it is largely isolated from the outside world.

 GEOGRAPHY
Mostly mountainous, with fertile plains in the southwest.

CLIMATE
Continental. Warm summers and cold winters, especially in the north, where snow is common.

PEOPLE AND SOCIETY
People live severely regulated lives. Divorce is nonexistent and extramarital sex highly frowned upon. Women form 57% of the work force, but are also expected to run the home. From an early age, children are looked after in state-run nurseries. Korean Workers' Party is only legal political party. Membership is essential for advancement. The political elite enjoy a privileged lifestyle.

◆ INSIGHT: *Private cars and telephones are forbidden in North Korea*

THE ECONOMY
Economy has suffered badly in 1990s, since end of aid from China and former Soviet Union. Manufacturing, agriculture, and mining all in decline. Electricity shortage is a problem.

FACT FILE

OFFICIAL NAME: Democratic People's Republic of Korea
DATE OF FORMATION: 1948
CAPITAL: Pyongyang
POPULATION: 23.1 million
TOTAL AREA: 46,540 sq miles
(120,540 sq km)

DENSITY: 496 people per sq mile
LANGUAGES: Korean*, Chinese
RELIGIONS: Traditional beliefs 16%, Ch'ondogyo 14%, Buddhist 2%, unaffiliated 68%
ETHNIC MIX: Korean 99%, other 1%
GOVERNMENT: Single-party republic
CURRENCY: Won = 100 chon

SOUTH KOREA

SOUTH KOREA occupies the southern half of the Korean peninsula. Under US sponsorship, it was separated from the communist North in 1948.

GEOGRAPHY
Over 80% is mountainous and two thirds is forested. Flattest and most populous parts lie along west coast and in the extreme south.

CLIMATE
Four distinct seasons. Winters are dry, and bitterly cold. Summers are hot and humid.

PEOPLE AND SOCIETY
Inhabited by a single ethnic group for the last 2,000 years. Tiny Chinese community. Family life is a central and clearly defined part of Korean society. Women's role is traditional; it is not respectable for those who are married to have jobs. Since the inconclusive Korean War (1950–1953), North and South Korea have remained mutually hostile.

◆ INSIGHT: Over 60% of Koreans are named Kim, Lee, or Park

THE ECONOMY
World's biggest shipbuilder. High demand from China for Korean goods, especially cars. Electronics, household appliances also important.

FACT FILE

OFFICIAL NAME: Republic of Korea
DATE OF FORMATION: 1948
CAPITAL: Seoul
POPULATION: 44.5 million
TOTAL AREA: 38,232 sq miles
(99,020 sq km)
DENSITY: 1,163 people per sq mile

LANGUAGES: Korean*, Chinese
RELIGIONS: Mahayana Buddhist 47%, Protestant 38%, Catholic 11%, Confucian 3%, other 1%
ETHNIC MIX: Korean 99.9%, other (mainly Chinese) 0.1%
GOVERNMENT: Multiparty republic
CURRENCY: Won = 100 chon

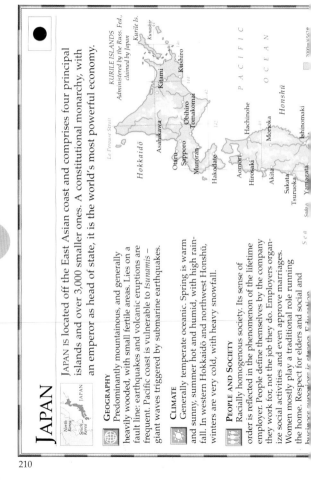

JAPAN

JAPAN IS located off the East Asian coast and comprises four principal islands and over 3,000 smaller ones. A constitutional monarchy, with an emperor as head of state, it is the world's most powerful economy.

GEOGRAPHY

Predominantly mountainous, and generally heavily wooded, with small fertile areas. Lies on a fault line: earthquakes and volcanic eruptions are frequent. Pacific coast is vulnerable to *tsunamis* – giant waves triggered by submarine earthquakes.

CLIMATE

Generally temperate oceanic. Spring is warm and sunny, summer hot and humid, with high rainfall. In western Hokkaidō and northwest Honshū, winters are very cold, with heavy snowfall.

PEOPLE AND SOCIETY

Racially homogenous society. Its sense of order is reflected in the phenomenon of the lifetime employer. People define themselves by the company they work for, not the job they do. Employers organize social activities and even approve marriages. Women mostly play a traditional role running the home. Respect for elders and social and

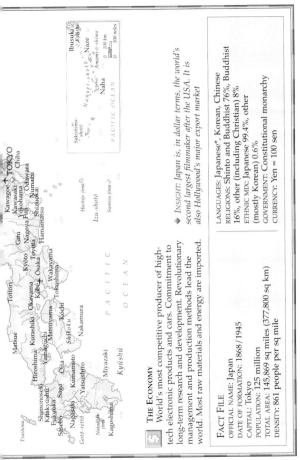

THE ECONOMY

World's most competitive producer of high-tech electronic products and cars. Commitment to long-term research and development. Revolutionary management and production methods lead the world. Most raw materials and energy are imported.

◆ INSIGHT: Japan is, in dollar terms, the world's second largest filmmaker after the USA. It is also Hollywood's major export market

FACT FILE

OFFICIAL NAME: Japan
DATE OF FORMATION: 1868/1945
CAPITAL: Tokyo
POPULATION: 125 million
TOTAL AREA: 145,869 sq miles (377,800 sq km)
DENSITY: 861 people per sq mile

LANGUAGES: Japanese*, Korean, Chinese
RELIGIONS: Shinto and Buddhist 76%, Buddhist 16%, other (including Christian) 8%
ETHNIC MIX: Japanese 99.4%, other (mostly Korean) 0.6%
GOVERNMENT: Constitutional monarchy
CURRENCY: Yen = 100 sen

211

AUSTRALASIA & OCEANIA

THIS REGION includes the world's smallest, flattest continent, Australia; large island groups such as New Zealand, Papua New Guinea, and Fiji; and myriad volcanic and coral islands scattered across the Pacific Ocean, which comprise three main groups: Micronesia, Melanesia, and Polynesia. The peoples of Oceania colonized the Pacific by 1500 A.D. Their insular farming and fishing communities have developed distinctive cultures. Owing to its isolation from other continents, Australia's flora and fauna have evolved many unique species.

Hawaii (to USA)
...ton Atoll (to USA)
Kingman Reef (to USA)
...a Atoll (to USA) *Teraina* *Tabuaeran*
Jarvis I. *Kiritimati*
KIRIBATI

Northern Cook Is.
...erican ...noa (to USA)
Cook Islands (to NZ)
Marquesas Is.
French Polynesia (to France)
Tahiti
Society Islands
Southern Cook Is.
Pitcairn Islands (to UK)

Equator

P A C I F I C
O C E A N

CONTINENTAL FACTS

HIGHEST POINT: Mt. Wilhelm, Papua New Guinea 14,794 ft (4,509 m)	LARGEST LAKE: Lake Eyre, Australia 3,700 sq miles (9,583 sq km)
LOWEST POINT: Lake Eyre, Australia 52 ft (16 m) below sea level	LONGEST RIVER: Murray-Darling, Australia 2,330 miles (3,750 km)

213

AUSTRALIA

AN ISLAND continent located between the Indian and Pacific oceans. European settlement, mainly from Britain and Ireland, began 200 years ago. Today, Australia's international focus has shifted away from Europe toward Asia.

GEOGRAPHY

Western half is mostly arid plateaus, ridges, and vast deserts. Central-eastern area comprises lowlands and river systems draining into Lake Eyre. To the east are the mountains of the Great Dividing Range. In the north are tropical rain forests.

CLIMATE

The interior, west, and south are arid and very hot in summer. Central desert areas can reach 120°F (50°C). The north is hot throughout the year, and humid during the summer monsoon. East, south-east, and southwest coastal areas are temperate.

PEOPLE AND SOCIETY

Immigration drives after 1945 brought many Europeans to Australia. Since 1970s, 50% of immigrants have been Asian. Aborigines, the first inhabitants, are sidelined economically and socially. They have made an increasingly organized stand over land rights in recent years. Wealth disparities are small, but 1990s recession increased gap between rich and poor.

THE ECONOMY

Efficient mining and agricultural industries. Successful tourist industry. Investor in booming Southeast Asian economies. High unemployment.

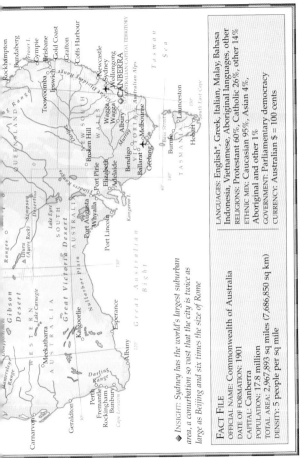

◆ INSIGHT: *Sydney has the world's largest suburban area, a conurbation so vast that the city is twice as large as Beijing and six times the size of Rome*

FACT FILE
OFFICIAL NAME: Commonwealth of Australia
DATE OF FORMATION: 1901
CAPITAL: Canberra
POPULATION: 17.8 million
TOTAL AREA: 2,967,893 sq miles (7,686,850 sq km)
DENSITY: 5 people per sq mile

LANGUAGES: English*, Greek, Italian, Malay, Bahasa Indonesia, Vietnamese, Aboriginal languages, other
RELIGIONS: Protestant 60%, Catholic 26%, other 14%
ETHNIC MIX: Caucasian 95%, Asian 4%, Aboriginal and other 1%
GOVERNMENT: Parliamentary democracy
CURRENCY: Australian $ = 100 cents

VANUATU

AN ARCHIPELAGO of 82 islands and islets in the Pacific Ocean, it was ruled jointly by Britain and France from 1906 until independence in 1980.

GEOGRAPHY
Mountainous and volcanic, with coral beaches and dense rain forest. Cultivated land along coasts.

CLIMATE
Tropical. Temperatures and rainfall decline from north to south.

PEOPLE AND SOCIETY
Indigenous Melanesians form a majority. 80% of the population live on 16 main islands. People are among the most traditional in the Pacific: local social and religious customs are strong, despite centuries of missionary influence. Subsistence farming and fishing are the main activities. Women have lower social status than men and payment of bride price is common.

◆ INSIGHT: *With 105 indigenous languages, Vanuatu has the world's highest per capita density of languages*

THE ECONOMY
Copra and cocoa are the largest exports. Recent upsurge in tourist industry. Offshore financial services are also important.

FACT FILE

OFFICIAL NAME: Republic of Vanuatu
DATE OF FORMATION: 1980
CAPITAL: Port-Vila
POPULATION: 155,000
TOTAL AREA: 4,706 sq miles
(12,190 sq km)
DENSITY: 34 people per sq mile

LANGUAGES: Bislama (Melanesian pidgin)*, English*, French*, other
RELIGIONS: Protestant 77%, Catholic 15%, traditional beliefs 8%
ETHNIC MIX: Ni-Vanuatu 98%, European 1%, other 1%
GOVERNMENT: Multiparty republic
CURRENCY: Vatu = 100 centimes

FIJI

A VOLCANIC archipelago in the southern Pacific
Ocean, Fiji comprises two large islands and 880
islets. From 1874 to 1970, it was a British colony.

 GEOGRAPHY
Main islands are mountainous,
fringed by coral reefs. Remainder
are limestone and coral formations.

 CLIMATE
Tropical. High temperatures
year round. Cyclones are a hazard.

PEOPLE AND SOCIETY
The British introduced
workers from India in the late
19th century, and by 1946 their
descendants outnumbered the
Native Fijian population. In 1987,
the Indian-dominated government
was overthrown by Native Fijians.
Many Indo-Fijians left the country.
Civilian rule returned in 1990, and
a new constitution discriminating
against Indo-Fijians was introduced.

◆ *INSIGHT: Both Fijians and Indians
practice fire-walking; Indians walk on
hot embers, Fijians on heated stones*

THE ECONOMY
Well-diversified economy
based on sugar production, gold
mining, timber, and commercial
fishing. Tourists are returning after
a drop in numbers after the coups.

FACT FILE

OFFICIAL NAME: Republic of Fiji
DATE OF FORMATION: 1970
CAPITAL: Suva
POPULATION: 700,000
TOTAL AREA: 7,054 sq miles
(18,270 sq km)
DENSITY: 99 people per sq mile

LANGUAGES: English*, Fijian*,
Hindi, Urdu, Tamil, Telugu
RELIGIONS: Christian 52%, Hindu
38%, Muslim 8%, other 2%
ETHNIC MIX: Native Fijian 49%,
Indo-Fijian 46%, other 5%
GOVERNMENT: Multiparty republic
CURRENCY: Fiji $ = 100 cents

PAPUA NEW GUINEA

ACHIEVING INDEPENDENCE from Australia in 1975 PNG occupies the eastern section of the island of New Guinea and several other island groups.

GEOGRAPHY

Mountainous and forested mainland, with broad, swampy river valleys. 40 active volcanoes in the north. Around 600 outer islands.

CLIMATE

Hot and humid in lowlands, cooling toward highlands, where snow can fall on highest peaks.

PEOPLE AND SOCIETY

Around 750 language groups – the highest number in the world – and even more tribes. Main social distinction is between lowlanders, who have frequent contact with the outside world, and the very isolated, but increasingly threatened, highlanders who live by hunter-gathering. Great tensions exist between highland tribes: any-one who is not a *wontok* (of one's tribe) is seen as potentially hostile.

THE ECONOMY

Significant quantities of gold, copper, silver. Oil and natural gas reserves. Secessionist violence on Bougainville deters investors.

◆ INSIGHT: *PNG is home to the only known poisonous birds; contact with the feathers produces skin blisters*

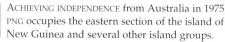

FACT FILE

OFFICIAL NAME: The Independent State of Papua New Guinea

DATE OF FORMATION: 1975

CAPITAL: Port Moresby

POPULATION: 4.1 million

TOTAL AREA: 178,700 sq miles (462,840 sq km)

DENSITY: 23 people per sq mile

LANGUAGES: Pidgin English*, Motu*, Papuan, 750 (est.) native languages

RELIGIONS: Christian 66%, other 34%

ETHNIC MIX: Papuan 85%, other 15%

GOVERNMENT: Parliamentary democracy

CURRENCY: Kina = 100 toea

SOLOMON ISLANDS

THE SOLOMONS archipelago comprises several hundred islands scattered in the southwestern Pacific. Independence from Britain came in 1978.

GEOGRAPHY
The six largest islands are volcanic, mountainous, and thickly forested. Flat coastal plains provide the only cultivable land.

CLIMATE
Northern islands are hot and humid all year round; farther south a cool season develops. November–April wet season brings cyclones.

PEOPLE AND SOCIETY
Most Solomon Islanders are Melanesian. Around 87 native languages are spoken, but Pidgin English is used as a contact language between tribes. Most people live on shifting, subsistence agriculture in small rural villages. Villagers work collectively on community projects and there is much sharing among clans. Animist beliefs are maintained alongside Christianity.

THE ECONOMY
Main products are palm oil, copra, cocoa, fish, and timber. Bauxite deposits found on Rennell Island, but islanders persuaded the government that exploiting them would destroy the island.

◆ INSIGHT: *The Solomons have no television service; the islanders oppose television as it might dilute their culture*

FACT FILE
OFFICIAL NAME: Solomon Islands
DATE OF FORMATION: 1978
CAPITAL: Honiara
POPULATION: 400,000
TOTAL AREA: 111,583 sq miles
(289,000 sq km)
DENSITY: 29 people per sq mile

LANGUAGES: English*, Pidgin English, 87 (est.) native languages
RELIGIONS: Christian 91%, other 9%
ETHNIC MIX: Melanesian 94%, other (Polynesian, Chinese, European) 6%
GOVERNMENT: Parliamentary democracy
CURRENCY: Solomon Is. $ = 100 cents

PALAU

THE PALAU archipelago, a group of over 300 islands, lies in the western Pacific Ocean. In 1994 it became the world's newest independent state.

GEOGRAPHY
Terrain varies from thickly forested mountains to limestone and coral reefs. Babelthuap, the largest island, is volcanic, with many rivers and waterfalls.

CLIMATE
Hot and wet. Little variation in daily and seasonal temperatures. February–April is the dry season.

PEOPLE AND SOCIETY
Palau was the last remaining US-administered UN Trust Territory of the Pacific Islands, until 1994. Only nine islands are inhabited and two thirds of the population live in Koror. Society is matrilineal; women choose which males will be the clan chiefs. Local traditions remain strong, despite US influence.

THE ECONOMY
Subsistence level. Main crops are coconuts and cassava. Revenue from fishing licenses and tourism. Heavily reliant on US aid.

Map of Palau showing:
134°30'
Ngaruangl
Kayangel Islands
8°
200m/656ft
Sea Level
0   30 km
0   30 miles
Konrei
PACIFIC
OCEAN
Ngardmau
Melekeiok
OREOR
Babelthu
Airai
Oreor
Urukthapel
Ell Malk
Peleliu
Angaur

◆ INSIGHT: *Palau's reefs contain 1,500 species of fish and 700 types of coral*

FACT FILE
OFFICIAL NAME: Republic of Palau
DATE OF FORMATION: 1994
CAPITAL: Oreor
POPULATION: 16,000
TOTAL AREA: 192 sq miles
(497 sq km)
DENSITY: 78 people per sq mile

LANGUAGES: Palauan*, English*, Sonsorolese-Tobian, other
RELIGIONS: Christian (mainly Catholic) 70%, traditional beliefs 30%
ETHNIC MIX: Palaun 99%, other (mainly Filipino) 1%
GOVERNMENT: Multiparty republic
CURRENCY: US $ = 100 cents

MICRONESIA

THE FEDERATED STATES of Micronesia, situated in the western Pacific, comprise 607 islands and atolls grouped into four main island states.

GEOGRAPHY

Mixture of high volcanic islands with forested interiors, and low-lying coral atolls. Some islands have coastal mangrove swamps.

CLIMATE

Tropical, with high humidity. Very heavy rainfall outside the January–March dry season.

◆ INSIGHT: *A major Japanese naval base during World War II, Chuuk's lagoon contains the sunken wrecks of over 100 Japanese ships and 270 planes*

PEOPLE AND SOCIETY

Part of the US-administered UN Trust Territory of the Pacific Islands, until independence in 1979, but it still relies on US aid, which funds food stamps, schools, and hospitals. Most islanders live without electricity or running water. Society is traditionally matrilineal.

THE ECONOMY

Fishing and copra production are the mainstays. Construction industry is largest private-sector activity. High unemployment.

FACT FILE

OFFICIAL NAME: Federated States of Micronesia

DATE OF FORMATION: 1986

CAPITAL: Palikir

POPULATION: 101,000

TOTAL AREA: 1,120 sq miles (2,900 sq km)

DENSITY: 374 people per sq mile

LANGUAGES: English*, Trukese, Pohnpeian, Mortlockese, other

RELIGIONS: Catholic 50%, Protestant 48%, other 2%

ETHNIC MIX: Micronesian 99%, other 1%

GOVERNMENT: Republic

CURRENCY: US $ = 100 cents

MARSHALL ISLANDS

UNDER US rule as part of the UN Trust Territory of the Pacific Islands until independence in 1986, the Marshall Islands comprise a group of 34 atolls.

GEOGRAPHY
Narrow coral rings with sandy beaches enclosing lagoons. Those in the south have thicker vegetation. Kwajalein is the world's largest atoll.

CLIMATE
Tropical oceanic, cooled year-round by northeast trade winds.

PEOPLE AND SOCIETY
Majuro, the capital and commercial center, is home to almost half the population. Tensions are high due to poor living conditions. Life on the outlying islands is still traditional, based around subsistence agriculture and fishing. Society is matrilineal: chiefly titles descend through the mother.

◆ INSIGHT: In 1954, Bikini atoll was the site for the testing of the largest US H-bomb – the 18–22 megaton Bravo

THE ECONOMY
Almost totally dependent on US aid and the rent paid by the US for its missile base on Kwajalein atoll. Revenue from Japan for use of Marshallese waters for tuna fishing. Copra and coconut oil are the only significant agricultural exports.

FACT FILE

OFFICIAL NAME: Republic of the Marshall Islands
DATE OF FORMATION: 1986
CAPITAL: Majuro
POPULATION: 48,000
TOTAL AREA: 70 sq miles (181 sq kms)

DENSITY: 689 people per sq mile
LANGUAGES: English*, Marshallese*
RELIGIONS: Protestant 80%, Catholic 15%, other 5%
ETHNIC MIX: Marshallese 90%, other Pacific islanders 10%
GOVERNMENT: Republic
CURRENCY: US $ = 100 cents

NAURU

NAURU LIES in the Pacific, 2,480 miles (4,000 km) northeast of Australia. Phosphate deposits have made its citizens among the richest in the world.

GEOGRAPHY
Low-lying coral atoll, with a rtile coastal belt. Coral cliffs enrcle an elevated interior plateau.

CLIMATE
Equatorial, moderated by sea reezes. Occasional long droughts.

PEOPLE AND SOCIETY
Native Nauruans are of mixed ficronesian and Polynesian origin. lost live in simple, traditional ouses and spend their money on uxury cars and consumer goods. overnment provides free welfare nd education. Diet of imported rocessed foods has caused widepread obesity and diabetes. Mining left to an imported labor force, ainly from Kiribati. Many young tend boarding school in Australia.

◆ INSIGHT: Phosphate mining has ft 80% of the island uninhabitable

THE ECONOMY
Phosphate, the only resource, is sold to Pacific Rim countries for use as a fertilizer. Deposits are near exhaustion. Huge investments in Australian and Hawaiian property. Possible future as a tax haven.

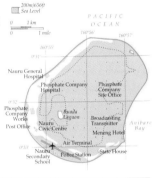

FACT FILE

OFFICIAL NAME: Republic of Nauru
DATE OF FORMATION: 1968
CAPITAL: No official capital
POPULATION: 10,000
TOTAL AREA: 8.2 sq miles
(21.2 sq km)
DENSITY: 1,113 people per sq mile

LANGUAGES: Nauruan*, English, other
RELIGIONS: Christian 95%, other 5%
ETHNIC MIX: Nauruan 58%, other
Pacific islanders 26%, Chinese
8%, European 8%
GOVERNMENT: Parliamentary
democracy
CURRENCY: Australian $ = 100 cents

KIRIBATI

PART OF the British colony of the Gilbert and Ellice Islands until independence in 1979, Kiriba comprises 33 islands in the mid-Pacific Ocean.

GEOGRAPHY
Three groups of tiny, very low-lying coral atolls scattered across 1,930,000 sq miles (5 million sq km) of ocean. Most have central lagoons.

CLIMATE
Central islands have maritime equatorial climate. Those to north and south are tropical, with constant high temperatures. Little rainfall.

PEOPLE AND SOCIETY
Locals still refer to themselves as Gilbertese. Apart from the inhabitants of Banaba, who employed anthropologists to establish their racial distinction, almost all people are Micronesian. Most are poor subsistence farmers. The islands are in effect ruled by traditional chiefs, though there is a party system based on the British model.

THE ECONOMY
Until 1980, when deposits ran out, phosphate from Banaba provided 80% of exports. Since the coconuts, copra, fish, have become main exports, but the islands are heavily dependent on foreign aid.

◆ INSIGHT: In 1981, the UK paid A$1 million in damages to Banabans for the destruction of their island by mining

FACT FILE
OFFICIAL NAME: Republic of Kiribati
DATE OF FORMATION: 1979
CAPITAL: Bairiki
POPULATION: 7,500
TOTAL AREA: 274 sq miles (710 sq km)

DENSITY: 242 people per sq mile
LANGUAGES: English*, Kiribati, other
RELIGIONS: Catholic 53%, Protestant (mainly Congregational) 40%, other Christian 4%, other 3%
ETHNIC MIX: I-Kiribati 98%, other 2%,
GOVERNMENT: Multiparty republic
CURRENCY: Australian $ = 100 cents

TUVALU

Kiribati

TUVALU

Solomon Is.

A TINY isolated state, linked to the Gilbert Islands as a British colony until independence in 1978, Tuvalu's nine islands lie in the central Pacific.

GEOGRAPHY
Coral atolls, none more than 15 feet (4.6 meters) above sea level. Poor soils restrict vegetation to bush, coconut palms, and breadfruit trees.

CLIMATE
Hot all year round. Heavy annual rainfall. Hurricane season brings many violent storms.

PEOPLE AND SOCIETY
People are mostly Polynesian, related to the Samoans and Tongans. Almost half the population live on Funafuti, where government jobs are centered. Life is communal and traditional. Most people live by subsistence farming, digging pits out of the coral to grow crops. Fresh water is precious due to frequent droughts.

THE ECONOMY
World's smallest economy. Fish stocks exploited mainly by foreign boats in return for licensing fees. Exports are few: copra, stamps, garments. Foreign aid is crucial.

Nanumea

Niutao

Nanumaga

Nui

Vaitupu

Nukufetau

FONGAFALE
Funafuti

Nukulaelae

Niulakita

PACIFIC OCEAN

PACIFIC OCEAN

200m/656ft
Sea Level

0   100 km
0   100 miles

INSIGHT: Tuvaluans have a reputation as excellent sailors. Many work overseas as merchant seamen on foreign ships

FACT FILE

OFFICIAL NAME: Tuvalu
DATE OF FORMATION: 1978
CAPITAL: Fongafale
POPULATION: 9,000
TOTAL AREA: 10 sq miles (26 sq km)
DENSITY: 900 people per sq mile

LANGUAGES: Tuvaluan, Kiribati, other (no official language)
RELIGIONS: Protestant 97%, other 3%
ETHNIC MIX: Tuvaluan 95%, other (inc. Micronesian, I-Kiribati) 5%
GOVERNMENT: Constitutional monarchy
CURRENCY: Australian $ = 100 cents

SAMOA

THE SOUTHERN Pacific islands of Samoa gained independence from New Zealand in 1962. Four of the nine islands are inhabited.

GEOGRAPHY
Comprises two large islands and seven smaller ones. Two largest islands have rain forested, mountainous interiors surrounded by coastal lowlands and coral reefs.

CLIMATE
Tropical, with high humidity. Cooler May–November. Hurricane season December–March.

PEOPLE AND SOCIETY
Ethnic Samoans are world's second largest Polynesian group, after the Maoris. Way of life is communal and formalized. Extended family groups own 80% of the land. Each family has an elected chief, who looks after its political and social interests. Large-scale migration to the US and New Zealand reflects lack of jobs and attractions of Western lifestyle.

THE ECONOMY
Agricultural products include taro, coconut cream, cocoa, and copra. Growth of service sector since 1989 launch of offshore banking. Dependent on aid and expatriate remittances. Rain forest increasingly exploited for timber.

◆ *INSIGHT: Samoa was named for the sacred (sa) chickens (moa) of Lu, son of Tagaloa, the god of creation*

1000m/3281ft
500m/1640ft
200m/656ft
Sea Level

FACT FILE
OFFICIAL NAME: Independent State of Samoa
DATE OF FORMATION: 1962
CAPITAL: Apia
POPULATION: 162,000
TOTAL AREA: 1,027 sq miles (2,840 sq km)

DENSITY: 156 people per sq mile
LANGUAGES: Samoan*, English*
RELIGIONS: Protestant (mainly Congregational) 74%, Catholic 26%
ETHNIC MIX: Samoan 93%, mixed European and Polynesian 7%
GOVERNMENT: Parliamentary state
CURRENCY: Tala = 100 sene

TONGA

TONGA IS an archipelago of 170 islands, 45 of which are inhabited, in the South Pacific. Politics is in effect controlled by the king.

GEOGRAPHY
Easterly islands are generally ow and fertile. Those in the west re higher and volcanic in origin.

CLIMATE
Tropical oceanic. Temperatures ange between 68°F (20°C) and 86°F 30°C) all year round. Heavy rain-all, especially February–March.

PEOPLE AND SOCIETY
The last remaining Polynesian monarchy, and the only Pacific state ever brought under foreign rule. All land is property of the crown, but is administered by nobles who allot it to the common people. Respect for traditional institutions and values remains high, although younger, Westernized Tongans are starting to question some attitudes.

THE ECONOMY
Most people are subsistence farmers. Commercial production of coconuts, cassava, and passion fruit. Tourism is increasing slowly.

▶ INSIGHT: Tonga has the world's owest annual death rate at one in 2,790

FACT FILE

OFFICIAL NAME: Kingdom of Tonga
DATE OF FORMATION: 1970
CAPITAL: Nuku'alofa
POPULATION: 101,000
TOTAL AREA: 290 sq miles (750 sq km)

DENSITY: 341 people per sq mile
LANGUAGES: Tongan*, English
RELIGIONS: Protestant 82% (mainly Methodist), Catholic 18%
ETHNIC MIX: Tongan 98%, mixed European and Polynesian 2%
GOVERNMENT: Constitutional monarchy
CURRENCY: Pa'anga = 100 seniti

NEW ZEALAND

LYING SOUTHEAST of Australia, New Zealand comprises the North and South Islands, separated by the Cook Strait, and many smaller islands.

GEOGRAPHY
North Island has mountain ranges, valleys, and volcanic central plateau. South Island is mostly mountainous, with eastern lowlands.

CLIMATE
Generally temperate and damp. Extreme north is almost sub-tropical; southern winters are cold.

PEOPLE AND SOCIETY
Maoris were the first settlers, 1,200 years ago. Today's majority European population is descended mainly from British migrants who settled after 1840. Maoris' living and education standards are generally lower than average. Tense relations beween the two groups in recent years. Government now negotiating settlement of Maori land claims.

THE ECONOMY
Modern agricultural sector; world's biggest exporter of wool, cheese, butter, and meat. Growing manufacturing industry. Tourism.

◆ INSIGHT: New Zealand women were the first in the world to get the vote

---

FACT FILE

OFFICIAL NAME: The Dominion of New Zealand
DATE OF FORMATION: 1947
CAPITAL: Wellington
POPULATION: 3.5 million
TOTAL AREA: 103,730 sq miles (268,680 sq km)

DENSITY: 34 people per sq mile
LANGUAGES: English*, Maori, other
RELIGIONS: Protestant 62%, Catholic 18%, other 20%
ETHNIC MIX: European 88%, Maori 9%, other (inc. Malay, Chinese) 3%
GOVERNMENT: Constitutional monarchy
CURRENCY: NZ $ = 100 cents

ANTARCTICA

THE CIRCUMPOLAR continent of Antarctica is almost entirely covered by ice over 1.2 miles (2 km) thick. It contains 90% of the Earth's fresh water reserves.

GEOGRAPHY & CLIMATE

The bulk of Antarctica's ice is contained in the Greater Antarctic Ice Sheet – a huge dome that rises steeply from the coast and flattens to a plateau in the interior. Powerful winds create a storm belt around the continent, which brings clouds, fog, and blizzards. Winter temperatures can fall to −112°F. (−80°C).

PEOPLE

No indigenous population. Scientists and logistical staff work at the 40 permanent, and as many as 100 temporary, research stations. A few Chilean settler families live on King George Island. Tourism is mostly by cruise ship to the Antarctic Peninsula. Tourist numbers increased by over 600% between 1985 and 1992.

TOTAL AREA:
5,366,790 sq miles
(13,900,000 sq km)

Ice Cap
Permanent Ice

1000 km
1000 miles

Territorial Claims:
Chilean claim
Argentinian claim
Brazilian zone of interest
British claim
Norwegian undefined limit
Australian claim
French claim
New Zealand claim

The Antarctic Treaty of 1959 holds all territorial claims in abeyance in the interest of international cooperation

◆ INSIGHT: If Antarctica's ice sheets were to melt, the world's oceans would rise by as much as 200–210 ft (60–65 m)

OVERSEAS TERRITORIES

DESPITE THE rapid process of decolonization since World War II, around 10 million people in 59 territories around the world continue to live under the protection of either France, Australia, Denmark, Norway, Portugal, New Zealand, the UK, the USA, or the Netherlands. These territories are administered in a wide variety of ways.

AUSTRALIA

Australia's overseas territories have not been an issue since Papua New Guinea became independent in 1975. Consequently, there is no overriding policy toward them. Norfolk Island is inhabited by descendants of the *HMS Bounty* mutineers and more recent Australian migrants. Phosphate is mined on Christmas Island.

ASHMORE & CARTIER ISLANDS (Indian Ocean)

STATUS: External territory
CLAIMED: 1978
AREA: 2 sq miles (5.2 sq km)

 CHRISTMAS ISLAND (Indian Ocean)

STATUS: External territory
CLAIMED: 1958
CAPITAL: Flying Fish Cove
POPULATION: 1,275
AREA: 52 sq miles (134.6 sq km)

COCOS ISLANDS (Indian Ocean)

STATUS: External territory
CLAIMED: 1955
CAPITAL: West Island
POPULATION: 647
AREA: 5.5 sq miles (14.24 sq km)

CORAL SEA ISLANDS (S. Pacific)

STATUS: External territory
CLAIMED: 1969
POPULATION: 3 (meteorologists)
AREA: Less than 1.16 sq miles (3 sq km)

HEARD & McDONALD ISLANDS (Indian Ocean)

STATUS: External territory
CLAIMED: 1947
AREA: 161 sq miles (417 sq km)

 NORFOLK ISLAND (S. Pacific)

STATUS: External territory
CLAIMED: 1913
CAPITAL: Kingston
POPULATION: 2,665
AREA: 13.3 sq miles (34.4 sq km)

DENMARK

The Faeroe Islands have been under Danish administration since Queen Margrethe I of Denmark inherited Norway in 1380. The Home Rule Act of 1948 gave the Faeroese control over all their internal affairs. Greenland first came under Danish rule in 1380. Today, Denmark remains responsible for the island's foreign affairs and defense.

FAEROE ISLANDS (N. Atlantic)

STATUS: External territory
CLAIMED: 1380
CAPITAL: Tórshavn
POPULATION: 48,065
AREA: 540 sq miles (1,399 sq km)

Strong sense of national identity. Voted against joining the EC with Denmark in 1973. Economy based on fishing, agriculture, Danish subsidies.

 ## GREENLAND (N. Atlantic)

STATUS: External territory
CLAIMED: 1380
CAPITAL: Nuuk
POPULATION: 55,385
AREA: 840,000 sq miles (2,175,516 sq km)

World's largest island. Much of the land is permanently ice-covered. Self-governing since 1979. Left the EU in 1985. Population is a mixture of Inuit and European in origin.

FRANCE

France has developed economic ties with its *Territoires d'Outre-Mer*, thereby stressing interdependence over independence. Overseas *départements*, officially part of France, have their own governments. Territorial *collectivités* and overseas *territoires* have varying degrees of autonomy.

CLIPPERTON ISLAND (E. Pacific)

STATUS: Dependency of French Polynesia
CLAIMED: 1930
AREA: 2.7 sq miles (7 sq km)

FRENCH GUIANA (S. America)

STATUS: Overseas department
CLAIMED: 1817
CAPITAL: Cayenne
POPULATION: 133,376
AREA: 35,135 sq miles (90,996 sq km)

The last colony in South America. Population is largely African and indigenous Indian. European Space Agency rocket launch facility.

 ## FRENCH POLYNESIA (S. Pacific)

STATUS: Overseas territory
CLAIMED: 1843
CAPITAL: Papeete
POPULATION: 210,333
AREA: 1,608 sq miles (4,165 sq km)

Most people live on Tahiti. Economy dependent on tourism and French military. Recent calls for autonomy.

GUADELOUPE (West Indies)

STATUS: Overseas department
CLAIMED: 1635
CAPITAL: Basse-Terre
POPULATION: 422,114
AREA: 687 sq miles (1,780 sq km)

Prospers from a strong infrastructure, plus French and EU aid. Indigenous population demands more autonomy.

MARTINIQUE (West Indies)

STATUS: Overseas department
CLAIMED: 1635
CAPITAL: Fort-de-France
POPULATION: 387,656
AREA: 425 sq miles (1,100 sq km)

Population largely of African origin. High living standards resulting from tourism and French subsidies.

MAYOTTE (Indian Ocean)

STATUS: Territorial collectivity
CLAIMED: 1843
CAPITAL: Mamoudzou
POPULATION: 89,938
AREA: 144 sq miles (374 sq km)

NEW CALEDONIA (S. Pacific)

STATUS: Overseas territory
CLAIMED: 1853
CAPITAL: Nouméa
POPULATION: 178,056
AREA: 7,374 sq miles (19,103 sq km)

Tensions between francophile expatriates and indigenous population over wealth inequalities and independence. Large nickel deposits.

RÉUNION (Indian Ocean)

STATUS: Overseas department
CLAIMED: 1638
CAPITAL: Saint-Denis
POPULATION: 639,622
AREA: 970 sq miles (2,512 sq km)

Wealth disparities between white and black communities. Ethnic tensions erupted into rioting in 1991. Large French military base.

ST PIERRE & MIQUELON (N. America)

STATUS: Territorial collectivity
CLAIMED: 1604
CAPITAL: Saint Pierre
POPULATION: 6,652
AREA: 93.4 sq miles (242 sq km)

WALLIS & FUTUNA (Pacific)

STATUS: Overseas territory
CLAIMED: 1842
CAPITAL: Mata-Utu
POPULATION: 14,175
AREA: 106 sq miles (274 sq km)

NETHERLANDS

The country's two remaining territories were formerly part of the Dutch West Indies. Both are now self-governing, but the Netherlands remains responsible for their defense.

ARUBA (West Indies)

STATUS: Autonomous part of the Netherlands
CLAIMED: 1643
CAPITAL: Oranjestad
POPULATION: 62,365
AREA: 75 sq miles (194 sq km)

In 1990, Aruba requested and received from the Netherlands cancellation of the agreement to automatically give independence to the island in 1996.

NETHERLANDS ANTILLES (West Indies)

STATUS: Autonomous part of the Netherlands
CLAIMED: 1816
CAPITAL: Willemstad
POPULATION: 191,311
AREA: 308 sq miles (800 sq km)

Economy based on tourism, oil refining, and offshore finance. Living standards are high. Political instability and allegations of drug-trafficking on smaller islands.

NEW ZEALAND

New Zealand's government has no desire to retain any overseas territories. However, the economic weakness of Tokelau, Niue, and the Cook Islands has forced it to remain responsible for their foreign policy and defense.

COOK ISLANDS (S. Pacific)

STATUS: Associated territory
CLAIMED: 1901
CAPITAL: Avarua
POPULATION: 18,903
AREA: 113 sq miles (293 sq km)

NIUE (S. Pacific)

STATUS: Associated territory
CLAIMED: 1901
CAPITAL: Alofi
POPULATION: 1,977
AREA: 102 sq miles (264 sq km)

TOKELAU (S. Pacific)

STATUS: Dependent territory
CLAIMED: 1926
POPULATION: 1,544
AREA: 4 sq miles (10.4 sq km)

NORWAY

In 1920, 41 nations signed the Spits-bergen treaty recognizing Norwegian sovereignty over Svalbard. There is a Nato base on Jan Mayen. Bouvet Island is a nature reserve.

BOUVET ISLAND (S. Atlantic)

STATUS: Dependency
CLAIMED: 1928
AREA: 22 sq miles (58 sq km)

JAN MAYEN (N. Atlantic)

STATUS: Dependency
CLAIMED: 1929
AREA: 147 sq miles (381 sq km)

PETER I ISLAND (Southern Ocean)

STATUS: Dependency
CLAIMED: 1931
AREA: 69 sq miles (180 sq km)

SVALBARD (Arctic Ocean)

STATUS: Dependency
CLAIMED: 1920
CAPITAL: Longyearbyen
POPULATION: 3,209
AREA: 62,906 sq km (24,289 sq miles)

In accordance with 1920 Spitsbergen Treaty, nationals of the treaty powers have equal rights to exploit Svalbard's coal deposits, subject to Norwegian regulation. The only companies still mining are Russian and Norwegian.

PORTUGAL

After a coup in 1974, Portugal's overseas possessions were rapidly granted sovereignty. By 1976, Macao was the only one remaining.

MACAO (S. China)

STATUS: Special territory
CLAIMED: 1557
CAPITAL: Macao
POPULATION: 477,850
AREA: 7 sq miles (18 sq km)

By agreement with Beijing in 1974, Macao is a Chinese territory under Portuguese administration. It is to become a Special Administrative Region of China in 1999. Macanese born before 1981 can claim a Portuguese passport.

UNITED KINGDOM

The UK has the largest number of overseas territories. Locally governed by a mixture of elected representatives and appointed officials, they all enjoy a large measure of internal self-government, but certain powers, such as foreign affairs and defense, are reserved for Governors of the British Crown.

ANGUILLA (West Indies)

STATUS: Dependent territory
CLAIMED: 1650
CAPITAL: The Valley
POPULATION: 8,960
AREA: 37 sq miles (96 sq km)

ASCENSION (Atlantic)

STATUS: Dependency of St Helena
CLAIMED: 1673
POPULATION: 1,099
AREA: 34 sq miles (88 sq km)

 BERMUDA (N. Atlantic)

STATUS: Crown colony
CLAIMED: 1612
CAPITAL: Hamilton
POPULATION: 60,686
AREA: 20.5 sq miles (53 sq km)

Britain's oldest colony. People are of African or European descent. 74% voted against independence in 1995. One of the world's highest *per capita* incomes. Financial services and tourism are main currency earners.

 BRITISH INDIAN OCEAN TERRITORY

STATUS: Dependent territory
CLAIMED: 1814
CAPITAL: Diego Garcia
POPULATION: 3,400
AREA: 23 sq miles (60 sq km)

 BRITISH VIRGIN ISLANDS (West Indies)

STATUS: Dependent territory
CLAIMED: 1672
CAPITAL: Road Town
POPULATION: 16,644
AREA: 59 sq miles (153 sq km)

 CAYMAN ISLANDS (West Indies)

STATUS: Dependent territory
CLAIMED: 1670
CAPITAL: George Town
POPULATION: 25,355
AREA: 100 sq km (259 sq km)

 FALKLAND ISLANDS (S. Atlantic)

STATUS: Dependent territory
CLAIMED: 1832
CAPITAL: Stanley
POPULATION: 2,121
AREA: 4,699 sq miles (12,173 sq km)

British sovereignty not recognized by Argentina, despite Falklands Wa in 1982. Economy based on sheep farming, sale of fishing licenses. Larg oil reserves have been discovered.

 GIBRALTAR (S.W. Europe)

STATUS: Crown colony
CLAIMED: 1713
CAPITAL: Gibraltar
POPULATION: 28,074
AREA: 2.5 sq miles (6.5 sq km)

Disputes over sovereignty between UK and Spain. The colony has traditionally survived on military and marine revenues, but cuts in defense spending by the UK have led to the development of an offshore banking industry.

 GUERNSEY (Channel Islands)

STATUS: Crown dependency
CLAIMED: 1066
CAPITAL: St Peter Port
POPULATION: 58,867
AREA: 25 sq miles (65 sq km)

ISLE OF MAN
(British Isles)

STATUS: Crown dependency
CLAIMED: 1765
CAPITAL: Douglas
POPULATION: 69,788
AREA: 221 sq miles (572 sq km)

 JERSEY
(Channel Islands)

STATUS: Crown dependency
CLAIMED: 1066
CAPITAL: St Helier
POPULATION: 82,809
AREA: 45 sq miles (116 sq km)

 MONTSERRAT
(West Indies)

STATUS: Dependent territory
CLAIMED: 1632
CAPITAL: Plymouth
POPULATION: 11,852
AREA: 40 sq miles (102 sq km)

 PITCAIRN ISLANDS (S. Pacific)

STATUS: Dependent territory
CLAIMED: 1887
CAPITAL: Adamstown
POPULATION: 52
AREA: 1.35 sq miles (3.5 sq km)

 ST HELENA
(Atlantic)

STATUS: Dependent territory
CLAIMED: 1673
CAPITAL: Jamestown
POPULATION: 6,720
AREA: 47 sq miles (122 sq km)

SOUTH GEORGIA & THE SANDWICH ISLANDS (S. Atlantic)

STATUS: Dependent territory
CLAIMED: 1775
POPULATION: No permanent residents
AREA: 1,387 sq miles (3,592 sq km)

TRISTAN DA CUNHA (S. Atlantic)

STATUS: Dependency of St Helena
CLAIMED: 1612
POPULATION: 297
AREA: 38 sq miles (98 sq km)

 TURKS & CAICOS ISLANDS (West Indies)

STATUS: Dependent territory
CLAIMED: 1766
CAPITAL: Cockburn Town
POPULATION: 12,350
AREA: 166 sq miles (430 sq km)

UNITED STATES OF AMERICA

US Commonwealth territories are self-governing incorporated territories that are an integral part of the US. Unincorporated territories have varying degrees of autonomy.

 AMERICAN SAMOA (S. Pacific)

STATUS: Unincorporated territory
CLAIMED: 1900
CAPITAL: Pago Pago
POPULATION: 50,923
AREA: 75 sq miles (195 sq km)

BAKER AND HOWLAND ISLANDS (S. Pacific)

STATUS: Unincorporated territory
CLAIMED: 1856
AREA: 0.54 sq miles (1.4 sq km)

GUAM (W. Pacific)

STATUS: Unincorporated territory
CLAIMED: 1898
CAPITAL: Agaña
POPULATION: 133,152
AREA: 212 sq miles (549 sq km)

JARVIS ISLAND (Pacific)

STATUS: Unincorporated territory
CLAIMED: 1856
AREA: 1.7 sq miles (4.5 sq km)

JOHNSTON ATOLL (Pacific)

STATUS: Unincorporated territory
CLAIMED: 1858
POPULATION: 1,375
AREA: 2.8 sq miles (4.5 sq km)

KINGMAN REEF (Pacific)

STATUS: Administered territory
CLAIMED: 1856
AREA: 0.4 sq miles (1 sq km)

MIDWAY ISLANDS (Pacific)

STATUS: Administered territory
CLAIMED: 1867
POPULATION: 453
AREA: 2 sq miles (5.2 sq km)

NAVASSA ISLAND (West Indies)

STATUS: Unincorporated territory
CLAIMED: 1856
AREA: 2 sq miles (5.2 sq km)

 NORTHERN MARIANA IS. (Pacific)

STATUS: Commonwealth territory
CLAIMED: 1947
CAPITAL: Saipan
POPULATION: 48,581
AREA: 177 sq miles (457 sq km)

PALMYRA ATOLL (Pacific)

STATUS: Unincorporated territory
CLAIMED: 1898
AREA: 5 sq miles (12 sq km)

 PUERTO RICO (West Indies)

STATUS: Commonwealth territory
CLAIMED: 1898
CAPITAL: San Juan
POPULATION: 3.6 million
AREA: 3,458 sq km (8,959 sq km)

Population voted in 1993 to maintain the current compromise between statehood and independence.

 VIRGIN ISLANDS (West Indies)

STATUS: Unincorporated territory
CLAIMED: 1917
CAPITAL: Charlotte Amalie
POPULATION: 101,809
AREA: 137 sq miles (355 sq km)

WAKE ISLAND (Pacific)

STATUS: Unincorporated territory
CLAIMED: 1898
POPULATION: 302
AREA: 2.5 sq miles (6.5 sq km)

INTERNATIONAL ORGANIZATIONS

THIS LISTING provides acronym definitions for the main international organizations concerned with economics, trade, and defense, plus an indication of membership.

ASEAN
Association of Southeast Asian Nations
ESTABLISHED: 1989 MEMBERS: Brunei, Indonesia, Malaysia, Singapore, Thailand

CIS
Commonwealth of Independent States
ESTABLISHED: 1991 MEMBERS: Armenia, Belarus, Kazakhstan, Kyrgyzstan, Moldova, Russia, Tajikistan, Turkmenistan, Ukraine, Uzbekistan

COMM
The Commonwealth
ESTABLISHED: 1931; evolved out of the British Empire. Formerly known as the British Commonwealth of Nations. MEMBERS: 53

EU
European Union
ESTABLISHED: 1965; formerly known as EEC (European Economic Community) and EC (Economic Community) MEMBERS: Belgium, Denmark, France, Germany, Greece, Ireland, Italy, Luxembourg, Netherlands, Portugal, Spain, UK, Austria, Finland, Sweden

GATT
General Agreement on Tariffs and Trade
ESTABLISHED: 1947 MEMBERS: 104

G7
Group of 7
ESTABLISHED: 1985 MEMBERS: Canada, France, Germany, Italy, Japan, UK, USA

IMF
International Monetary Fund (UN agency)
ESTABLISHED: 1944 MEMBERS: 175

NAFTA
North American Free Trade Agreement
ESTABLISHED: 1994 MEMBERS: Canada, Mexico, USA

NATO
North Atlantic Treaty Organization
ESTABLISHED: 1949 MEMBERS: Belgium, Canada, Denmark, France, Germany, Greece, Iceland, Italy, Luxembourg, Netherlands, Norway, Spain, Turkey, UK, USA

OPEC
Organization of Petroleum Exporting Countries
ESTABLISHED: 1960 MEMBERS: Algeria, Gabon, Indonesia, Iran, Iraq, Kuwait, Libya, Nigeria, Qatar, Saudi Arabia, United Arab Emirates, Venezuela

UN
United Nations
ESTABLISHED: 1945 MEMBERS: 184; all nations are represented, except Palau, Kiribati, Nauru, Taiwan, Tonga, and Tuvalu. Switzerland and Vatican City have "observer status" only

KEY

~~	*International border*
------	*Disputed border*
······	*Claimed border*
········	*Ceasefire line*
	State/Province border
	River
	Lake
	Canal
	Seasonal river
	Seasonal lake
	Waterfall
◇	*Capital city*
○	*Other towns*
✈	*International airport*
△	*Spot height - feet*
•	*Spot depth - feet*

The asterisk in the Fact File denotes the country's official language(s)

DATE OF FORMATION in the Fact File denotes the date of political origin or independence; the second date (if any) identifies when its current borders were established

ABBREVIATIONS

Abbreviations used throughout this book are listed below:

abbrev. abbreviation
Afgh. Afghanistan
Arm. Armenia
Aus. Austria
Aust. Australia
Az. Azerbaijan

Bel. Belarus
Belg. Belgium
Bos. & Herz. Bosnia & Herzegovina
Bulg. Bulgaria

C. Central
C. Cape
Cam. Cambodia
CAR Central African Republic
Czech Rep. Czech Republic

D.C. District of Columbia
Dominican Rep. Dominican Republic

E. East
EQ. Equatorial
Est. Estonia
est. estimated

Fr. France
ft feet

Geo. Georgia
Ger. Germany

Hung. Hungary

I. Island
Is. Islands
inc. including

Kaz. Kazakhstan
km kilometers
Kyrgy. Kyrgyzstan

L. Lake, Lago
Lat. Latvia
Leb. Lebanon
Liech. Liechtenstein
Lith. Lithuania
Lux. Luxembourg

m meters
mi. miles
Mac. Macedonia
Med. Sea Mediterranean Sea
Mold. Moldova
Mt. Mount/Mountain
Mts. Mountains

N. North
N. Korea North Korea
Neth. Netherlands
NZ New Zealand

Peg. Pegunungan (Indonesian/Malay for mountain range)
Pol. Poland

R. River, Rio, Rio
Rep. Republic
Res. Reservoir
Rom. Romania
Russ. Fed. Russian Federation

S. South/Southern
S. Korea South Korea
SA South Africa
Slvka. Slovakia
Slvna. Slovenia
St. Saint
Str. Strait
Switz. Switzerland

Tajik. Tajikistan
Turkmen. Turkmenistan

UAE United Arab Emirates
UK United Kingdom
USA/US United States of America
Uzbek. Uzbekistan

Ven. Venezuela

W. West
W. Sahara Western Sahara

yds yards
Yugo. Yugoslavia

INDEX

KEY:
○ = Country
□ = Overseas territory